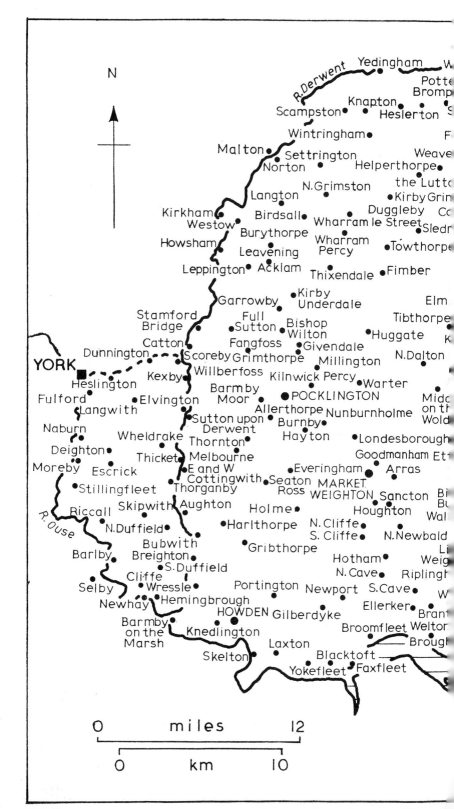

Ilkton Muston FILEY
Flotmanby
axton
on
Hunmanby
Fordon Reighton
Wold Newton Speeton
Buckton
Burton Fleming Bempton Flamborough Head
Thwing Argam Grindale
n Flamborough
Swaythorpe Boynton Sewerby
Rudston BRIDLINGTON
angtoft Bessingby Hilderthorpe
Kilham Carnaby
am Burton Agnes
Ruston Harpham Fraisthorpe
Parva Lowthorpe
on Nafferton Barmston
olds
Gt.Kelk
GT. Gembling
DRIFFIELD Ulrome
Wansford Skipsea
erne Brigham
Hutton Beeford
Cranswick N. Frodingham
Watton Hempholme Bewholme
Beswick Brandesburton
kington HORNSEA
Leven Catwick Wassand
Scorborough Sigglesthorne
nfield Eske Long Riston
ry Rise
on Tickton Withernwick
BEVERLEY
Meaux Skirlaugh Aldbrough
Woodmansey Ellerby
Wawne Burton
Swine Constable
kidby Bilton
Cottingham Grimston
Eppleworth Sutton
on Hull Preston Burton
Willerby Pidsea Waxholme
Kirk Ella Drypool HEDON
Marfleet Burstwick Withernsea
anland
HULL Thorngumbald
Hessle Paull Keyingham
by Ottringham Winestead
Patrington
R. Humber
Welwick
Sunk Island Easington

Spurn
Head

THE MAKING OF THE ENGLISH LANDSCAPE

THE EAST RIDING OF YORKSHIRE LANDSCAPE

THE MAKING OF THE ENGLISH LANDSCAPE
Edited by W. G. Hoskins and Roy Millward

THE MAKING OF THE WELSH LANDSCAPE
Edited by W. G. Hoskins and Roy Millward

The East Riding of Yorkshire Landscape

by

K. J. ALLISON

HOWDEN

MR. PYE (BOOKS)

© 1976 by K. J. Allison
Originally published 1976 by Hodder and Stoughton Ltd.
Reprinted 1998 with permission by
Mr. Pye (Books)
The Howden Bookshop
5b Vicar Lane
Howden, Goole
East Riding
DN14 7BP

ISBN 0 946289 36 0

Printed and bound by
Smith Settle
Otley, West Yorkshire LS21 3JP

Preface

AFTER TWENTY-FIVE years of exile in Yorkshire a
Norfolkman may perhaps be forgiven for writing about his
adopted county, and the newly-created counties of Humberside and North Yorkshire must forgive him, too, for
perpetuating the memory of Yorkshire and its ridings.
Inevitably this view of the making of the East Riding
landscape is a personal one, in which some features have
more forcefully caught the eye than others. It is nevertheless
an attempt at a balanced view, for in a general survey of
this kind it would surely be wrong to dwell upon any
aspect of the history of the landscape simply because it is
fashionable or because it has been hitherto neglected. In
the shaping of the East Riding landscape, prehistoric
farmers and Anglian colonists played important parts,
more so, perhaps, than has sometimes been supposed.
But their contributions must not be over-emphasised at the
expense of those of medieval husbandmen or Tudor landlords, and the work of eighteenth-century enclosure commissioners and Victorian engineers is no less significant
because it is so comparatively well known.

To describe the gradual fashioning of the landscape over
several thousand years is one of the objects of this book.
A broad division into periods seems best to serve the
purpose, though industry and communications and towns
have been placed in separate chapters in order to avoid an
unduly fragmented story. The second object of the book
is to describe some of the features that survive and to
offer guidance in their interpretation. Much remains in the
present-day landscape by which the past may be reconstructed, and our enjoyment of both town and country is
greatly increased by a combination of fieldwork and a

delving into books and documents. Enjoyment and recording should, moreover, go hand-in-hand, for it must be acknowledged that historical evidence is constantly being erased from the landscape at the present time. Indeed, anyone who follows in my footsteps should be prepared to find that the plough or the bulldozer has got there first.

This is not a work of reference and footnotes giving sources of information have therefore been largely excluded. Further information on some topics will be found in the works listed in the select bibliographies at the end of each chapter. It soon becomes apparent to the student of the East Riding landscape, however, that many aspects have yet to be properly studied and described. In a modest way this book may help to stimulate further research.

My first debt is to Professor Maurice Beresford, of the University of Leeds, to whom above all I owe my enthusiasm for the exploration of the landscape. My familiarity with the East Riding has been gained in the company of many people, among them members of the East Yorkshire Local History Society, students in the Adult Education Department at the University of Hull, and colleagues with the Victoria County History. I am especially grateful to Dr Alan Harris, Mr David Neave, Dr Graham Kent and Mr Herman Ramm for their advice and for comments upon the manuscript of the book. I must also thank Mr Norman Higson, formerly East Riding County Archivist and now Hull University Archivist, and Mr K. D. Holt, Humberside County Archivist, for giving constant access to their records and Professor R. B. Pugh, who has allowed me to use unpublished material collected for the Victoria History of the East Riding. Finally, I am greatly indebted to the general editors of this series: to Dr W. G. Hoskins, whose writings encourage and guide all his fellow-travellers in the English landscape, and to Mr Roy Millward, who has dealt so helpfully with this particular volume.

Cottingham, North Humberside   K. J. ALLISON

Contents

List of plates

ACKNOWLEDGMENTS

The author wishes to thank the following for permission to use their photographs:

The Hull *Daily Mail*: Plates 18, 24, 31, 35, 40, 41, 42
Mrs Margaret Tomlinson: Plates 4, 15, 27
The Victoria County History: Plate 37

C. H. Wood (Bradford) Ltd: Plates 36, 38

The National Monuments Record of the Royal Commission on Historical Monuments (England): Plates 2, 3, 5, 6, 7, 8, 9, 12 (Crown copyright reserved)

The Committee for Aerial Photography, Cambridge: Plates 1, 10, 11, 13, 14 (photographs by Dr J. K. St Joseph, Cambridge University Collection, copyright reserved)

Aerofilms Ltd: Plates 25, 29, 33, 39

The Ordnance Survey: Plates 17, 32 (Crown copyright reserved)

Hunting Surveys Ltd: Plates 22, 23

The Yorkshire Post: Plate 26

Mr A. P. Baggs: Plate 30

Beverley Borough Council: Plate 34 (photograph by H. Tempest, Cardiff, Ltd)

Mr Peter Mulholland: Plates 16, 28

Mr Alan Marshall, University of Hull: Plate 20

Mrs H. M. King and Dr A. Harris: Plate 19

The Librarian, Brynmor Jones Library, University of Hull: Plate 21

The architects of the University of York (Robert Matthew, Johnson-Marshall & Partners): Plate 43 (photograph by Keith Gibson, Keighley)

The photographic service, Department of Geography, University of Hull: Plate 44

Plates 27 and 30 first appeared in volumes of the Victoria County History

List of maps and plans

The maps and plans were drawn by Mr K. J. Wass from drafts by the author.

List of Abbreviations

A.H.R.	*Agricultural History Review*
E.Y.L.H.S.	East Yorkshire Local History Society
I.B.G. Trans.	*Transactions and Papers of the Institute of British Geographers*
V.C.H.	Victoria County History
Y.A.J.	*Yorkshire Archaeological Journal*
Y.A.S.R.S.	Yorkshire Archaeological Society Record Series

Editor's Introduction

THIS SERIES OF books on The Making of the English Landscape originated in 1955 with my own pioneer book under that title. A few county volumes were published under the same format (Cornwall, Leicestershire, Gloucestershire, and Lancashire), but a new and better format was worked out from 1970 onwards, beginning with Arthur Raistrick's *West Riding of Yorkshire* and Christopher Taylor's *Dorset*. Since then there has been a steady flow of such county studies, aiming at covering the whole country eventually. Already there have been volumes as far apart as Northumberland and Sussex; and books are in preparation ranging from Kent in the east to a revised edition of Cornwall in the far west.

Purists might object that the geographical county has no particular unity except for administrative purposes, that the 'region' would be more appropriate. Apart from the fact that few would agree about what constituted a 'region', the primary fact is that the geographical county is a unity so far as the documentary material is concerned; but, more than that, it evokes local patriotism, and again each English county (one ought to say 'British' in view of the fact that Wales has been brought within the orbit of the series) contains a wide variety of landscapes each interesting and appealing in its own right. Every county presents a multitude of problems of Landscape History and their very contrast is illuminating. Even little Rutland has such contrasts, though naturally on a more limited scale; and a large county like Devon has almost every kind of landscape. One other point: when the reorganisation of local government took place a few years ago, and some entirely new names appeared on the administration map of England, such as Avon and Cleveland, I had to consider whether we should stick to the old counties as we have always known them or adopt the new set-up. As the series was by then so far advanced under the old and well-loved names, we decided to retain them and go on as before. There were other good reasons, besides the sentimental one, for sticking to the original plan.

It is a well-worn truism that England is a very small country with an almost infinite variety of rocks, soils, topography, and watercourses by the tens of thousands: all these things create what one might call micro-landscapes at the risk of importing a little professional jargon into something which is meant to be enjoyed and explained in plain English. One look at the coloured map of the geology of England and Wales and above all the way in which the colours change every few miles, is enough to excite the visual imagination. This is especially true when one crosses the grain of a piece of country, instead of travelling along it. There is for example the major grain, so to speak, which runs from the south-west coast in Dorset north-eastwards to the Yorkshire coast round Whitby. If you cut *across* this geological grain, going from south-east to north-west the landscapes change every few miles. On a smaller scale but nearly as complicated, the south-eastern corner of England, running from say Newhaven northwards to the Thames estuary, presents rapid and very contrasted changes of landscape—in soils, building stones (and hence buildings themselves), in vernacular building—the architectural equivalent of the once-rich variety of local dialects in this country—in land-forms, in farming, in almost everything that is visible.

Most of us enjoy some widespread view from a hilltop or on some grand coast: we enjoy it as 'scenery' but this is really a superficial enjoyment. What I prefer to call 'landscape' as distinct from 'scenery' is that a landscape to me asks questions: why is something like this at all, why does it differ from another view a few miles away? It is the difference perhaps between what an amateur portrait painter sees and puts on paper and what a skilled surgeon sees when he contemplates and reflects over a human body. He sees things, even on a superficial examination, because of his training and his long experience, that the layman never sees. So it is with *landscape*. To see it thus, seeing beneath the surface and the obvious, is to increase one's enjoyment of the English countryside enormously. The great English painter John Constable makes this point in one simple sentence in one of his *Discourses on Landscape*, a sentence I shall never tire of quoting: "*We see nothing till we truly understand it.*" Constable's *Discourses* were an attempt to justify landscape-painting as an end in itself. If we take his great dictum as our text, Landscape History becomes an end in itself, transmuting the textbook facts of rocks and soils, landforms, economic history, industrial archaeology—words calculated to deter all but the most determined reader—into a different way of looking at perhaps commonplace things, into a different language. The art is to use these academic disciplines in a concealed way, never to let them obtrude or, if so, to some essential purpose so that the visual is always paramount.

When I wrote my own book now more than twenty years ago I did not answer all the possible questions by a long way, though it still stands as a good introduction to a new field of history. Landscape History is now, I think, a well-accepted and respectable discipline, taught in some universities and in schools, and the subject of theses. I did not answer all the questions for the simple reason that I did not then know what they all were. And even now, after so many books and articles and theses have been written, there is so much that remains unknown, and no doubt questions that I, and others, have still not perceived. This, to me, is one of the great values of these landscape books, treated county by county. Local studies in depth, to use a fashionable phrase, but for once a useful one, will not only enlarge our generalisations about the major changes in the landscape, but also because of their detail bring new lights into the picture. Ideally, as editor of this series, I would like each writer on a particular county to pick out an even smaller area for special examination under the microscope, having in mind such revealing studies as Professor Harry Thorpe's masterly essay on Wormleighton in Warwickshire (*The Lord and the Landscape,* published in 1965) and Dr Jack Ravensdale's *Liable to Floods* (1974) which deals with three Fen-Edge villages in Cambridgeshire. Not only are the topographical settings of these two studies so completely different, but one is concerned with 'peasant villages' and the landscapes they created. So social structure also enters into the many hidden creators of a particular bit of England and the vision it presents.

Some major problems remain virtually unsolved. I myself in my first book fell into the trap, or rather accepted the current doctrine, that until the Old English Conquest most of this country was uncleared woodland or undrained marsh or in many parts primaeval moorland. To a large extent I was deceived by the overwhelming evidence of the number of Old English place-names on the map, or, if not these, then the powerful Scandinavian element in the eastern parts of England. I am no longer deceived, or perhaps I should say that I have become much more sceptical about the ultimate value of this treacherous evidence. Thanks to archaeological advances in the past twenty years (and partly thanks to the opportunities offered by the odious onwards march of the motorways—their only value in my

eyes) we know very much more about the density of
settlement and of population in prehistoric times right back
to the Mesolithic of seven or eight thousand years ago.
There is evidence for forest clearance and to some extent for
settled farming as early as this, and to an even greater
extent by Neolithic times when one thinks of the axe-
factories two thousand or more feet up on the wildest
mountains of Lakeland. Forest clearance was going on at
this height, and axes were being exported as far south as
the coast of Hampshire. We now need a completely fresh
study of the distribution of woodland by, say, Romano-
British times. Not only woodland clearance, but the river
gravels which have been exploited by modern man for his
new roads have changed our whole concept of prehistoric
settlement. The gravels of the Welland valley, almost in the
heart of the Midlands, have been particularly intensively
studied and have changed our entire thinking in these parts.

That is one aspect of the English landscape which I
greatly under-estimated when I first wrote and I welcome
every fresh piece of evidence that proves me misguided. Yet
all the same the outlines of the main picture remain unchanged, and I stand by that first book subject to such
changes of emphasis as I have mentioned.

There are other problems waiting to be worked out,
some special to particular bits of England, others of a more
general nature. Of the special problems I think of the
number of isolated parish churches in the beautiful county
of Norfolk: why are they there, stuck out all alone in the
fields? Somebody could write a wonderful book on
Churches in the Landscape. And there are other special
aspects of the landscape wherever one walks in this most
beloved of all countries: so much to do, so little done.
These closer studies of England county by county will add
enormously to our knowledge. Already the study of
Landscape History has attracted a growing literature of its

own, a great deal of it scattered in local journals and periodicals. Soon, perhaps in ten years' time, we shall need a Bibliography of the subject. This makes it sound dull and academic, but in the end I look upon it as an enlargement of consciousness, a new way of looking at familiar scenes which adds to the enjoyment of life. For those who have eyes to see, the face of Britain will never look the same again.

Exeter, 1976   W. G. HOSKINS

1. The East Riding scene

WHEN THE EAST RIDING was abruptly abolished by local government reorganisation in 1974 it had enjoyed a life of only eighty-five years as an administrative county, but the 'three parts' of Yorkshire—the Danish *thridings*—had been created long before the Norman Conquest. For many people, historians among them, the East Riding cannot be so easily set aside, and this will not be the last book to adhere to the old boundaries and the old name. Let the facts be briefly stated, however, that most of the former East Riding now forms part of the county of Humberside and that the rest lies in North Yorkshire.

Visitors to the East Riding have never praised it highly for the beauty of its landscape. Rarely can it be compared to the grandeur of the hills and dales of the other ridings, but lying as it does within lowland England it is in counties of the east and the south that comparisons should perhaps be sought. Even then the East Riding landscape often seems undistinguished. As J. E. Morris perceptively wrote in his *Little Guide* in 1906, Nature has wrought in this district not only with minor materials but also with lack of definite stamp. Some other lowland counties possess a stronger local colour, a more distinctive landscape, by which they are unmistakably known. But, in Morris's words, "we can hardly speak of East Riding scenery . . . as of something of immediate and unfailing recognition". The riding nevertheless has much to delight the eye of the traveller and to hold the attention of the landscape historian, and within a mere 750,000 acres it reveals an unsuspected variety of both rural and urban landscapes.

William Camden, writing of the East Riding in his *Britannia* in 1695, described the low-lying areas as "pretty fruitful", but he was disparaging of the rest: "the middle is nothing but a heap of mountains, called Yorkeswold, which signifies Yorkshire hills". These chalk hills, stretching in crescent fashion from the sea at Flamborough Head to the Humber estuary (Fig. 1), only occasionally exceed 600 feet above sea-level. And for all their deeply-cut dry valleys, they are modest and gently rolling, highly farmed and absolutely tamed by many centuries of settlement. The most prominent feature within the Wolds is the long trough known as the Wold Valley, through which the Gypsey Race makes its way to the sea at Bridlington. To the north and west the Wolds end in a high but generally gentle escarpment, looking northwards over the Vale of Pickering (a small part of which lies in the East Riding) and westwards across the Vale of York.

The Wolds contain the best-known scenery of any part of the riding. At their seaward end the chalk rises sheer for up to 400 feet in the cliffs of Buckton, Bempton and Flamborough, with their swirling thousands of seabirds. Inland the Wolds landscape presents wide vistas of open farmland, dotted with isolated farmsteads, broken by shelter belts and plantations, and interwoven with steep-sided dry valleys, where many of the villages lie (Plate 1). The dry valleys are countless, but they are nowhere more impressive than around Thixendale, a village which takes its name from the six valleys that converge there. Often the valley sides have resisted the plough, but for the most part the Wolds have a highly cultivated landscape. They possess, nevertheless, a stark beauty of their own, verging on the picturesque only where wealthy landlords at such places as Boynton, Sledmere or Warter have lavished special attention upon the setting for their mansions.

Between the Wolds and the Vale of York lies a distinctive stretch of countryside, underlain by a series of Jurassic limestones and sandstones. In the north these much

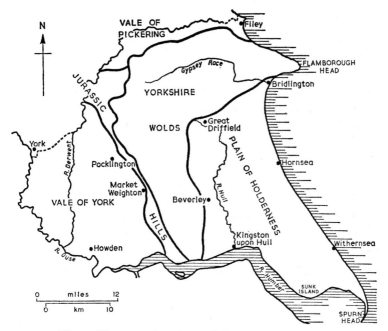

Fig. 1. The natural regions of the East Riding.

dissected 'hills'—mostly a mere 100 to 200 feet in height—stretch for several miles west of the chalk escarpment, while in the south they form a narrow bench which points its own small escarpment towards the Vale beyond. The Jurassic hills are less well known than the Wolds, but with their numerous streams and valleys, stone-built villages, and plentiful pastures and plantations they contain perhaps the most intimate and attractive landscape in the East Riding (Plate 2).

From the hills westwards to the boundaries of the riding stretch the level expanses of the Vale of York. Much of it is covered by a mantle of glacial deposits—sands and gravels, silts and clays—some of them dropped by the glacier which moved southwards down the Vale during the Ice Age, others washed out from it as the ice melted and retreated. Successive limits of the ice sheet are marked by two terminal moraines, where accumulated glacial deposits stand up to 100 feet high, almost the only prominent features in the Vale. The York and Escrick moraines have provided routeways across the marshy Vale since prehistoric times, as well as sites for several villages. Near the rivers Ouse and Derwent and alongside the Humber there are also extensive post-glacial deposits of silt, warp, peat and alluvium.

Though parts of the Vale of York were soon colonised, much of it was inhospitable to early settlers. Some areas were successfully drained only in the eighteenth century and later, and elsewhere flooding is frequent still. The Derwent, for example, as in Camden's time, "is apt to overflow the banks, and lay all the neighbouring meadows afloat". The Vale is thus a district of highly varied natural conditions and equally varied landscape history, but it is a rather dull countryside, enlivened mainly by the waters of the Ouse and the Derwent.

On the eastern side of the Wolds the chalk dips gently towards the wide valley of the river Hull and the undulating

Plate 1 Fordon. This Wolds hamlet, with its pond, lies in a deep dry valley. Beyond the still uncultivated valley sides stretch the regular fields of a typical parliamentary enclosure landscape. Ridge-and-furrow (centre) suggests, however, that even the valley bottom was cultivated in the Middle Ages.

Plate 2 Mount Ferrant, Birdsall. Looking north-west from the Wolds escarpment across the rolling country of the so-called Jurassic hills. The concentric earthworks around the spur of high ground in the centre of the picture mark the site of a castle belonging to the Fossard family; it was destroyed in 1150.

Plate 3 Willy Howe. A great burial mound, perhaps late Neolithic in date, standing in the valley of the Gypsey Race on the northern Wolds. The fence on the left marks the parish boundary between Thwing and Burton Fleming, and it seems clear that this boundary was aligned upon the barrow. Boundaries on the Wolds often make use of prehistoric features.

Plate 4 Rudston. The village takes its name from the 'rood stone', the Bronze Age monolith standing in the churchyard. A cross-head may have been affixed to the stone in an attempt to Christianise an already venerated site. The stone, made of grit from North Yorkshire, stands more than twenty-five feet high.

Plate 5   Staple Howe, Knapton. Looking north from the Wolds escarpment across the flat ground of the Vale of Pickering. The bare knoll in the centre of the picture is the site of an early Iron Age farmstead. The tall white building in the distance is a modern malting.

Plate 6   Langton dikes. The triple banks seen here form one of the most impressive surviving examples of the hundreds of prehistoric linear earthworks that once criss-crossed the Wolds. Some may have been boundaries, others were probably droveways.

country of Holderness. Like the Vale of York, Holderness is formed of a great variety of glacial and post-glacial deposits. But its hummocky landscape of boulder clay, often rising above fifty feet and interspersed with winding streams and once-marshy hollows, is quite distinctive. Holderness is less flat than the Vale, more thickly sprinkled with villages; it is also, perhaps, more austere, less well-endowed with trees and hedgerows. Only in the woods and parkland around such houses as Burton Constable and Wassand or beside the waters of Hornsea Mere—the last of the once numerous meres of Holderness—is there a hint of the picturesque. The coastline is no more inviting. Daniel Defoe, writing in the 1720s, was harsh in his judgment on the Holderness coast: "the most that I find remarkable here is that there is nothing remarkable . . . for above thirty miles together; not a port, not a gentleman's seat, not a town of note".

The low clay cliffs of this coastline are still gradually yielding to the sea, and since medieval times a score of villages have been slowly washed away. At the southern tip of Holderness, however, the sea has created the gravel spit of Spurn Head, extending into the mouth of the Humber estuary. As the coast further north has receded, so over the centuries has Spurn gone through a cycle of alternating deposition and destruction; indeed, only artificial sea defences prevent the spit from being destroyed once again.

The river Hull and a host of dikes now effectively drain the flat silt- and peat-covered lands through which the river flows. Until modern times, however, there was much marshy 'carr' ground in the middle and upper parts of the valley which inhibited settlement, and the few villages and old farmsteads of the area were placed on the higher 'islands' of sand and clay. To the south the wide expanse of silts around the confluence of the Hull and the Humber is now largely covered by the surburban sprawl of Kingston upon Hull. From the Hull valley the reclaimed silt-lands extend eastwards along the shore of the estuary, where Sunk Island contributes an area of truly flat land to the East Riding scene. It is a landscape without villages, a bare countryside marked only by drains, embankments and lonely farm-houses.

Over most of the riding, village houses and scattered farmsteads alike are built of a ubiquitous brown or mottled brick, baked from the plentiful clays of Holderness and the Vale of York. Largely replaced are the timber frames and the mud and chalk walls which must formerly have abounded. For all the subtle attractiveness of that brickwork, the modern landscape is impaired by the lack of good building stone in the riding. As a rule the easily weather-damaged chalk survives only in farm buildings, and little use has been made of the flint which contributes so much to the buildings of chalk areas in south-east England. A little variety is given to the villages of Holderness by the use of cobbles— the 'boulders' of the boulder clay—especially near the coast where they are washed out in large quantities. The only 'superior' stone, and the term is only a relative one, found in the East Riding is the Jurassic limestone. In many villages, from the Humber near Brough northwards to the river Derwent, this pleasing grey or brown stone is used in most of the older buildings. For village churches, however, medieval builders often looked outside the riding to the finer and whiter Magnesian limestone found near Tadcaster in west Yorkshire.

The visitor from more southerly parts of lowland England is frequently struck by another characteristic of the domestic buildings in the East Riding landscape, and that is the scarcity of houses earlier than Georgian. There are virtually none from the Middle Ages and few from the sixteenth and seventeenth centuries, though the latter include several, like Burton Agnes Hall, that are gems by most standards. The paucity of early houses no doubt reflects the relative poverty of the East Riding among English counties. Picturesque houses of yeoman farmers, lesser gentry, and wealthy craftsmen and tradesmen are therefore rare. Even the agricultural improvements which in the eighteenth century began to bring wealth to the Wolds did not extend the ability to build impressive houses far down the social scale. The visitor is better impressed by the medieval churches of the riding, though even here it is on the strength of a dozen outstanding buildings rather than the general quality of village churches. Many of the more humble country churches were rebuilt in the nine-teenth century, and the East Riding offers a wealth of Victorian ecclesiastical architecture.

Large towns are few in the East Riding's overwhelm-ingly rural landscape. York, as the county town of Yorkshire, lay in none of the ridings, but in *The Making of the English Landscape* it will be treated along with the North Riding. Its presence has nevertheless been strongly felt in the adjoining parts of east Yorkshire. The oldest town in the riding is Beverley, a thriving community in medieval times and from 1889 the seat of government for the East Riding. Beverley still has very much the appearance of an 'historic town', with many visible reminders of its former prosperity. In contrast the great seaport of Kingston upon Hull has lost much of its ancient central townscape, a victim of its own commercial success and of the ravages of war and neglect. For the urban-landscape historian the riding also offers the contrasts of several small market towns, a decayed medieval port, Hedon, and four seaside resorts, Bridlington the most conspicuous of them.

The generally unspoilt rural character of the East Riding is no doubt partly the result of that remoteness which much of it has long possessed. The approach from the south is hindered by the barrier of the Humber estuary. The traveller

27

has always been obliged to make a long detour to avoid the two-mile crossing from Lincolnshire. Celia Fiennes in 1697 described the estuary as "more turbulent than the Thames at Gravesend", Camden thought it "not without great danger to sailors and passengers", and Defoe was "near four hours tossed about" going from Barton to Hull. From the west the Humber and the river Ouse formed a great artery of trade, the basis of Hull's commercial success, but they were peripheral to the riding as a whole. Improved roads from the eighteenth century onwards and then railways, transient though most of them have proved to be, helped to lessen the riding's remoteness. Only now, however, is the long-discussed bridging of the Humber being attempted, and at the same time a motorway from the west has been driven across the Vale of York. The opening of them both may well herald far-reaching changes in the riding's landscape.

SELECT BIBLIOGRAPHY

Dickens, A. G., *The East Riding of Yorkshire* (1955).
Fairfax-Blakeborough, J., *Yorkshire East Riding* (1951).
The Geology and Mineral Resources of Yorkshire, ed. D. H. Rayner and J. E. Hemingway (1974).
Pevsner, N., *Yorkshire: York & the East Riding* (1972).
Stamp, L. D., *The Land of Britain: Yorkshire East Riding* (1942).
Wilson, V., *East Yorkshire and Lincolnshire* (British Regional Geology) (1948).

2. Prehistoric and Roman landscapes

Prehistoric peoples. The Romano-British landscape

Prehistoric peoples

FOR SEVERAL THOUSANDS of years the East Riding was inhabited by a succession of prehistoric peoples whose contribution to the making of the landscape is extremely difficult to assess. The size of the prehistoric population at different periods, the variation in intensity of settlement from one part of the riding to another, and the extent to which the natural vegetation was cleared for grazing and cultivation—these are imponderable problems and yet they are vital to our story. Archaeological evidence nevertheless allows some useful suggestions to be made. Standing earthworks, artifacts found by chance or by deliberate excavation, and a variety of sites discovered more recently by the patient study of aerial photographs all suggest that prehistoric and Romano-British peoples made a greater contribution than has sometimes been supposed. In some parts of the riding, indeed, the wild landscape had probably been substantially tamed long before the Anglian settlers began to arrive in the fifth century A.D. Especially on the Wolds the prehistoric peoples also raised countless earthen banks and burial mounds which were to remain prominent features of the country scene until laid flat by twentieth-century plough and bulldozer. Enough of these banks and barrows still stand, however, to remind us of the prehistoric foundations underlying the present landscape.

With sophisticated modern methods of investigation,

29

above all by the use of aerial photography, it is likely that more remains to be discovered about the prehistoric and Romano-British impact on the landscape than about any later period. Our current conclusions must therefore be cautious, and even so they will be subject to constant reassessment. On the basis of the work of the older school of archaeologists, such as Mortimer and Greenwell, it has long been held that prehistoric man in the East Riding lived mainly on the Wolds, where the vegetation was more easily cleared and the light soils more readily tilled. The denser vegetation and heavier soils of the lowlands have been seen as essentially unattractive to settlement. These views were partly based on the prevalence of earthworks on the Wolds and their virtual absence from Holderness and the Vale of York. Already we must be prepared to revise such a clear-cut interpretation. To some extent it may be accepted that earthworks were numerous on the Wolds because they were preserved in the commons and sheepwalks that survived there until modern times. In contrast, parts of the lowlands have been cultivated for so long that similar earthworks have been erased. Where an extensive common *has* survived in the Vale of York, at Skipwith, there is significantly a large group of Iron Age barrows still in existence. Air photography is already revealing that the lowlands were not so completely intractable to prehistoric settlement as was once believed, though the discovery of crop-marks by this means is far more difficult on the heavy clay soils there than on sand, gravel or chalk.

Beyond that it would at present be incautious to go. It is now being suggested that in some parts of England the lowlands were quite as attractive to prehistoric man as the chalk and limestone hills. It would be unwise, however, in the East Riding to suggest that prehistoric and Romano-British peoples were attracted to the marshy carr-lands of the Hull valley or the flooded expanses of the southern parts of the Vale of York; or indeed, until they had adequate equipment—perhaps in the later Bronze Age—to the heavy wooded clay-lands of Holderness. What does seem increasingly clear is that on the Wolds, especially on the lower eastern slopes of the Wolds, and on the lighter well-drained soils of the Jurassic hills and certain parts of the lowlands, considerable progress had been made in taming the natural landscape by the time that the first Anglian invaders arrived. With these tentative conclusions in mind we may look a little more closely at the first millennia of settlement in the riding.

There is no certain trace here of the earliest prehistoric people known in Britain, the Palaeolithic hunters who roamed the country during and after the Ice Age. Subsequently, as climatic conditions changed, tundra and scrub gave way to forest and swamp, and new groups of people migrated into Britain to lead a life of fishing, hunting and collecting. Some of these Mesolithic peoples, in the period from around 10,000 to 4,000 B.C., settled in the low-lying parts of the riding where they opened up small clearings for their huts beside lakes and meres. They are best known in east Yorkshire from a settlement site excavated at Star Carr in the Vale of Pickering, a few yards beyond the East Riding boundary. But their bone points and harpoon heads have also been found at half a dozen places in Holderness, north and west of Hornsea, and other implements have come to light near Everingham, in the Vale of York. Much more shadowy figures from the Mesolithic period are those people who preferred firmer ground and whose flint implements have been found on and around the Wolds. All the Mesolithic peoples, however, were few in number and they can have had little lasting effect upon the landscape. During this period one far-reaching natural change took place with the separation of Britain from the Continent, probably about 6,000 B.C.; later migrants would have to cross not swamp and forest but the North Sea in order to reach east Yorkshire.

From about 4,000 to 2,000 B.C. fresh invaders reached the East Riding, many of them technically far more advanced than their predecessors. This was probably a region of primary settlement, the newcomers moving in directly from the east rather than working their way up from southern England. These Neolithic peoples knew the making of pottery, kept domesticated animals, possessed the rudiments of tillage, and practised an elaborate ritual of burial. In the East Riding, so far as we yet can tell, it was mainly on the Wolds that they lived and were buried. There, the light soils supported open woodland, scrub and grassland which were more easily cleared for their cultivated plots and more readily grazed by their animals. Few Neolithic settlement sites have been discovered, but traces of occupation during this period were uncovered on Beacon Hill at Flamborough, and an exciting discovery of many small pits containing pottery and high-quality flint implements has been made on the lower Wold slopes at Carnaby. Scattered flint and stone axes, many of them Neolithic, have been found in large numbers on the Wolds, and there too were the great mounds, or long barrows, in which the dead were placed. About a dozen such barrows have been found but none is clearly recognisable on the ground today. The outstanding barrow to survive is, in contrast, circular in shape—Howe Hill at Duggleby; this mound is late Neolithic in date, as may also be Willy Howe, between Thwing and Burton Fleming. Seen from Duggleby village, beside the Gypsey Race, the first of these barrows stands out boldly on the valley side. The tree-covered Willy Howe is even more prominent, rising from the floor of the same valley where it widens out downstream (Plate 3). The Neolithic peoples did not entirely avoid the lowlands, for a few of their flint implements have been found in Holderness and in the

Vales of York and Pickering. In the Vale of York it was characteristically the dry sandy margins, together with the York and Escrick moraines, which attracted them.

The gradual clearance of the natural vegetation was continued by a series of new invaders from about 2,000 B.C. onwards, some arriving from the south and others across the North Sea. Stone and flint implements were still used by these Bronze Age peoples, but axes and other tools of bronze became increasingly common. With this new equipment, Bronze Age man was a more proficient huntsman, a better-equipped deforester, and a more able cultivator than his predecessors, and the grazing of his domesticated animals also played an important part in reducing the vegetation.

The clearance of scrub and woodland on the Wolds was no doubt greatly extended as the population grew, for in the early and mid Bronze Age preference continued to be shown for the higher ground. The settlement sites of these people have mostly eluded discovery, but their scattered implements are found on the Wolds, as well as the numerous round barrows in which the dead were buried. The ritual of burial constantly changed and the beakers which the earlier Bronze Age people placed in their barrows gave way successively to food vessels and cremation urns; perhaps as many as 600 of these various pots have been found in Wolds barrows. Many of the smaller round barrows have been ploughed down in modern times. Some are still prominent, however, and dozens more are visible at certain times of the year as slight humps in the cultivated fields.

Other round barrows have been identified from the air on the lower ground, for example around Driffield and continuing southwards down the Hull valley. Some bronze axes, one or two dug-out canoes, and a few food vessels provide further evidence that the early and mid Bronze Age folk did not completely shun the lowlands of Holderness.

C

A flat cremation cemetery—without barrows—belonging to the urn people has, moreover, been discovered west of Hornsea. Several boats, found on the shore at North Ferriby and made of carefully jointed planks sewn together with yew withies, suggest that in the mid Bronze Age there was also free movement along and across the Humber. But in the later Bronze Age the pattern of finds changes radically and it is clear that a new wave of invaders showed a marked preference for the lowlands. The newcomers brought a wealth of superior bronze weapons and implements, more especially a type of axe which enabled the denser lowland forests to be cleared. Late Bronze Age finds are consequently abundant in Holderness, and also along the eastern margins of the Vale of York and on the Jurassic hills which link the Wolds with the Howardian Hills of the North Riding.

The culture which thus developed in east Yorkshire continued from about the thirteenth to the sixth century B.C., bridging the late Bronze and early Iron Ages, with new influences like the use of iron entering about 700 B.C. Several settlement sites of these peoples are known: pottery of the period has been found, for example, on the Wolds at Fimber, hutted encampments (the so-called 'lake villages') at Barmston and Ulrome, and several hill-forts on the Wolds. The first fort to be discovered was at Grimthorpe, near the western escarpment, and half a dozen others have been recognised from aerial photographs, for example at Thwing. The forts suggest that stresses were developing among the growing population. From late in the period come several early Iron Age settlement sites found on the Wolds, in the upper Hull valley, and on two prominent knolls beneath the northern Wolds escarpment. On one of these knolls, at Staple Howe, Knapton, a palisade enclosed several huts and what was probably a granary. It seems likely that the occupants were growing grain and rearing animals on the Wolds, and hunting and fishing on the lower ground of the Vale of Pickering. Staple Howe, bare and hog-backed, is a place to stir the imagination, rising gauntly now from the plantations that clothe the escarpment (Plate 5).

The improved equipment of the late Bronze Age had no doubt been developed in response to similarly difficult conditions on the Continent and it suggests that easier country such as the Wolds was becoming fully settled, if not indeed over-populated. Without doubt the clearance of vegetation and the development of a peopled countryside were spreading to all but the least attractive parts of the East Riding before the end of the Bronze Age. The analysis of peat deposits at the Barmston settlement site shows, for example, a substantial amount of grass pollen and bracken spores, suggesting that there was no longer an unbroken woodland cover there. Pollen analysis also indicates growing human activity in the southern Vale of York, for example at Faxfleet, and this is clearly another valuable method of enquiry into prehistoric conditions.

The Wolds were next conquered by warrior bands of invaders who originated in the Marne region of France and made east Yorkshire one of their main strongholds in Britain. Their chieftains apparently maintained a firm rule over their own followers and over the existing population. These La Tène people were both cultivators and herdsmen. Traces of huts and ditches at their farmsteads have been found, for example at Langton, Rudston and Elmswell, and many of the linear earthworks and small enclosures on the Wolds may have been connected with their cattle-rearing. The once extensive network of earthworks, or dikes, has been much reduced during the last century, but many short stretches of single, double, and sometimes triple dikes can still be seen. One of the most prominent sets of earthworks, now diminished to a few sad remnants, was that known as

Argam Dikes, stretching for several miles across the base of Flamborough Head. Other good examples remain in and beside the dry valleys near Huggate and Millington, and part of a fine triple dike survives near Langton (Plate 6).

These later Iron Age tribesmen were apparently responsible, moreover, for the great cemeteries of small square barrows that have been found on the Wolds, often on the lower slopes, at places like Arras, Garton on the Wolds, Rudston, Driffield and Eastburn. Scores of barrows may still be seen at Danes' Graves, near Driffield, and others survive in parkland at Scorborough. About ten chariot burials of La Tène chieftains have been discovered in such barrows, the finest—at Garton—as recently as 1971. Other surviving barrows, such as those at Skipwith, in the Vale of York, as well as cemeteries found in north Holderness, show that these people extended their influence far beyond the Wolds, covering most of the East Riding and going a little further north and west.

In all probability the La Tène people were the ancestors of the tribe known as the Parisi, which was in occupation of the East Riding when the Romans arrived in the first century A.D. The Belgic tribes which occupied some of the more southerly parts of Britain in the late Iron Age apparently did not reach east Yorkshire, though Belgic pottery, imported across the Humber, has been found at a settlement site near North Ferriby.

The expanding population of the Iron Age no doubt extended and accelerated the process of clearing the natural vegetation in many parts of the riding. Reclamation and farming may have reached a peak after about 200 B.C., making further inroads into the lowland forests as well as the long-favoured Wolds. On the higher ground prehistoric man had shaped a landscape of extensive rough pastures and smaller cultivated fields, pock-marked with burial mounds, and criss-crossed by scores of miles of embankments which marked the boundaries of estates or served as droveways for moving stock. Long-distance trackways had also been established, certainly by the Bronze Age, which formed part of routes connecting western Britain with the Continent; these trackways crossed the Vale of York by the natural bridges provided by the moraines, ran over the Wolds, and reached the sea in the region of Flamborough Head and Bridlington Bay. And if standing stones are rare in east Yorkshire there is neverthe-less the great Bronze Age monolith at Rudston (Plate 4), standing twenty-five feet and more in height and extending deep into the ground. This massive lump of sandstone, dwarfed now by the parish church, must have been carried at least ten miles from beyond the Vale of Pickering. Only two or three miles away, in Burton Fleming, and now visible only from the air, is an oval-shaped 'henge' which was probably a Bronze Age meeting-place. Clearly these sites were monuments of considerable religious significance.

Arable farming on the Wolds, especially in recent centuries, has so reduced the area of rough grassland remaining in the riding that there are now few places where traces of prehistoric fields might survive, as they sometimes do on the downland of southern England. The largest grassland area left to us, the great Westwood common at Beverley, does, however, retain traces, albeit faint traces, of prehistoric enclosures as well as barrows. Other enclosures may be seen in old pasture near Arden Fleets, an isolated farmstead between Warter and North Dalton, and fragments survive here and there in roadside verges. For the rest, only soil- and crop-marks, seen from the air, now reveal the pattern of prehistoric field boundaries.

The effects of the prehistoric effort must not be exagger-ated. Much remained to be done, especially among the wetter woodlands and swamps, but the way had been prepared, more thoroughly or less from one area to another, for further progress under the Romans, and later by the Angles and Danes.

The Romano-British landscape

It was not until A.D. 71, nearly thirty years after they had landed in Britain, that the Romans pushed forward beyond the Humber to meet the threat of the rebellious Brigantes in the north. The resistance of the Parisi to this advance was perhaps stronger than was once thought. To the well-known forts at Brough and Malton we can add another recently found at Hayton, and several of the Romano-British villa farms in the riding had to be fortified. There are also possible signs, on the Wolds south of Ganton and Staxton, of a regular pattern of land-partition which suggests the need to impose Roman control in the area.

The Roman communications network in east Yorkshire was, so far as is yet known, a comparatively simple one. From their first foothold in the riding, at the fort of Brough (*Petuaria*), the Romans moved along the brow of the Wolds as far as the Vale of Pickering, where they established another base at Malton (*Derventio*). The ninth legion then struck across the Vale of York, following the more northerly of the moraines, to set up its headquarters at York (*Eboracum*). A second route from Brough to York ran to the west of the Wolds escarpment, reaching the moraine at Stamford Bridge. Other roads evidently led eastwards to the coast, one from Malton to the Filey area, others across the Wolds to Bridlington Bay, where the Romans may well have had a harbour; any Roman settlement in the neighbourhood of Bridlington, however, has inevitably been eroded by the sea.

Within this framework, many of the settlements of the Parisi were probably little disturbed during the Roman occupation. But some of the native population, especially those living close to the chief centres of Roman influence, adopted Roman customs and enjoyed in greater or lesser degree the material civilisation of their conquerors. There must have been great variety among the Romano-British settlements, from primitive encampments like that excavated at Bessingby to comparatively wealthy farms like the one found at Elmswell. What does seem clear, in the light of repeated finds of pottery from these centuries, is that settlements were multiplying in many parts of the East Riding during the Roman period.

The most distinctive features of Roman civilisation were no doubt to be found at Brough, at Malton, and in a handful of wealthy villas. During the Roman occupation Brough seems to have become the tribal capital of the Parisi. The civil town there, with its amphitheatre, enjoyed a heyday during the second century A.D., later declining long before the departure of the Romans from east Yorkshire. Malton is, of course, outside the East Riding, though the civil settlement that grew up beside the military base produced activity on the south side of the river Derwent, at Norton. In the countryside, fewer than a dozen villas have been discovered in the East Riding, though the buildings excavated at Langton and Rudston suggest that some of them were the centres of large and prosperous estates. The Langton, Rudston and Welton villas were all built on the sites of Iron Age farmsteads. Here it seems likely that native chieftains, gradually adopting Roman customs, had turned earlier mainly stock-rearing farms into mixed-farming or corn-growing estates.

The examination of many air photographs of the Burton Fleming–Rudston–Kilham area has made it possible to reconstruct "an almost complete Romano-British landscape with fields, trackways and native farms" (Plate 7).[1] A few

[1] Reported by the Royal Commission on Historical Monuments, in *Y.A.J.*, xliii, p. 194.

miles away, in a valley known as Garton Slack, a Romano-British farmstead has been found alongside plentiful evidence of Iron Age settlement. Similar evidence of extensive Iron Age and Romano-British fields is being found from other areas, too. Complex systems of crop-marks have, for example, been seen from the air in the sandy soils along the eastern margin of the Vale of York, at such places as South Cliffe and Hotham. Others have been photographed on slightly elevated ground in the Hull valley near Woodmansey.

Evidence of Romano-British settlement is widespread, extending into south Holderness, for example, at places like Sutton on Hull, Keyingham and Easington. Along the banks of the Ouse and the Humber—much used as a waterway—there have been Roman finds at Blacktoft, Faxfleet, Broomfleet and elsewhere. There, Romano-British settlers may have begun the long process of drainage which will be discussed in a later chapter, though towards the end of the fourth century flooding seems to have resulted in the abandonment of their riverside sites. A little to the north, at several places around Holme upon Spalding Moor, pottery kilns have been found which probably sent their wares over a wide area of northern England.

The peaceful Roman occupation of the riding made military posts largely unnecessary, and it was only in the fourth century, with threats from northern tribes and Anglo-Saxon seaborne raiders, that such posts were again strengthened. Signal stations were established after A.D. 370 on Carr Nase at Filey, on Beacon Hill at Flamborough, and perhaps at unknown sites on the Holderness coast. Inland stations were needed to convey signals to Malton and Brough. One of these was probably located at Staxton, and another may have been placed upon a Bronze Age barrow near Walkington. The remains of twelve bodies, mostly decapitated, found on the Walkington site suggest that raiders were already penetrating inland before the end of the fourth century.

The native population continued to follow its Romanised way of life long after the Roman withdrawal around A.D. 400. Many Romano-British farmsteads and villages were still inhabited, and their land occupied, throughout the century of intermittent Anglian raids that followed the withdrawal. At Elmswell, for example, there is evidence of settlement from about A.D. 50 until at least A.D. 500. When the Anglians finally came to settle rather than to raid they frequently placed their farmsteads and villages near Romano-British settlements, and must as frequently have taken over existing farmland. The chance discovery of Romano-British pottery near Anglian villages increasingly suggests this continuity of land-use from the Roman period to the Anglian. We shall have to consider this question further when describing the Anglian settlement. At this point it is sufficient to emphasise that the Anglians were confronted by a landscape in the East Riding which was the culmination of many centuries of work by prehistoric and Romano-British settlers.

SELECT BIBLIOGRAPHY

Brewster, T. C. M., *The Excavation of Staple Howe* (1963).

Clark, J. G. D., *Excavations at Starr Carr* (1954).

Elgee, F. and H. W., *The Archaeology of Yorkshire* (1933).

Greenwell, W., *British Barrows* (1877).

Kitson Clark, Mary, *A Gazetteer of Roman Remains in East Yorkshire* (1935).

Longworth, I. H., *Yorkshire* (Regional Archaeologies) (1965).

Manby, T. J., 'Neolithic Occupation Sites on the Yorkshire Wolds', *Y.A.J.*, xlvii (1975), pp. 23–59.

Mortimer, J. R., *Forty Years' Researches in British and Saxon Burial Mounds* (1905).

Norman, A. F., *The Romans in East Yorkshire* (E.Y.L.H.S. 12) (1960).

Stead, I. N., *The La Tène Cultures of Eastern Yorkshire* (1965).

Stead, I. N., 'Yorkshire before the Romans: some recent discoveries', in R. M. Butler, ed., *Soldier and Civilian in Roman Yorkshire* (1971), pp. 21–43.

V.C.H., *Yorkshire*, I (1907) (early man).

Wacher, J. S., 'Yorkshire Towns in the Fourth Century', in Butler, *Soldier and Civilian*, pp. 165–77.

Wacher, J. S., *The Towns of Roman Britain* (1975).

3. The Anglian and Scandinavian settlement

Angles and Danes. The question of continuity. Villages and churches. Boundaries

FOR MORE THAN FIVE centuries after about A.D. 450 the East Riding was settled by invading bands of Angles and Scandinavians. It can no longer be believed, as it formerly was, that the invaders drove out the remaining British population and established their own villages and fields where they chose. The early Anglian settlement was, rather, a gradual infiltration into the British countryside. New settlers coexisted with old, sharing existing village sites or finding fresh ones as best they could. Nor were all the early sites to be permanently occupied. Some were probably abandoned and replaced during the centuries of Anglian settlement so that an established pattern of villages and scattered farmsteads only gradually emerged. The Danes who began to arrive in the ninth century moved by a similar process of infiltration, sharing or taking over existing settlements, founding new ones where space could be found. By the end of the Dark Ages, however, the Angles and Scandinavians had established a pattern of landscape which contained some of the most basic features of the present-day countryside. Most of the villages in the East Riding, for example, were in existence by 1066, and bore recognisable names, even though their shape and layout were in many cases destined to be greatly changed later on.

The detailed character of the Anglo-Saxon settlement, all

over the country, is now being reappraised by historians
and archaeologists, and firm conclusions have not yet been
reached. The concept of a landscape gradually taking shape
during Romano-British and Anglo-Saxon times is, however,
now generally accepted, and it is much more plausible than
the old notions of the English settlers starting almost from
scratch amidst the wreckage of Romano-British rural life.
In the East Riding, as elsewhere, traditional types of
evidence, especially place-names, still have much to tell us,
and we must consider them for the contributions made by
both Angles and Danes to the emerging landscape.
Evidence for a continuity of settlement and land-use
between Romano-British and Anglian times is provided by
an ever-increasing volume of archaeological finds and by the
growing use of aerial photography. Other work on the
settlement history of these centuries involves a new
assessment of the available documentary evidence. By these
various means we can gain an impression of the way in
which the Anglian and Scandinavian settlers, working
within an already old-established framework, left their own
firm imprint upon the East Riding landscape.

Angles and Danes

During the last years of the Romans' occupation, and in the
period following their withdrawal, small groups of troops
were brought from the continent to help in the defence of
Romanised Britain against northern tribes and Anglo-Saxon
raiders. These 'mercenaries' represent the earliest Germanic
settlement in this country, and there is evidence of their
presence at York and other important Roman centres in
Yorkshire. They were probably also placed at strategic
points to defend the Roman road network, one such group
apparently being established at Sancton, near the road from
Brough to Malton. A large cemetery there has been found

to contain pottery of the very early fifth century, possibly even dating from before 400, and the mixed styles of the pottery also suggest the organised introduction of a mercenary force from various districts on the continent.

By the second half of the fifth century, however, independent settlement by Anglian invaders was already taking place in various parts of eastern Yorkshire. In the East Riding the Angles seem to have made little early penetration of the comparatively inhospitable country of Holderness. Instead it appears that they chose two main points of entry: at the eastern end of the Wolds, around Flamborough Head, and in the south, where the Wolds meet the Humber. From these landing places they pushed inland, along or close to the higher ground. Former Roman roads guided some of the invaders along well-worn paths, and many early pagan cemeteries have been found near the roads running north from Brough and west from Bridlington Bay (Fig. 2).[1]

Especially significant in the early Anglian settlement was the area along the western margin of the Wolds, close to the old roads from Brough to Malton and York. This may well have been the nucleus of the Anglian kingdom of Deira, with its royal seat at Goodmanham. It was at Goodmanham that, according to Bede, a pagan Anglian temple was destroyed in 627 after Paulinus had converted King Edwin to Christianity. Several large pagan cemeteries lie in this area, at North Newbald, Nunburnholme and Londesborough, as well as at Sancton where the cemetery begun by the mercenaries continued in use until about 650. There was apparently another concentration of early Anglian settlement in the Driffield area, again not far from the old Roman routeways and in a district heavily settled in Romano-

---

[1] Based on a map in Gillian F. Jensen, *Scandinavian Settlement Names in Yorkshire*, p. 172. See also the map in Margaret L. Faull, 'Roman and Anglian Settlements in Yorkshire', in *Northern History*, ix, p. 3.

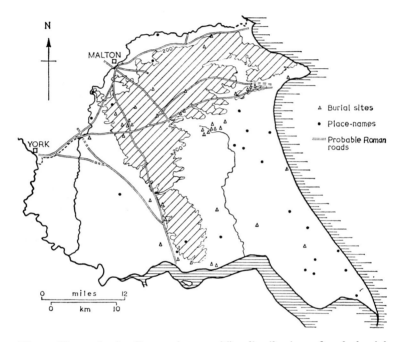

Fig. 2. The early Anglian settlement. The distribution of early burial sites and place-names in the East Riding. The names are those incorporating -ing, -ingham or -ham.

British times. Driffield may also have been a royal seat, for Aldfrith of Northumbria is said to have died there in 705.

With the spread of Christianity from the seventh century onwards, several cemeteries—like one at Garton on the Wolds—show evidence of the abandonment of pagan burial practices, with their emphasis on grave-goods for the after-life. Not all Anglian burials were grouped in cemeteries. Some were placed in prehistoric barrows, at Duggleby and Rudston, for example, while at Garton burials were set into prehistoric embankments. Cemeteries and other burials are a valuable guide to the areas of early settlement. Often, as at Garton, they were situated away from the settlement sites themselves and close to later parish boundaries. It may well be that the cemeteries each served a group of small scattered settlements, both British and Anglian, during these first centuries of infiltration.

The distribution of Anglian burials on and around the Wolds suggests that settlers were spreading widely into the most favoured areas of Romano-British habitation. We must no longer suppose that the existing population was displaced or wiped out, even though few British place-names were retained, apart from such river names as Ouse and Derwent. Otherwise, only a handful of British names were borrowed and reused by the Angles.

The earliest purely Anglian village names are probably those containing the elements *-ing, -ingham,* or *-ham*. These are now believed to represent a slightly later settlement phase than the early cemeteries, but it is hardly surprising that some of them are found in the same districts as the burial sites. In the important area centred on Goodmanham, for example, there are Brantingham, Everingham and Riplingham. Goodmanham itself is a name of special interest, for it was recorded by Bede as 'Godmundingaham' and the element *-ing* had already been lost by the time that Domesday Book was compiled. The early place-names also suggest a more energetic settlement of Holderness than in the initial phase, both in the south, within easy reach of the banks of the Humber, and in the north, at no great distance from the Wolds.

Cemeteries and place-names provide most of the evidence for the earliest phases of the Anglian settlement. It is possible, however, that Danes' Dyke (Plate 8), one of the most spectacular earthworks in the East Riding, forms part of the same picture. The bank runs for nearly three miles across Flamborough Head, from cliff top to cliff top, with a deep ditch along the landward side. Its date has never been firmly established by excavation. It may well have been constructed, however, during the Anglian invasions, either defensively by a beleaguered British population or by Angles gaining a foothold on the promontory. Responsibility may conceivably lie with Ida, the first king of the Anglian kingdom of Bernicia, who was said by Symeon of Durham to have landed at Flamborough with sixty ships, before proceeding further north.[2]

From the areas of their earliest settlement the Angles moved into almost all parts of the riding during the sixth, seventh and eighth centuries. Some of the later Anglian village names were those incorporating *-ton* or *-ington*, and there are many such names in both Holderness and the Vale of York, as well as in parts of the Wolds. Anglian names of all kinds account for nearly 300 of the 440 settlement names recorded in Domesday Book. Certain districts nevertheless appear to have been relatively lightly settled by the Angles, including some of the higher parts of the Wolds and some of the wettest areas of the lowlands. But everywhere there was still room for many new villages and hamlets to be founded by the Danes.

[2] I am indebted to Mr H. G. Ramm for these suggestions. The dike might alternatively have been built during the Roman attempt to subdue the Brigantes before A.D. 70. A pre-Roman date is unlikely.

In A.D. 867 the great Danish army, which had landed in East Anglia two years before, captured the Anglian town of York, and it was not until the death of Eric Bloodaxe, the last Viking King of York, in 954 that Scandinavian rule in the area came to an end. During this 'Viking century' the East Riding landscape was endowed with many new settlements, and further inroads were made into the remaining areas of forest and marsh.

The remnants of the Danish army settled down in Yorkshire in 876, when their king, Halfdan, is said to have shared out the land among them and "they were engaged in ploughing and in making a living for themselves". No doubt Danish leaders often established their families in existing Anglian villages, and sometimes they changed the original names of the settlements. Nearly seventy hybrid or Scandinavianised names have been identified in the riding. Around existing centres the Danes also founded new villages and hamlets where space and opportunity allowed, and this process continued long after the initial Danish settlement. The earlier of these secondary Danish villages often bear names ending in *-by,* with names ending in *-thorpe* coming a little later on. There are about forty *-bys* in the East Riding and about seventy *-thorpes,* as well as forty Scandinavian names of various other kinds. With the hybrids these make a total of some 220 Scandinavian names.

Scandinavian place-names are to be found all over the riding, but they are more plentiful in some areas than others. There are many of them on the Wolds, especially in the northern part, and a considerable scattering in Holderness. They are common, too, in and around the Vale of York: many *-bys* and *-thorpes* occur on the low ground in the south, around the Ouse and the Derwent, and many others on the higher ground of the Jurassic hills further north. In the south, Howden is an interesting case of the substitution of a Scandinavian form of the Anglian name, and within the

D

territory belonging to that village the Danes added Belby and Thorpe to the existing hamlets. Both in the Vale of York and in the Hull valley the part played by the Danes in colonising marshy land is emphasised by the frequency of minor names incorporating *-holm* and *-carr,* both deriving from Scandinavian words.

The detail of local siting is perhaps of more significance than the general pattern of Danish settlement. When the distribution of villages is examined in relation to the local geology and soils it becomes clear that those with purely Scandinavian names usually occupy relatively poor and unattractive soils. The Danes were obliged to use the best vacant land that was available and so to push colonisation into less hospitable country. An area around Bubwith in the Vale of York, on either side of the river Derwent, will serve as an illustration. Apart from the wet alluvial valley bottom, where there are naturally no settlements, the country here consists of limited spreads of easily-worked sand and gravel in a wide expanse of heavy ill-drained clay. Most of the villages with Anglian names, including some showing the results of Scandinavian linguistic influence, are situated on the more attractive soils of the sand and gravel. In contrast almost all those with purely Scandinavian names, including several *-bys* and *-thorpes,* lie on the clay, in areas which had probably been left empty by the Anglians. Areas in other parts of the riding have been examined to provide similar illustrations.[3]

The question of continuity

All over the riding, and more especially in those areas where Iron Age and Romano-British settlement had been most intensive, the Angles must have found much improved land

[3] For maps and discussion see Jensen, *Scandinavian Settlement Names in Yorkshire.*

which could be incorporated in their own fields. Even allowing for some reversion of farmland during the unsettled period that followed the Roman withdrawal, it was often an hospitable landscape that confronted the new settlers. The Angles worked their fields either from existing farmsteads and villages, or from others newly-established among the British population. As this fluctuating pattern of settlement gradually took more lasting shape, it was no doubt the most attractive sites that were used for permanent villages. The Anglian and Danish settlers thus at first infiltrated into the British countryside, and then gradually absorbed both fields and settlements into a new pattern.

In a general way, then, there is no reason to doubt that continuity of settlement from Romano-British to Anglo-Danish times was widespread in the riding. Continuity of a more precise kind will be proved only by painstaking research. It is not yet possible to point to any East Riding site where evidence of unbroken settlement by Britons and Angles has been found, though such sites are beginning to be identified in other parts of the country. Nor have examples yet been found of Anglian fields exactly coinciding with British. Even at Elmswell, where excavation suggests that there was continuous settlement of a native village for 400 years before the Anglian invasion, there seems nevertheless to have been a break thereafter. The Anglians eventually chose a new site a short distance away for their village at 'Helm's spring'.

When evidence for exact continuity of settlement is eventually discovered, it will be no surprise if it comes first from the area stretching northwards from Brough, or from the Driffield region, or from the valley of the Gypsey Race. As already suggested, these were among the areas of the riding where evidence of prehistoric, Roman and early Anglian settlement is most abundant. Already there is good reason to suspect a general continuity of land-use around such villages as Kilham, Rudston and Garton on the Wolds. Kilham lies in a shallow valley, on the southern slopes of the Wolds, where several springs feed a constant stream. A long barrow and several round ones show that there was settlement in the locality in Neolithic and Bronze Age times. In one branch of the valley there is an Iron Age cemetery, recently discovered by aerial photography, and one of the probable east–west Roman roads leading towards Bridlington Bay passed across the valley. Near by, moreover, were two Roman villas. On one side of the valley a pagan cemetery suggests Anglian settlement in the fifth or sixth century, and on the other side there is a later Christian cemetery. In the heart of this area the Angles established their village 'at the kilns', or perhaps more plausibly 'at the springs', choosing a site on the line of the Roman road and close to the springs and stream. Only careful excavation of all the sites in the area could confirm that settlements and fields around Kilham were continuously occupied from the Iron Age to the later Anglian period, but the likelihood is strong.

Many of the same elements are to be found near by at Rudston, in the valley of the Gypsey Race. Neolithic long barrows, Bronze Age barrows, the henge known as Maiden's Grave at Burton Fleming, and the monolith at Rudston itself are all within easy reach of one another. Several ceremonial avenues lead into the valley here, as do the far-ranging embankments called Argam Dikes. North of Rudston is an extensive later Iron Age cemetery, and to the south-west lay a Roman villa on the site of an Iron Age settlement. Wold Gate skirts the valley to the south, and another probable Roman road runs into and along the valley bottom, while Romano-British pottery has been found on the site of the Anglian village. Evidence for pagan Anglian settlement is at present lacking. When eventually the village itself was established, the Angles chose a site by the stream, close to a reliable spring and to the Bronze Age monolith; they presumably attempted to Christianise the monolith, hence the naming of the village 'at the rood stone', or cross stone. The very use of the monolith in this way strongly suggests that the Angles were cohabiting with pagan British people who continued to venerate their ancient stone and were thus led towards Christianity. In due course the village church was built alongside the stone (Plate 4). Again the possibility of continuous settlement seems strong.

At Garton a similar pattern is emerging. Neolithic and Bronze Age burials, an Iron Age cemetery and settlement, a Romano-British farmstead of the second and third centuries B.C., and an Anglian cemetery apparently with both pagan and Christian sectors—all these lay within a mile or so of the later Anglian village. Garton is the village 'in or near the triangular piece of ground', an obscure name which perhaps refers to the space around a spring or pond supplying water; a mere still exists at Garton, together with the remains of a former 'green' around it.

These are outstanding examples of the way in which an accumulation of evidence suggests that there may have been continuity of settlement within a small area. Many other, less dramatic, examples are being provided as archaeological finds multiply. At Boynton, for instance, a fourth-century Romano-British settlement and a probable Anglian cemetery have been found near the Gypsey Race half a mile from the later village. Romano-British pottery has also turned up close to Burton Agnes village, on the southern edge of the Wolds, while at Ganton, beneath the northern escarpment, similar pottery and an Anglian cemetery have come to light. A few miles east of Ganton, at Staxton, a sequence of Iron Age, Romano-British and Anglian discoveries has been made near the site of 'Stakk's farmstead', and high on the Wolds evidence for at least one Romano-British farmstead has been found at Wharram Percy. At Wharram, indeed, there are signs that the basic layout of the medieval village may have been to some extent determined by the lines of Romano-British field boundaries and trackways. The continuing study of this deserted medieval village promises to throw significant light on the problem of continuity.

A further possibility to emerge from recent research is that the continuing settlement of the Iron Age and the Romano-British and Anglian periods took place within a framework of long-lasting estates.[4] It is suggested that in east Yorkshire, as in many other parts of the country, Iron Age farmsteads and villages may already have been organised into these large federal groupings. The estates may sometimes have been separated from one another by the familiar linear earthworks of the Wolds, and their chieftains may have been laid to rest in the chariot burials of our La Tène cemeteries. Later on, the same estates may have become the basis of large Romano-British villa farms, from which outlying farmsteads and hamlets were controlled. These may in turn have been taken over by Angles and Danes to provide the basis for an organisation of dependent hamlets under the control of large 'capital' villages. Support for this suggestion is adduced from the Domesday Survey, where large manors are frequently described with numerous subsidiary berewicks and sokelands. Places like Hunmanby, Driffield, Bridlington and Pocklington are likely foci of such federal estates, and as we shall see it was also at these larger villages that early churches were built. While some of the large estates thus survived until the Norman Conquest, and even later, many others had by then already been split up into smaller units.

---

[4] See, for example, G. R. J. Jones, 'Basic Patterns of Settlement Distribution in Northern England', *The Advancement of Science*, xviii (1961–2), p. 192.

The fragmentation of federal estates is, indeed, now seen by historians as the chief means by which new villages were added to the landscape during the Anglo-Saxon period. The theory of long-lasting federal estates has yet to be carefully tested in the East Riding, but it would help to explain the continuity of settlement which seems so likely here.

Villages and churches

The patterning of villages and hamlets which eventually emerged from the centuries of Anglian and Danish settlement is essentially that with which we are still familiar today. The new settlers were able to plough the heavier soils which had been less readily cultivated by prehistoric and Romano-British farmers. There were nevertheless areas which were still relatively unfavourable to colonisation, and the density of settlement varied with drainage and water supply, as well as with soils.

Most densely settled were the heavier and inherently more fertile soils of Holderness, the lower eastern slopes of the Wolds, and the drier parts of the Vale of York. In all these areas there was a plentiful supply of surface water. Villages are consequently numerous on the hummocky boulder clay of Holderness; on the Wolds slopes they tend to lie in two lines, one near the upper and one the lower margins of the boulder clay that mantles the chalk; and in the Vale of York many settlements were sited on the higher clay and gravel of the moraines and on the more gentle swells of the outwash sands. A string of villages also lies beneath the chalk escarpment, where many springs feed streams flowing towards the Vales of York and Pickering.

Paradoxically, on the higher parts of the Wolds villages are less thick on the ground: though the lighter soils there had favoured prehistoric settlement, their natural fertility was less than that of the heavier soils and water supply was often also a problem. There were comparatively few streams there, though it may be supposed that during the Anglian and Danish settlement water flowed in some of the many valleys that are now permanently dry. The disappearance of such streams is to be attributed to a gradual lowering of the water table, both by climatic change and by the extensive pumping out of water to meet modern demands. Anglian and Danish settlers no doubt sought out reliable springs, as well as the occasional streams and natural ponds. The valley of the Gypsey Race provides an obvious example. Though this Wolds stream was erratic in its flow, the springs along its course nevertheless attracted such Anglian settlements as Wold Newton and the Luttons, and several Danish villages were later interspersed with them, including Duggleby and Weaverthorpe.

Natural ponds were probably few on the high Wolds, for clay rarely existed *in situ* to form a seal over the chalk or the valley-bottom gravels. Yet village names occasionally suggest that ponds provided the initial attraction: Sledmere took its name from a pond, as did Fimber, a name with such early spellings as Fimmar and Fimmere. The pond survives at Fimber, but there is now only a grassy hollow in 'Capability' Brown's parkland at Sledmere. Other high Wolds villages have long possessed ponds which were probably created artificially, and Anglo-Danish settlers may well have known the technique of making an impervious saucer of mud or clay to hold dew and rainwater. Some Wolds villages had, and still have, two ponds, one for domestic water and one for the use of animals. Many of these ponds have been filled in in recent years, but they are still a prominent part of the village scene at places like Wetwang, Huggate and Fridaythorpe (Plate 26). Ponds are also common in villages alongside the Gypsey Race, as well as on the lower clay-covered parts of the Wolds, where they

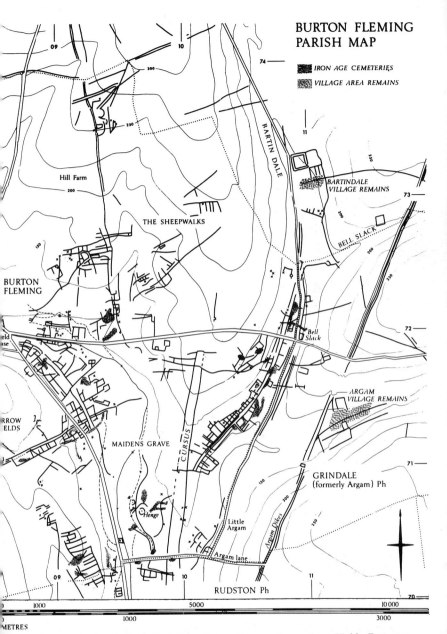

BURTON FLEMING
PARISH MAP

███ *IRON AGE CEMETERIES*
▒▒▒ *VILLAGE AREA REMAINS*

Hill Farm

BARTIN DALE

BARTINDALE
VILLAGE REMAINS

BELL SLACK

THE SHEEPWALKS

BURTON
FLEMING

Bell
Slack

ARGAM
VILLAGE REMAINS

RROW
ELDS

MAIDENS GRAVE

C
U
R
S
U
S

GRINDALE
(formerly Argam) Ph

Henge

Little
Argam

Argam lane

RUDSTON Ph

| 1000 | 5000 | 10 000 |

METRES

| 1000 | 3000 |

Plate 7 Burton Fleming, in the valley of the Gypsey Race on the northern Wolds. By means
of aerial photography it has been possible to reconstruct a dense pattern of fields, settlements
and boundaries, mainly dating from the Iron Age and the Romano-British period. The henge
and cursus (bottom centre) are probably Bronze Age. Argam and Bartindale villages were
depopulated during the Middle Ages.

Plate 8 Danes' Dyke, Flamborough. This massive embankment runs right across Flamborough Head. It is seen here from the seaward side and the trees mark the line of the ditch beyond. The embankment may have been the work of Anglian invaders establishing a foothold on the promontory, but its date has yet to be proved by excavation.

Plate 9 Lynchets at Croom, near Sledmere. This terraced effect was produced by ploughing along the contours of relatively steep slopes on the Wolds. Lynchets probably date from the 'High Middle Ages' of the twelfth and thirteenth centuries, when the open fields were at their greatest extent.

Plate 10 Skipsea Castle. The great motte of Drew de Bevrere's castle was in its heyday surrounded by the waters of one of the many meres of Holderness. The bailey, with its protective ramparts, lay on a ridge of higher ground. The hamlet of Skipsea Brough, in the foreground, was the scene of an unsuccessful attempt at town plantation in the late eleventh century. Ridge-and-furrow preserves the pattern of open-field strips at the top left.

Plate 11 Meaux Abbey. The site of the best-known religious house in the riding, founded about 1150. The outline of the abbey church (centre) is picked out by robber trenches where the foundation stones have been removed. Ridge-and-furrow indicates open-field cultivation all around the precinct, perhaps by the peasants whose small village was removed when the abbey was established.

include such picturesque examples as those at Bishop Burton, Burton Agnes, Swanland and Walkington.

If the siting of villages can usually be explained, it is much more difficult to describe the shape or plan of the early settlements. Alterations during the succeeding thousand years have naturally obscured the original layout, and it is impossible without the aid of archaeology to judge the appearance of an Anglian settlement or to tell whether Angles and Danes laid out their villages differently from one another. The simple wooden or earthen huts probably lay in straggling or huddling groups, together with their church, close to the water supply on which they relied. It is unlikely that the layout of such settlements would survive the growth in population that occurred later in the Dark Ages or in post-Conquest times. Villages were then, as we shall see, laid out anew or expanded far beyond their original bounds. The many East Riding 'street' villages, the less common 'green' villages, and even the large amorphous settlements all tell us little about the villages of the early settlers.

The gradual adoption of Christianity was accompanied by the building of many churches in the riding during the centuries before the Norman Conquest. The earliest churches—'minster' churches from which missionary work was conducted over a wide area—are difficult to identify, though Beverley Minster was presumably one of them. A monastery at Beverley was founded by John, Bishop of York, about A.D. 705, and a nunnery apparently existed not far away at Watton soon after. These early monasteries were no doubt destroyed by the Danes, but a religious community was re-established at Beverley by King Athelstan. Crosses were probably set up at preaching posts within the territories of the minster churches, and some of the fragments of pre-Conquest crosses that survive may indicate such posts; often the stones have been built into the fabric of the churches that were later erected in their stead. Other minster churches may have included Bridlington and Hunmanby, at the eastern end of the Wolds, and Pocklington, Hemingbrough and Howden, in the Vale of York. All of these formerly had huge parishes with numerous dependent townships and chapelries; the medieval parish of Bridlington, for example, stretched from north to south for eight miles and included ten villages, all at one time served from the mother church. From these examples it seems likely that some at least of the minster churches were built at the capital villages of old federal estates.

To the early minster churches many others were later added, often built by local Anglian chiefs. In the years 705–718, for example, churches were consecrated at Bishop Burton and Cherry Burton, both near Beverley, built by Puch and Addi respectively. Most of the village churches in the riding were probably built in the tenth and eleventh centuries, and Domesday Book records churches at about fifty places and priests at half a dozen more; no doubt there were others that went unmentioned. The 'kirk' element in the names of Kirby Grindalythe and Kirby Underdale suggests an early church, but at neither place was a church or priest recorded in 1086. And none was recorded at Wharram le Street, where part of the surviving tower is pre-Conquest in date, or at Aldbrough, where inscription on a mid-eleventh-century sundial tells us that "Ulf ordered the church built for himself and for Gunvor's souls".

There is little other noteworthy Anglo-Scandinavian work to be seen in the churches of the East Riding, though another pre-Conquest tower exists at Skipwith, in the Vale of York. One carved stone that deserves mention is the tall cross shaft, elaborately carved, which now stands inside the church at Nunburnholme. The subject matter of its carving is partly Viking in origin, partly German and partly

Norman, and the stone is of interest in revealing a Norman influence in Yorkshire before the Conquest. At Stillingfleet the ironwork decorating the church door includes an undoubted Viking ship, but though pre-Conquest in style the work probably dates from the twelfth century.

In some cases churches were apparently placed close to objects or sites that were venerated by the indigenous British population or by the early pagan Anglian settlers. The outstanding case of Rudston, where the church stands beside a Bronze Age monolith, has already been mentioned, and at Goodmanham the church stands on a natural knoll which was no doubt the site of the destroyed heathen temple. Fimber church was planted exactly upon a Bronze Age barrow, in the side of which pagan Anglian burials had been placed. We can only guess at the antiquity of the sites on which other churches stand. Fraisthorpe, Kilham and Nafferton are but three examples of churches standing on prominent mounds which may already have attracted earlier monuments.

Boundaries

Around the Anglian and Scandinavian villages, arable fields were brought into cultivation and meadows and pastures were mown and grazed. Beyond these farmlands there were, in most cases, areas of unimproved waste, marsh or woodland. The way in which the farmlands were laid out and the fields cultivated in these early centuries is not clearly understood, but both Angles and Danes probably employed a communal form of husbandry which was later to develop into the fully-fledged open-field system of the Middle Ages. The extent to which the Anglo-Scandinavian field patterns were influenced by earlier, Romano-British, farm boundaries can only be guessed at; it seems likely, however, that the first English settlers sometimes used and extended the small squarish fields laid out by their predecessors, and that the well-known open-field arrangements were only gradually developed during subsequent centuries.

Whatever the detailed layout of farmland may have been, it is certain that by 1066 the English and Scandinavian settlers in the East Riding had made great progress in dividing up the countryside, and in demarcating the estates of neighbouring landlords and the territories of adjoining villages. At the same time, the building of churches was accompanied by the establishment of parishes, usually coextensive with the territory belonging to one or more villages. Thus by the late eleventh century a pattern of townships and parishes had gradually crystallised, and a web of clearly-marked boundaries had been woven around them.

The Anglo-Saxon land charters that exist in large numbers for parts of southern England are unhappily almost unknown in the East Riding. They would doubtless have shown that the boundaries of many of our present parishes had already been worked out by the ninth or tenth centuries, and a tantalising glimpse of the landscape revealed by such documents is given by the single detailed land charter for this county. In A.D. 963, King Edgar granted an estate at Newbald to a man called Gunner, and the boundaries of the estate were described in detail in the king's charter. Newbald lies on the western edge of the Wolds and stretches from the high chalk lands down to the ground at the foot of the escarpment. On the Wolds the tenth-century boundary followed dry valleys, ran along a 'dyke'—probably a prehistoric embankment, and was aligned upon various prehistoric burial mounds; on the lower ground it mostly followed ditches and streams, and at several points ran along the limits of the arable fields. Twice the boundary crossed the 'street'—the old Roman road running north from Brough. From these details there is little doubt that the boundaries of Newbald as we now know them were well-established by 963, and a similar conclusion may be confidently surmised for most East Riding townships.[5]

The features that marked the boundary of Newbald are typical of those used elsewhere. The boundaries of Wolds townships frequently follow prehistoric embankments for long distances, and many stretches of boundary are aligned upon barrows. Between Ruston Parva and Lowthorpe, for example, the boundary runs obliquely up the Wolds slopes towards a barrow known as Fox Hill, and then passes close by it, before continuing down into the valley beyond. Again, on the southern flank of the valley of the Gypsey Race the boundary between Thwing and Burton Fleming is aligned upon Willy Howe; and there are many other barrows on the Wolds which provided guide-lines for Anglian and Scandinavian settlers. Natural features, such as prominent hilltops, often served the same purpose, and in the lower-lying areas of Holderness and the Vale of York streams and ditches were, of course, used for many boundaries.

The use made by boundaries of the old lines of Roman roads suggests that some of those roads were still of practical significance during the later centuries of the Anglian and Scandinavian settlement. As already suggested, the road from Brough to Malton may have guided early Anglian invaders northwards from the Humber; but when townships and parish boundaries were being fixed the line of that road was largely ignored. The same is true of the road from Brough to Stamford Bridge. In marked contrast, extensive use as a boundary was made of one of the east–west roads leading from the vicinity of Bridlington towards

---

[5] There are also land charters for Howden and Patrington, but they are couched in general terms, and detailed comparison with modern boundaries is not possible: see *Early Yorkshire Charters*, i, pp. 12–15 (Howden), 15–18 (Newbald) and 23–7 (Patrington).

York: indeed, for much of its length it was used to separate the parishes that lay on either side. To some extent, failure to utilise certain of the Roman roads may be explained by the fact that villages were often sited close to the roads, so that their territories naturally extended to either side of them. This is true, for example, of Newbald, where the boundary crossed rather than followed the 'street', and of several other villages between Brough and Pocklington. The names of Thorpe le Street and Wharram le Street indicate the continuing prominence of the Roman roads besides which those villages were established.

SELECT BIBLIOGRAPHY

Binns, A. L., *The Viking Century in East Yorkshire* (E.Y.L.H.S. 15) (1963).

Brooks, F. W., *Domesday Book and the East Riding* (E.Y.L.H.S. 21) (1966).

Darby, H. C., and Maxwell, I., *The Domesday Geography of Northern England* (1962).

De Boer, G., 'Eastern Yorkshire: the Geographical Background to Early Settlement', *The Fourth Viking Congress* (1965), pp. 197–210.

Elgee, F. and H. W., *The Archaeology of Yorkshire* (1933).

Faull, Margaret L., 'Roman and Anglian Settlements in Yorkshire', *Northern History*, ix (1974), pp. 1–25.

Jensen, Gillian F., *Scandinavian Settlement Names in Yorkshire* (1972).

Jensen, Gillian F., 'Place-name Research and Northern History', *Northern History*, viii (1973), pp. 1–23.

Meaney, Audrey, *A Gazetteer of Early Anglo-Saxon Burial Sites* (1964).

Myres, J. N. L., and Southern, W. H., *The Anglo-Saxon Cremation Cemetery at Sancton, East Yorkshire* (Hull Museums Publication 218) (1973).

Palmer, J., 'Landforms, Settlement and Drainage in the Vale of York', in *Geography as Human Ecology*, eds. S. R. Eyre and G. R. J. Jones (1966).

Pattison, I. R., 'The Nunburnholme Cross and Anglo-Danish Sculpture in York', *Archaeologia*, civ (1973), pp. 209–34.

Pevsner, N., *Yorkshire: York & the East Riding* (1972).

Rowley, R. T., ed., *Anglo-Saxon Settlement and Landscape* (British Archaeological Reports, 6) (1974).

Smith, A. H., *The Place-names of the East Riding of Yorkshire* (1937).

Swanton, M., 'An Anglian Cemetery at Londesborough', *Y.A.J.*, xli (1964), pp. 262–86.

Versey, H. C., 'The Hydrology of the East Riding of Yorkshire', *Proceedings of the Yorkshire Geological Society*, xxvii (1949).

V.C.H., *Yorkshire*, II (1912) (Anglo-Saxon remains, and Domesday Book).

4. The early medieval landscape

Expansion and colonisation. The replanning of villages.
Domestic buildings, parks and churches

Expansion and colonisation

FOR THE CENTURIES of Anglo-Scandinavian settlement
there is ample indication of the steady reclamation of land
that was taking place around scores of villages and hamlets
in the riding. It is impossible, however, to give any precise
quantifications to that general picture. Domesday Book
tells us that about 2,400 people, most of them no doubt
heads of households, were living in some 440 villages, and
that there were about 1,850 ploughlands available for
cultivation. For some places Domesday fills in details of
woodland and meadow, of water-mills, churches and
fisheries, but all we suspect in a way that is far from com-
prehensive. It was not, of course, the purpose of the
Domesday commissioners to give an accurate topographical
description of the towns and villages that existed in 1086.
But in a general and incomplete way their survey does
give an impression of what had already been achieved and
what remained to be done.

In broad terms the landscape of the late eleventh century
consisted of small groups of huts and farmsteads, each
surrounded by an area of farmland but all separated from
each other by expanses of wasteland, marsh or forest.
Already before the Norman Conquest, the wastes were
being broken up, the marshland diked and drained, and the
timber cleared, and that continual process of reclamation

64

was to go on, with gathering momentum, for some two centuries more. Before the tide of colonisation turned, perhaps about 1300, the growing population of the East Riding had added dozens of new settlements to the map and turned many thousands of acres to profitable use.

To speak of a continuing process of colonisation from pre-Conquest to post-Conquest times is, however, to overlook the serious, if temporary, setback which many districts suffered at the hands of William the Conqueror. Rebellions in Yorkshire led William in the winter of 1069–70 to undertake his well-known 'harrying of the North', during which many villages were wholly or partially emptied of people and much land was laid waste. The Domesday Survey shows that in 1086 sixty-seven East Riding villages were wholly and ninety-three partially wasted: that is to say over a third of the settlements in the riding. Wasting appears from the Survey to have been most severe on the Wolds, less intensive in the Vale of York and in Holderness. It is possible, however, that this evidence is misleading, for it has been suggested that after the harrying many of the surviving inhabitants may have been deliberately moved from the Wolds by lords of the manor down to wasted but inherently more fertile land on the lower ground. Reclamation of the wasted land may thus have already begun by 1086, and for the next fifty years there is much evidence of recovery all over the riding.

It is as well at the outset to emphasise the uncertain nature of some of the evidence for the founding of new settlements after the Conquest. The names of many East Riding hamlets first appear in the written record in the twelfth and thirteenth centuries simply because there are so few documents of an earlier date. Some of those hamlets may in fact have existed before the Conquest but have escaped notice in Domesday Book. Others were indeed new post-Conquest settlements which appeared in the

E

landscape at some time before their first documentary mention. The balance of probability is that many new settlements were founded during these colonising centuries, but there can be no certainty in individual cases.

On the higher parts of the Wolds colonisation from the late eleventh century onwards was largely concerned with the clearing of scrub, heath and the ubiquitous furze, or whins, which abounded on the thin soils that barely covered the chalk. More of the earlier woodland cover no doubt remained to be cleared on the lower, boulder-clay-covered, slopes and below the escarpment to the north and west of the Wolds. The Domesday Survey is strangely silent, however, about woodland in most of these areas, perhaps because the commissioners were concerned only with 'pasturable' woodland and not with that which was economically less valuable. The Survey does nevertheless record notable areas of woodland in the country near Beverley, on the eastern Wold slopes. At Beverley itself, and at such places as Bentley, Etton and Leconfield, appreciable amounts of woodland were indeed mentioned.

Some woodland was to survive throughout the Middle Ages, valuable for its herbage and pannage as well as for its timber. At Cottingham, not far from Beverley, for example, the manor in 1276 included North, South, West and Bentley Woods, and at Settrington, on the northern edge of the Wolds, there were eighty acres of wood in 1305. But much of the early woodland was cleared and added to the arable fields and pastures. This activity may be glimpsed on the lands of North Ferriby Priory, which had estates at the southern end of the Wolds, near the river Humber. In the late twelfth and early thirteenth centuries the priory was given arable land near Hessle Wood and nine acres in Wood Ridding, a name deriving from the Old English 'hryding', a clearing. And by 1262 the priory had been given a third of Hessle Wood itself, with the right to reclaim and enclose it and sow it with corn. It seems likely that several new villages and isolated farmsteads were established during the colonisation of these wooded areas around the Wolds. In the neighbourhood of Hessle, Cottingham and Beverley the twelfth and thirteenth centuries thus saw the appearance of such names as Swanland, 'Svan's wood', Braffords, 'the broad clearing', Eppleworth, 'apple wood', Loatleys, 'the dirty clearing', and Woodhall.

The clearings, or assarts, made on the Wolds were less often described as riddings than as ovenhams, from the Middle English 'ofnam'. In the thirteenth and early four-teenth centuries Bridlington Priory created ovenhams on many of its Wolds estates, at Bempton, Buckton, Fordon, Flotmanby, Marton and Staxton, for example. At Burton Fleming in 1299 the priory had ovenhams in the east and west fields of the township, and the fields were said to extend to the bounds of six neighbouring villages—a clear sign that reclamation and cultivation had been pushed as far as they could go. Burton Fleming was probably typical of many Wolds townships at this time: the arable land, now farmed in several large common fields, dominated the landscape, leaving a relatively small area of waste for common pasture and in some cases, as at Burton, a stretch of meadow land as well.

Burton Fleming's fields lay on the Wold slopes on either side of the valley of the Gypsey Race. On the highest parts of the Wolds, however, the landscape was less completely dominated by arable strips and furlongs. There, the most remote parts of a township may have been left to the rabbit and the sheep. The value of Wolds sheep pastures was indeed such that it was even necessary in some cases to safeguard sheepwalks from encroachment. Ganton, Staxton and Willerby all included high Wolds ground near the northern escarpment, and they illustrate the determined assarting which took place at this period: ploughs were working on the edge of the escarpment, in the steep-sided dry valleys, and alongside the prehistoric embankments which were used to delimit and identify the parcels of arable land. But Bridlington Priory was also given rights of pasture for 500 sheep in Willerby, beyond the arable fields, and Adelard of Willerby, the donor's son, agreed "that he will not plough any land except what was ploughed in the time of his father, nor will he allow that anyone should plough whom he is reasonably able to restrain". The priory was, moreover, always to have access to its sheepfold, whatever land might be ploughed each year. Prior Moor, as that pasture became known, was not broken up until modern farming methods changed the face of the high Wolds.

Colonisation was as actively pursued by lay landlords as by monastic, though the examples already drawn from the cartularies of North Ferriby and Bridlington show the reliance that we often must place upon monastic documents. The monasteries are frequently credited with the establishment of great sheep-runs on their Wolds granges, but Bridlington's record clearly shows that it was much concerned with corn growing, too. Granges like those of Bridlington Priory at Speeton and Burton Fleming, of Malton Priory at Mowthorpe, and of Meaux Abbey at Wharram, Octon and Dalton all shared in the creation of a predominantly arable landscape in which sheep ranged over the cultivated land whenever it was unsown, as well as over the wastes and commons.[1]

Monastic farming on the Wolds rarely involved that depopulation of villages which sometimes marked the establishment of Cistercian monasteries and granges elsewhere in England. The Cistercians required complete solitude, but here, with the help of grants of land from

[1] B. Waites, 'Aspects of Thirteenth and Fourteenth Century Arable Farming on the Yorkshire Wolds', *Y.A.J.*, xlii (1968), pp. 136–42.

benefactors, they found it without the need to empty existing settlements. At Octon, for example, Meaux was able to establish its grange about 1150–60 half a mile from the settlement, and though Octon is now a much shrunken hamlet there is no reason to think that it was depleted by the lay brethren at the grange. It has, indeed, been suggested that soon after its foundation the grange had a consolidated estate quite separate from the fields of the neighbouring villages. Octon Grange eventually comprised 400 acres and more, and another of Meaux's Wolds granges, at Wharram le Street, had as many as 1,300 acres. Earthworks still mark the site of the grange buildings at Octon.

In the Vale of York woodland and especially marsh presented the greatest obstacles to colonisation, though there were marked contrasts from one district to another. Woodland was most widespread in an area stretching from the river Ouse in the west to and a little beyond the river Derwent in the east. It was there that the Domesday commissioners had noticed much more wood than anywhere else in the riding. Thus woodland was valued for its pasture in 1086 at places like Elvington, Osgodby and Skipwith in the area between the two rivers, and at Catton, Howden, Kirkham and Melbourne on the east side of the Derwent. The largest individual entry records woodland two leagues long and two broad which in all probability was centred on Escrick. The country between Ouse and Derwent became during the twelfth century the only royal hunting forest in the East Riding, and it remained under the forest law until 1235.[2] Like other royal forests it was by no means continuously wooded, but the farmlands of the forest villages were often closely hemmed in by woodland and waste.

Some of this woodland survived the medieval clearances. The 260-acre wood at Escrick, for example, that was

[2] J. C. Cox, 'The Forest of Ouse and Derwent', in *Memorials of Old Yorkshire*, ed. T. M. Fallow (1909), pp. 64–76.

mentioned in 1291 was largely intact five centuries later, and the 180-acre wood at Catton, valued for pasture in 1260 though it "bears no fruit", was probably incorporated in the deer park there. Woodland also survived at Langwith, which remained as a 'hay', or forest enclosure, after 1235. In 1270 there were estimated to be 400 oaks in the hay, which contained about 400 acres "in covert" and 100 acres "in plain".

A large part of the wood and scrub in the country between Ouse and Derwent was, however, gradually assarted during the early Middle Ages. A start was made even before 1235, though royal licence was normally required to encroach upon the forest. At Wheldrake, for example, small additions to the original arable nucleus of the village were being made in the later twelfth century, and larger assarts were taken out of South Wood there about 1200.[3] But it was after the removal of the forest law that extensive reclamation began. By 1300 the woods and moors of Wheldrake had been reduced by the taking in of much new arable land, some of it used in common by the inhabitants and some kept in single ownership. It may not have been until the early fourteenth century that the two or three distinct fields normally associated with open-field farming became established at Wheldrake, and even then much of the assarted arable land remained outside the fields and was known as 'forland'. The same situation is to be seen in neighbouring Escrick where, by 1290, there were 450 acres of forland as well as much land in the fields. The elements 'ridding', 'thwaite', 'wood', 'hag' and 'hurst' in the names of so many of the Escrick assarts that were described in 1323 clearly indicate their woodland origin. A different

---

[3] June A. Sheppard's detailed study of this village provides a basis for understanding landscape changes in the area: see 'Wheldrake: Pre-Enclosure Field and Settlement Patterns in an English Township', *Geografiska Annaler*, xlviii, Series B (1966), pp. 59–77.

landscape was thus emerging here from that of the Wolds: the common fields occupied much less of the village territory, individual closes were far more numerous, and the remaining trees and extensive pastures gave this the unmistakable air of a 'bocage' countryside.

The colonisation of the wooded parts of the Vale of York, both in the former forest of Ouse and Derwent and in areas to the east of the Derwent, seems to have been carried out for the most part from existing, pre-Conquest, settlements. There are, nevertheless, some examples of new hamlets with significant names: Woodhall in Hemingbrough, Woodhouses in Sutton upon Derwent, Storthwaite in Melbourne, Blackwood in North Duffield, and Thicket in Thorganby. All these names made their appearance in twelfth- and thirteenth-century documents, though the hamlets probably came into existence even earlier.

The more southerly parts of the Vale of York, towards the Ouse and the Humber, were of a different character. Marsh and carr, only occasionally interrupted by islands of drier ground, stretched almost to the foot of the Wolds. In the extreme south there were also salt-marshes in a broad belt that was frequently inundated by the tidal rivers. Inland were the waterlogged carrs which included the great tract later known as Wallingfen, and everywhere there were streams carrying superabundant fresh water from the Wolds. Diking and draining were here the only means by which reclamation could be extended beyond the limits of the widely-scattered pre-Conquest settlements.

Reclamation of the salt-marshes had been started by Anglian and Scandinavian settlers mainly in the west of the Vale, around Howden and towards Selby, where flooding was less severe. Improvement there continued in the twelfth century, and Newhay in Hemingbrough, close by the river Ouse, typifies the kind of 'new enclosure' that was being created. It may have been about this time that a change in the course of the Ouse left Newhay on the East Riding side of the river.[4] The old course was slow to run completely dry and centuries later it was still known as 'Old Ways', but the movement of the Ouse left Hemingbrough and Cliffe no longer riverside villages.

Further east the raising of substantial river banks to exclude the tidal waters may have been longer delayed. There had, it is true, been modest beginnings before the Conquest, for places like Faxfleet and Broomfleet have names deriving from Scandinavian personal names; Faxi and Brungar must already in the tenth century have settled beside their 'fleets'—stretches of the Humber itself or perhaps streams draining into it. River banks begin to be mentioned in the twelfth century and the 'fleet' villages soon appear in documents, perhaps indicating a more systematic reclamation of the marshes as the population increased. The result of embanking is well illustrated by an estate at Broomfleet belonging to St Leonards' Hospital, York, which in 1287 included 358 acres of 'lucrative' arable and sixty-eight acres of 'fresh' pasture, while beyond the banks there were still thirty-two acres of salt pasture.[5]

Reclamation may have been assisted in the twelfth century by a gradual fall in the relative sea-level, but it seems that by the mid thirteenth century the level was slowly rising again. The banks must have needed constant attention, and the appointment from about 1300 onwards of commissioners to survey the river banks shows increasing concern with the problem of drainage. In places the present-day river banks may lie on approximately the same line as those early defences, but at Broomfleet, where modern reclamation has been extensive, the medieval banks have been left far inland where stretches of them can still be seen (Fig. 16).

[4] It was only in 1883, however, that Newhay was transferred to the East Riding for administrative purposes.
[5] Eleanor M. Reader, *Broomfleet and Faxfleet* (1972).

Banks were also needed on the north side of the newly-reclaimed marshes to keep out drainage water from the inland parts of the Vale. These banks have long since become obsolete, but some of the winding lanes of north Howdenshire may indicate their courses. Through the reclaimed tracts dikes were dug to drain into the Ouse and Humber, and many of the straight modern dikes doubtless follow ancient lines. In all of this work the Abbot of Selby and the Bishop of Durham, the latter as lord of Howdenshire, were among the busiest landlords.

Three examples of the drainage dikes were those constructed before 1200 by the lords of the manors of Blacktoft, Thornton Land and Faxfleet, beside the Ouse. Hansardam was the work of Gilbert Hansard, Thornton Dam that of Thornton Abbey, and Temple Dam that of the Knights Templar. A host of small hamlets, like Gowthorpe, Bellasize, Greenoak and Bennetland, sprang up alongside these main dikes and beside the cross dikes which ran between them, and the modern pattern of lanes linking the villages partly preserves the medieval drainage pattern. The dikes also began to improve the condition of the inland carrs, and a new straight course for the old Foulney stream was soon constructed and named Langdike. The changing landscape of areas bordering the Foulney is shown by twelfth- and thirteenth-century documents relating to Holme upon Spalding Moor. Besides surviving marsh and woodland, they speak of dikes and ditches, of assarts and enclosures, and of the hamlets of Bursea and Hasholme, already founded among the newly-won grounds.

Reclamation of marshes and carrs was also a feature of the Vale of Pickering, for all the villages lying beneath the chalk escarpment had low-lying land as well as wold ground. Drainage channels were dug by the thirteenth century, like Newdike and Redike in Flotmanby, and marsh was improved for meadow, like New Ing in Staxton, New

Meadow in Potter Brompton, and meadow beside the river
Derwent in Willerby and Ganton. Bridlington Priory was
an active reclaimer in these villages, but lay landlords also
took their part; in Flotmanby, for example, the priory and
Fulk Constable separated their pasture and marsh in 1278
so that both could enclose their shares. Extensive earthworks mark the site of Bridlington's grange at Willerby,
close to the parish church and the few remaining houses of
the village; the shrinkage of Willerby and the expansion of
its hamlet of Staxton may well reflect the presence of the
grange.

The face of Holderness had something in common with
that of the Vale of York: numerous meres lying on the
undulating surface of the boulder clay, countless streams,
extensive carrs bordering the Hull valley, and a salt-marsh
tract alongside the Humber. Drainage was the major task
facing the medieval colonists. And yet more had been
achieved here before the Conquest than in the Vale of York,
especially in the boulder-clay areas where villages and
arable fields had reduced the watery aspect of the landscape.
The low-lying tracts around those fields were gradually
reclaimed, but some of the meres and their surrounding
reed beds were slow to yield and were long of value only for
their fisheries. In the mid thirteenth century Meaux Abbey
was in dispute over such fisheries at Hornsea and Wassand,
and Hornsea Mere survives today as the largest expanse of
inland water in the riding. The other meres were in due
course drained. There was still a fishery called Pidsea in
1285, but only a village name commemorates it now. The
'marr' at Sutton, an eel-pond at Brandesburton, the fishery
of 'Eumerske' at Burstwick, meres at Skipsea, Lambwath,
Withernsea and elsewhere—all these have gone, though the
dates of their final drainage are uncertain.[6]

[6] June A. Sheppard, 'The Medieval Meres of Holderness', *I.B.G. Trans.*,
xxiii (1957), pp. 75–86.

By the end of the thirteenth century there were many villages in Holderness with extensive open arable fields of a conventional kind; but references to areas of 'forland', to enclosed meadows and carrs, and to marshy closes all remind us of the forms which reclamation was taking in the forest of Ouse and Derwent. The landscape of Holderness was clearly full of variety. There were, too, some small remnants of woodland, at Swine, Bewholme, Burton Constable, Routh and elsewhere.

Fraisthorpe, a few miles south of Bridlington, was typical of those Holderness villages where the open fields never came to dominate the landscape. In the thirteenth century the priors of Bridlington, as lords of the manor, kept a sheepfold at Fraisthorpe and had much meadow land and numerous closes there. Marshy ground in the township was gradually drained, and in 1307 the prior had the permission of the lord of a neighbouring manor to enclose the marsh of the township with a fosse, or dike. Along the southern boundary of Fraisthorpe is the Earl's Dike, named after the Earls of Aumale, lords of Holderness, and it too was mentioned in the thirteenth century. Another religious house prominent in colonising the plain was Meaux Abbey. Several of the Meaux granges had extensive estates, like the 400 acres taken in at Moor Grange from the waste ground "outside the ditches of the town" (of Beeford). The moated site of the grange survives at Moor and at other sites like Croo, near Beeford, and Dringhoe.

Clearly not all the newly-colonised land was being added to the territories of the older villages. As well as the monastic granges there were many new hamlets which gave the Holderness landscape a dimension largely absent from the Wolds. Some of the new names bear the marks of colonising settlement, like Woodhouse in North Skirlaugh, Woodhall in Ellerby, Newsome near Winestead, and Newland in Benningholme. And Ruddens in Withernwick recalls the assarts already noted in other parts of the riding. Between the old villages and new hamlets, and around the fields, marshes and meres, there was also developing a network of winding lanes that provides another contrast to the Wolds, with its more straightforward road pattern.

Further west, between the Holderness claylands and the Wolds, the Hull valley presented even greater problems of drainage. The southern part of the valley was occupied by marshland that was frequently flooded by tidal waters, and further up the valley the marshes and carrs were regularly turned into freshwater swamps. These wet grounds had been used to some degree, often seasonally, before the Conquest, and Anglian and Scandinavian hamlets had been planted on some of the islands of drier land and along the margins of the valley. The attack upon the swamps in the twelfth and thirteenth centuries was two-fold: banks were built to keep out the tides, and dikes were dug to remove land-water into the river.

Sea-banks were raised alongside both the Humber and the Hull. Reclamation by this means, as in the Vale of York, may at first have been facilitated by the relative lowering of the sea-level, but after about 1200 that situation was reversed. By the mid thirteenth century there was serious flooding around Sutton and Drypool, and the waters are said to have reached as far as Cottingham. Reclamation nevertheless made it possible for new settlements to be established in the lower Hull valley, among them Newland, Sculcoates and Stoneferry; and Wyke—the forerunner of Kingston upon Hull—was also founded in the twelfth century. By 1282 the manor of Cottingham included a hamlet on the banks of the Hull as well as Newland, and ings, pastures and sheep-cotes had replaced much of the former marshland in the parish.

The Abbot of Meaux was prominent among the improving landowners higher up the river Hull, as well as around its confluence with the Humber, for the monastery itself and many of its lands lay in the valley. There were Meaux granges at Wawne, Heigholme near Leven, Skerne, Cranswick and elsewhere, and in several cases their sites are still marked by moats and mounds. Dikes were cut by the monks to serve as canals as well as for drainage. Thus Eschedike had been cut by the later twelfth century, and Monkdike, Skernedike and Forthdike were all mentioned in the early thirteenth. This early drainage pattern has been overlaid by many other, more recent, improvements, but the names and to some extent the lines of the Meaux dikes survive in the present landscape.

Other drainage work in the Hull valley was carried out by Bridlington Priory, which had meadows and marshes near the river at Brandesburton. The priory made a fosse around a marsh called Witheland, for example, and a grant to the priory significantly spoke of "all the marsh and all the firm ground" beside the river and between two dikes. Farms called Hempholme and Hallytreeholme perpetuate the names of two of the priory's meadows, and Mickley and Weedland Dikes those of two of the fosses. Also part of the early medieval landscape are the winding lanes which still follow the ridges of slightly higher ground around Heigholme and Hempholme.

Along the southern margin of Holderness, as in the lower Hull valley, sea-banks were raised to keep out the waters of the Humber. Here, however, both the gains of the twelfth and earlier thirteenth centuries and the losses that began around 1250 were more dramatic. A belt of land up to three miles wide was reclaimed by the embanking of the silts that accumulated along the shore of the Humber, and several new settlements were established. One of these villages, Tharlesthorpe, was certainly in existence by 1086 and others, like Frismersk, Penisthorpe and Orwithfleet, were probably founded about the same time, though not mentioned in documents until later. Some of the reclaimed land was given to Meaux Abbey, and monastic granges were built like those at Saltaugh, Keyingham and Tharlesthorpe. Another of these siltland farms was Little Humber, belonging to the Earls of Aumale, and Bridlington Priory had property here, too.

At Ottringham the canons of Bridlington had closes of arable land called Aselcroft and Newcroft, both enclosed by fosses and the latter lying beside 'Sedyk'—the Humber bank itself. Other parts of the marsh there were protected by 'Mersk Newland Dik', 'Sumergangdik', and various other drainage channels. As in the south of the Vale of York, a complex pattern of dikes and banks marked out the Humberside landscape.

The floods which hit the lower Hull valley in the mid thirteenth century also began the protracted erosion of nearly all the newly-won land in south Holderness. Much of the land at Tharlesthorpe grange and Orwithfleet was lost in the 1250s, and Meaux was forced to rebuild Saltaugh grange further inland. Thenceforth old sea-banks were periodically heightened and new ones made further inland, but by the end of the fourteenth century the new villages, the granges, and hundreds of acres of land had gone. A whole new landscape was lost.[7]

Parallel changes took place at Spurn Head, at the seaward extremity of Holderness. An earlier sand spit, which had been formed during the two centuries before 1086, was probably eroded by the sea soon afterwards. A new spit was subsequently built up further to the west, but by the late fourteenth century that too had been lost and the cycle was beginning once again.[8] As Spurn Head was pushed westwards, so too was the eastern coastline of Holderness, and

[7] J. R. Boyle, *The Lost Towns of the Humber* (1889).

[8] G. De Boer, 'Spurn Head: its Evolution and History', *I.B.G. Trans.*, xxxiv (1964), pp. 71–87.

erosion has proceeded steadily there since at least the thirteenth century. A strip of land perhaps a mile wide and a score of villages have been lost.[9] As will be seen later, another new landscape was eventually to be created along the Humber bank, but the seaward cliffs of Holderness have continued to recede.

The replanning of villages

The increase of population during the centuries of colonisation naturally led to the growth of most pre-Conquest villages. That growth was often not of a haphazard kind but rather took the form of a deliberate replanning of older settlements. It seems natural to suppose that the huddles of cottages established by Anglians or Danes would in due course be replaced by more carefully laid out villages. The 'green' villages so common in Durham and other parts of England and the 'street' villages which are so characteristic of the East Riding are probably two of the more obvious forms which replanning took. Such formal changes were not, of course, universal and other villages seem to have expanded more or less haphazardly.

The period when the replanning of a village took place is usually hard to establish. It has been argued, from the evidence of maps and other documents, that the street village of Wheldrake, in the Vale of York, may have been laid out in the tenth or earlier eleventh century, or alternatively very soon after the Conquest. William's harrying in 1069–70 could have provided the opportunity for new Norman lords to make such changes in the latter years of the eleventh century.

In other cases replanning is more likely to have occurred in the twelfth or thirteenth century, and Wharram Percy provides an example. The Anglian settlement probably lay

[9] T. Sheppard, *The Lost Towns of the Yorkshire Coast* (1912).

in the bottom of the deep Wolds valley where the church still stands and where springs fed a stream supplying the village with water. On either side of the valley, at the top of the slope, is a bank and ditch which may have marked the boundary of the village. In the twelfth century a group of houses was built on the shoulder of the valley above the church, and beyond the boundary bank, where there was more space than in the confined valley bottom. Thorough excavation of part of this area has revealed a succession of peasant houses dating from the twelfth to the fifteenth centuries, but none earlier. A short distance beyond this group of houses stood the twelfth-century manor-house. Further expansion took place in the thirteenth century, when a row of tofts and crofts was laid out beyond the earlier manor-house, and again excavation has revealed a series of houses ending in the late fifteenth century shortly before Wharram Percy was depopulated. A new manor-house was also built, standing as before just beyond the row of peasant houses. In addition to these large-scale changes in the layout of the village there were also detailed changes in the position of the houses and even in the boundaries of the tofts. The site of the twelfth-century manor-house provides a good illustration of these points. In the thirteenth century it was occupied by two houses in separate tofts, both houses side-on to the street but one set back from it; then in the fourteenth century a house lying obliquely to the street occupied a single toft; and in the fifteenth the house was rebuilt end-on to the street.

A differing sequence of changes has been revealed by excavations at Wawne, in the Hull valley. There, an informally-arranged group of houses of the twelfth to fourteenth centuries was replaced in the fifteenth century by a completely new and regular 'street' layout. By the seventeenth century, however, the houses along the street had been replaced by two farmsteads, but by then the village was perhaps concentrated on its modern site, a short distance to the north.[10]

Two stages of replanning have been suggested for Wharram Percy, and in many other cases it is likely that the replanned village was subsequently enlarged by the addition of further regular rows of houses. A street village like Wheldrake or Barmby on the Marsh, Wetwang or Walkington, North Frodingham or Beeford may have begun as a single row of houses, later enlarged to the familiar two rows, and perhaps further enlarged by the lengthening of the rows.[11] Occasionally a one-row village was not changed for centuries. The houses of Great Kelk, for example, almost all lie on one side of the village street, hence the local saying that it is impossible to pass through the village, only along it. The large village of North Frodingham, closely built up for three-quarters of a mile, was perhaps more than once enlarged. Here there is also the intriguing possibility that the Anglian village lay near the now isolated church by the river Hull. It is possible that Frodingham was founded beside a bridge over the river, which incidentally gave its name to Brigham on the opposite bank, and that it was later moved to a drier situation.

Isolated churches, like that at Frodingham, are unusual in the East Riding, but a similar village migration is suggested by the church at Westow, standing alone among the fields half a mile from the village. Again, at Holme upon Spalding Moor we must suspect that the village has moved down from its isolated hill-top church. The antiquity of the site on Holme Hill is undoubted, for the church contains Norman masonry and a recently-discovered pre-Conquest carved stone. Other villages may have been replanned at a

---

[10] For Wharram Percy and Wawne see J. G. Hurst, 'The Changing Medieval Village in England', in *Man, Settlement and Urbanism*, ed. P. J. Ucko, Ruth Tringham and G. W. Dimbleby (1972), pp. 531–40.

[11] June A. Sheppard, 'Metrological Analysis of Regular Village Plans in Yorkshire', *A.H.R.*, xxii (part II) (1974), pp. 118–35.

shorter but still significant distance from their churches: were Burythorpe and Walkington, for example, moved a few hundred yards, perhaps to the streams and ponds that supplied their water? Such villages might repay the kind of investigation which has revealed Anglo-Saxon pottery in the ploughed fields around isolated churches in Norfolk, and only later pottery near the new settlement sites.

The date and the form of village replanning and growth may often have been influenced by special local circumstances. One possible example is provided by the hamlet of Cliffe, in Hemingbrough parish. Both were riverside settlements, founded on small islands of high ground beside the Ouse, and Cliffe was named from the steep slope down to the river bank. We have already seen that a change in the course of the Ouse deprived these villages of the benefits of a riverside location. Hemingbrough subsequently remained a compact village but Cliffe, with farmland and commons stretching well away from the river, later extended so far along its new main street that it was sometimes called 'Long Cliffe'.

Simple or modified street villages are to be seen in all parts of the riding. The arrangement of houses around a village green is, in contrast, rare, being most clearly represented by Cranswick, Full Sutton and Gembling. The distinction between a narrow green and a wide street is, however, not easily drawn. Harlthorpe and Allerthorpe are both street villages which had wide green verges, though at Harlthorpe they were divided into gardens when the township was enclosed in 1838. At other places, such as Fangfoss, greens have been reduced in size by encroachment for houses and gardens. Small greens also form part of a more complicated village layout at such places as Bishop Burton and North Newbald.

Some greens and other open spaces in villages may have arisen as market-places and fairgrounds. Dozens of East

Riding villages acquired markets and fairs in the thirteenth and fourteenth centuries as lords of the manor, with an eye to tolls, sought to profit from the growing trade of the time. Some markets became established by custom, many more were granted by royal charter. In the majority of cases little more is heard of them, but some prospered. The market and fairs at Hunmanby, for example, which were set up without a charter, lasted into the present century, and the medieval market cross still stands in a triangular open space known as Cross Hill, close to the main village street and the church. Of special interest are those villages whose layout may have been changed to accommodate fairs or a market, and possible examples in the riding include South Cave, Kilham and North Duffield.

It is probable that the early village at South Cave lay near the church, and that the place grew after the acquisition of a market in the twelfth century and the granting of markets and fairs in 1291 and 1314. The market eventually came to be held on the main road half a mile to the east, the former Roman road from Brough to York (Fig. 3). The market survived into modern times and a market hall still stands on the stretch of the main road called Market Place. At Kilham a market and fairs were granted in 1227 and stalls are known in later centuries to have been set up in the main village street, near the church. The sale of animals, however, especially at the fairs, may have taken place on ground that was called the Greens in the eighteenth century. Running up to the Greens is part of the village known as West End: it is separate from the main street and less closely built up, with many earthworks and empty crofts between the surviving houses. West End may have been a post-1227 extension of Kilham which eventually dwindled when the market and fairs declined around 1800. The Greens has long since been enclosed and in part built upon, but Green Lane still joins the two parts of the village. North Duffield is

83

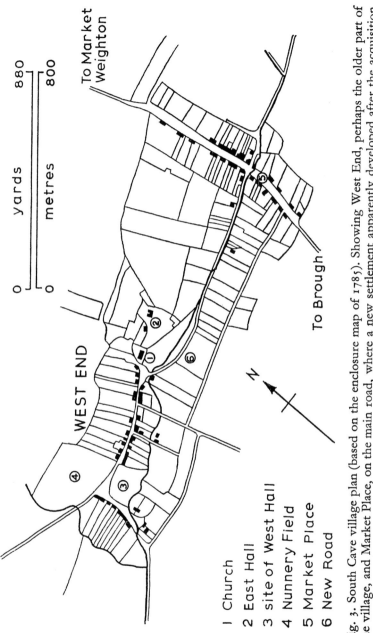

WEST END

To Market Weighton

To Brough

N

yards
metres

0   800
0   880

1 Church
2 East Hall
3 site of West Hall
4 Nunnery Field
5 Market Place
6 New Road

Fig. 3. South Cave village plan (based on the enclosure map of 1785). Showing West End, perhaps the older part of the village, and Market Place, on the main road, where a new settlement apparently developed after the acquisition of markets and fairs.

another village of two distinct parts—a typical street and a triangular green with a large pond. Here again the green and the house sites around it may have originated after the grant of market and fairs in the thirteenth century, and this is another market which continued long after the Middle Ages.

The expansion of trade and the development of markets encouraged individual efforts to improve communications during these centuries. But small-scale and piecemeal improvements made no radical difference to the poor roads which wound their way between towns and villages. Attempts were made early in the fourteenth century to construct new roads towards the port of Kingston upon Hull, but it is not clear how far they succeeded. Perhaps of more significance for the landscape was the construction of bridges, for it was during this period that many of them made their appearance. The Hull and the Derwent alone among East Riding rivers called for bridges of any size. The Hull was bridged at Tickton, near Beverley, by the mid thirteenth century and the Derwent at Buttercrambe by 1282, at Elvington by 1396, at Kexby in the 1420s, and at Stamford Bridge.

The Derwent crossing at Stamford Bridge has long influenced the pattern of roads and settlement near by. There is no evidence to show whether the Romans had a bridge there or relied on the natural ford provided by an outcrop of sandstone. By 1066, however, there was a narrow wooden bridge which played a part in the battle in which King Harold defeated a Norse army before marching to his death at Hastings. It perhaps stood downstream from the ford at the point where a more substantial timber and stone bridge was built, first mentioned in the late thirteenth century. The latter bridge survived until 1727, when a new one was built still further downstream. The movement of the river crossing necessitated the realignment of the approach roads, and the street pattern of Stamford Bridge still preserves the curious double bends which mark both the medieval and the eighteenth-century improvements (Plate 17).[12]

The movement of the crossing at Stamford Bridge away from the ford may have followed the building of a water-mill, for the creation of a head of water to drive a mill would have deepened the river upstream. The medieval bridge, and perhaps its Anglian predecessor too, were also positioned to avoid the pool that was formed below the mill. There was probably already a mill there by 1086, mentioned in Domesday Book under Catton, the manor in which Stamford Bridge lay. In 1258-9 there were said to be seven 'mills' on the pond—perhaps seven pairs of grindstones in one or two buildings. Water-mills, with their dams and races, became common features of the landscape during the twelfth and thirteenth centuries, and many of the early sites are easily recognised today, for once a head of water had been created the mill itself was constantly rebuilt in the same position. Even if a mill no longer exists there may be traces of the site, like the earthworks beside the stream between Great and Little Givendale.

Windmills were being built in these centuries, too, and that mentioned at Weedley, near South Cave, in 1185 is the earliest yet known in England. These were post mills, and excavation has shown that foundation timbers set cross-wise in the ground helped to support the main post. Some of the mills have left their mark on the landscape in the circular mounds which covered the foundations, as at Thorganby and Kexby. In other cases earth was heaped over the timbers to form an embankment cross, but though many of these were recorded in the nineteenth century few

[12] H. G. Ramm, 'The Derwent Crossing at Stamford Bridge', *Y.A.J.*, xli (1965), pp. 368–76.

still survive.[13] One was ploughed out in recent years close to the site of the deserted village of Swaythorpe, near Kilham.

Domestic buildings, parks and churches

Few castles of any size were built in the East Riding after the Conquest to control the estates of the king's barons or those of their under-tenants. No grand ruins survive to compare with those that grace the landscape of the other ridings, and the most impressive remains are the earthworks at Skipsea, in Holderness (Plate 10). Here the massive motte of Drew de Bevrere's castle rises nearly fifty feet from the level fields, just as it once rose abruptly from the waters of one of the Holderness meres. A causeway linked the motte with a ridge of rising ground, where high banks still surround the eight-acre bailey. Henry III ordered the destruction of the castle in 1221 after its owner's rebellion, and it was soon abandoned. Only a small fragment of masonry is left, but seen across the waterlogged fields through the mists of a winter's day the motte at Skipsea still makes a lasting impression.

Among the smaller castles were several built on manors that were held in 1086 by Niel Fossard. One stood on a spur below the main Wolds escarpment at Mount Ferrant, near Birdsall, where its banks and ditches are still to be seen (Plate 2). The castle was destroyed by the Earl of Aumale about 1150 to punish the infidelity of William Fossard and its timber was given to construct the first buildings at Meaux Abbey. Two small motte-and-bailey castles, the mottes thirteen or fourteen feet high, stood at the Fossard manors of Lockington, on the eastern slopes of the Wolds, and Aughton, beside the river Derwent (Plate 12). The

[13] J. R. Earnshaw, 'The Site of a Medieval Post Mill and Prehistoric Site at Bridlington', *Y.A.J.*, xlv (1973), pp. 19–40.

remains of other mottes can still be seen at Hunmanby, raised by the Gant family, at Leppington, and at Great Driffield.

The fortified manor-houses of these centuries were more numerous, and they were usually surrounded by moats, though whether for reasons of defence, drainage or amenity it is hard to say. The so-called Baynard Castle at Cottingham was one of the finer examples. Already in 1282 the house was "well constructed with a double ditch enclosed by a wall", and in 1327 the king gave licence for it to be strengthened and crenellated. Parts of the ditches and the high mound within are still prominent among the encroaching suburban houses. At Leconfield, too, a large moat still surrounds the site of the manor-house or 'castle' of the Percies, for which licence to fortify was granted in 1308.

In some cases there is reason to think that manor-houses were moved to new and less cramped sites during the Middle Ages, as we have seen happening at Wharram Percy, and occasionally there are signs that a moated house replaced an earlier castle. At Aughton, for example, the moat overlaps the site of the former bailey (Plate 12). Something similar may have happened at Bilton and Paull Holme, to the east of Hull. At Leconfield the manor-house was possibly moved from Hall Field, close to the village, to a more distant site, and ridge-and-furrow still lapping around the sides of the moat suggests that the house was replanted in the open fields. Other early manor-houses and their gardens, like those mentioned at Burton Constable in 1294, have probably been buried beneath their grander successors of later centuries.

Moated sites are still common in the landscape of all the lowland parts of the riding, where they were easily supplied with water, less so on the Wolds. Well over a hundred have recently been listed and others could certainly be added

Plate 12   Aughton. The church stands at the end of the village, on the edge of the flood plain of the river Derwent. On the right in this view is the motte of a small castle, and on the left the moat surrounding the site of the manor-house of the Aske family, well known for their part in the Pilgrimage of Grace in 1536.

Plate 13   Little Givendale. An aerial view of the site of the deserted village. Several house-sites are clearly visible. There is some evidence that abandonment took place during the economic contraction of the fifteenth century. A flight of lynchets, not visible in this picture, lies on the steep valley side to the right.

Plate 14 Argam. The earthworks of the deserted village site are clearly picked out by the low sun. Individual house-sites can be identified along and behind the main street. The prominent rectangular enclosure may have been an animal pound. By 1632 only a shepherd lived at Argam, and the church had been demolished. Depopulation for sheep farming is a possible explanation here.

Plate 15 Garton on the Wolds. An essentially simple Norman church consisting of chancel, nave and west tower. Much of the building, including the tower, is original work of the twelfth century, but other details are from a restoration—still in the Norman style—for Sir Tatton Sykes in 1856–7. Inside, the walls and woodwork are adorned with a riot of Victorian painting.

te 16 Cottingham. One of the st grand of the village churches the riding. The nave (not seen this view) is in the Decorated le of the early fourteenth cen- y; the chancel was built in the quarter of the century, fol- ved by the transepts, and in the eenth century by the tower.

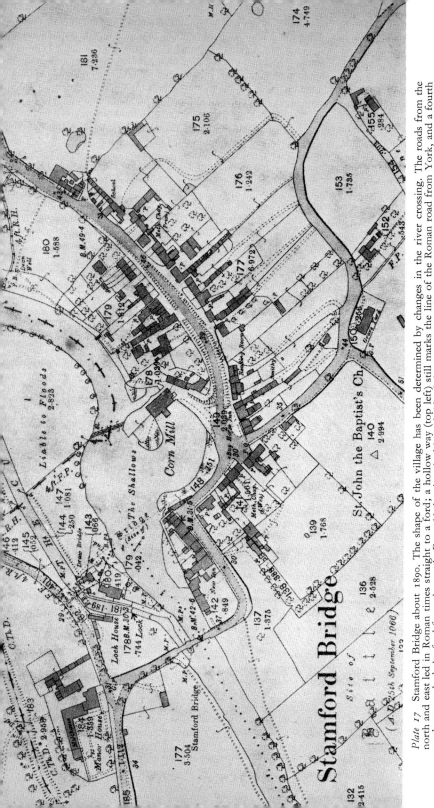

Plate 17 Stamford Bridge about 1890. The shape of the village has been determined by changes in the river crossing. The roads from the north and east led in Roman times straight to a ford; a hollow way (top left) still marks the line of the Roman road from York, and a fourth road approached the ford from the south. By 1066 the river had been bridged downstream, perhaps at the point where a later medieval bridge stood, the site of which is shown on the map. The first water-mill on the site may have caused the crossing to be moved from the ford. The mill

(Fig. 4).[14] Most often, it is thought, they date from the late twelfth, thirteenth and early fourteenth centuries. Many, in or close to villages, were certainly the sites of manor-houses. Some, more remote, apparently surrounded the houses built by colonists who reclaimed the new lands and for whom moats were probably fashionable 'status symbols'. Such no doubt were the still existing isolated moated farms called Barnhill, near Howden in the Vale of York, Barfhill, at Lockington in the Hull valley, and Old Little Humber, beside the siltlands in south Holderness. As we have seen, other moats were dug at monastic granges and farms. Two fine moats of this kind survive at Lingcroft, near Naburn, and at St Loy's, near Sutton upon Derwent, both of which were farms belonging to Warter Priory. At Lingcroft the moat is still wet but that at St Loy's, like so many others, is silted and grass-grown.

Another distinctive feature of the seigneurial landscape in most parts of the riding was the deer park, sometimes adjoining the manor-house but often at a little distance from it. Landlords great and small were attracted by the pleasure and utility of the chase, and dozens of small parks were created. Usually they were surrounded by a park pale, consisting of a ditch and a bank topped by a fence. Baldwin Wake's park at Cottingham, "well enclosed" and four leagues around in 1282, may have been one of the larger examples. So may Tottelay Park at Burstwick, into which the king took ninety acres in 1296 and which has left its mark on the present-day countryside in Totleys Farm. In 1260, before the manor passed to the Crown, the Earl of Aumale already had two other small parks at Burstwick, and the names North Park and South Park still show where they lay. Altogether, at least thirty medieval parks are known from documentary evidence.

[14] Based on the map and gazetteer in H. E. Jean Le Patourel, *The Moated Sites of Yorkshire*, Society for Medieval Archaeology, Monograph 5 (1973).

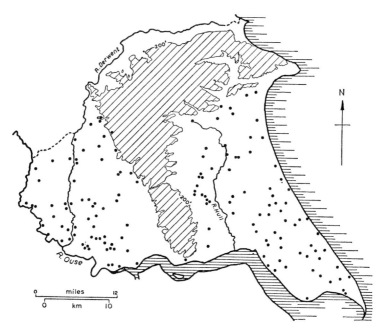

Fig. 4. Moated sites in the East Riding. Most of the moats surrounded manor-houses and substantial farmsteads, and the majority of them probably date from the twelfth, thirteenth and early fourteenth centuries.

90

In the field the signs of parks are now usually slight. At Catton, in the Vale of York, there are traces of the pale of the Percy family's park, which in the sixteenth century was surveyed at 350 acres. The park was first explicitly mentioned in 1352, but it was apparently made in the previous century when the villagers of neighbouring Wilberfoss agreed to give up their right of common in Richard de Percy's wood. During a later dispute the Percies recalled that Richard had in return allowed the park pale to run an inconvenient twisting course so as not to disturb the arable lands that had been reclaimed from the woodland. Modern field boundaries, and the parish boundary too, still follow that same sinuous course (Fig. 5). There are also probable traces of a park pale at Etton, where the lord of the manor made a deer park in the thirteenth century. Contemporary descriptions of its boundaries mention Park Dike and identify adjoining grounds as the fields of Lockington, Etton Moor, the Templars' wood, and the fields of Belaugh, this last being a monastic grange in Lockington parish. Stretches of a bank and ditch can still be seen in the eastern part of Etton, where the documentary evidence clearly locates the park.

The one prominent park pale in the riding is at Bishop Burton. The high bank and deep ditch, together called the Reins, run for about a mile around part of the modern park, which is now the home of an agricultural college. In all probability there has been a park there since the thirteenth century, when it belonged to the Archbishop of York as lord of the manor. Seventeenth-century material has been found in the ditch and so the pale is clearly very old, perhaps as old as the park itself.

At least some of the parks contained hunting lodges, perhaps moated or standing on artificial mounds. This may be the explanation of a small motte at Rise, situated in the park that was mentioned in 1304. A moated site lies in North

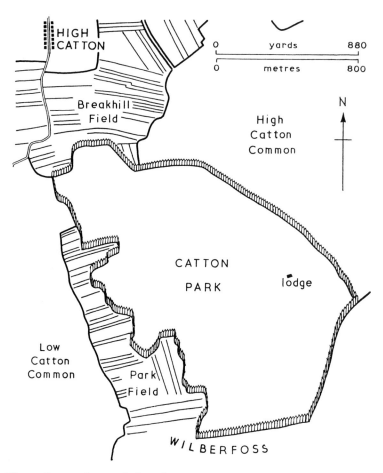

Fig. 5. Catton deer park (based on maps of 1616 and later, at Petworth House, Sussex). The irregular boundary of the park on the west was said to result from an agreement between the lord of the manor and his tenants whereby their land in Park Field was not encroached upon.

Park at Burstwick and another at Escrick near the park made by the Abbot of St Mary's, York, about 1276. A farm called Langwith Lodge, in the former Hay of Langwith, still has the remains of a moat beside it. Other mounds may have served simply as look-out points in connection with hunting and fowling. This is at least a possible explanation of the so-called 'Giants' Hills' at North Duffield and Thorganby, close to the river Derwent, and of another mound of the same name at Swine, in the Hull valley. A mound beside the waters of Hornsea Mere could have been intended for a similar purpose.

If many moated sites of manor-houses survive, together with traces of their deer parks, there is little to be seen of the houses themselves. Even the striking undercroft of Burton Agnes manor-house, built about 1175, is mostly encased in later brickwork. The vaulted undercroft, with its sturdy piers and carved water-leaf capitals, is a fine example of the domestic buildings of the period. A similar if plainer undercroft of the same period was uncovered during excavation of the manor-house at the deserted village of Wharram Percy, and substantial twelfth- and thirteenth-century buildings have been excavated at the sites of Weaverthorpe and Sherburn manors. For the rest we must rely on documentary descriptions, such as those of the great royal manor-house at Burstwick, in Holderness, with its two chapels and many halls and chambers. The homes of lesser landowners and peasants are also, of course, known only from excavations, but the sequence of houses found at Wharram Percy and elsewhere gives some impression of the changes that were taking place during these centuries. The twelfth- and thirteenth-century houses at Wharram had no more than a slight timber framework resting on posts and sleepers set directly into the ground, but from the late thirteenth century onwards they had substantial walls built of chalk to full height. In the fifteenth century, however, some houses had timber walls resting upon narrow chalk foundations. The earliest houses were small and squarish, perhaps with only a single room, but from the fourteenth century they began to be replaced by typical long-houses, with opposing doorways and a central cross passage dividing the living room from the byre.

It has already been shown that a number of religious houses, some of them situated outside the riding, played a significant part in the development of the landscape by their agricultural activities. Some of the monasteries made a more immediate impact upon their surroundings, for their buildings were extensive and their churches were the grandest edifices in the East Riding during these centuries. In the cases of St John's College at Beverley and the Augustinian priory at Bridlington they clearly had a great influence on the economic and social life of the towns in which they stood. At Beverley the pre-Conquest buildings were doubtless embellished by the Normans, but it was the new church of the thirteenth and fourteenth centuries which was of such outstanding size and beauty. No other monastic church could rival Beverley Minster, though Bridlington Priory, founded in the early twelfth century, nevertheless possessed a magnificent church, of which the nave survives. Remaining fragments of a cloister arcade make it clear, moreover, that the thirteenth-century church replaced a fine Norman building. Of the other small towns only Howden benefited from the presence of a religious house: the splendid church there was rebuilt in the half century after it was made collegiate in 1267.

In the countryside the most wealthy of the monasteries were the Cistercian abbey at Meaux and the double house of Gilbertine nuns and canons at Watton, both in the Hull valley and both founded about 1150. The building programme of the thirteenth and early fourteenth centuries at Meaux is well chronicled, but only moats and earthworks are visible now to show where the church, cloisters and various conventual buildings stood (Plate 11). Some fourteenth-century work survives at Watton, but the highly-attractive building still standing there is largely of later date. On the other side of the Wolds Kirkham Priory was founded about 1130, close by the river Derwent, and the beautiful late-thirteenth-century work of its gatehouse has been preserved together with extensive ruins.

For the rest, the riding's monastic houses were comparatively small and their remains have a minor place in the present-day landscape. Several village churches, however, contain impressive portions of monastic predecessors, Lowthorpe and Swine among them. East Riding villages seem rarely to have grown large under the influence of a nearby religious house, but conversely there is rarely good reason to suppose that the foundation of a monastery brought about the desertion of a village. At Meaux, however, a small village was removed, and in Cottingham the hamlet of Newton gave way to the 'great enterprise' of Haltemprice Priory, which—in 1320—was almost the last house to be founded in Yorkshire. Some reduction of the village also seems to have taken place at Kirkham.

The centuries after the Conquest witnessed the building of some new village churches, as well as the rebuilding of many of the humble churches that were put up before 1066. Doubtless the Norman structures were mostly simple, small and without aisles, but few of the riding's churches now retain much of the atmosphere of these early buildings. The aisleless Norman churches at Garton on the Wolds (Plate 15), Kirkburn and Weaverthorpe are perhaps too grand to be typical. More modest is Wharram le Street, where twelfth-century alterations were made to the pre-Conquest church, but here an aisle was added in the fourteenth century. Where a populous village or a wealthy manorial family provided the means, Norman churches may have been more elaborate and North Newbald provides an outstanding example; here the nave, the crossing and the transepts of a cruciform church all survive largely unaltered. Many other East Riding churches incorporate fragments of Norman work.

During the twelfth and thirteenth centuries growing population and wealth enabled many village churches to be enlarged by the addition of aisles or to be partially, even wholly, rebuilt. Aisles were added, for example, to the Norman nave at Wharram Percy, where excavation has shown a succession of alterations to the Anglian church. Among other Early English churches mention must be made of Filey and Sigglesthorne, and the most complete examples of the Decorated style are Bainton and Patrington. The beautiful church at Patrington would, indeed, be outstanding in any company; it surely attests not only to the ownership of the manor by the Archbishop of York but also to the growing wealth of the surrounding Holderness countryside, and perhaps to the development of trade at Patrington Haven. The other outstanding parish churches of these centuries were in the towns: St Mary's at Beverley, St Augustine's at Hedon, and Holy Trinity at Hull, which all reflect a life and a landscape of a very different kind (see Chapter 10).

Notable churches were undoubtedly one feature of the early medieval landscape, but to dwell upon them would be to obscure the fact that many twelfth- and thirteenth-century villages possessed no fully-fledged parish church at all. Some had only a chapel dependent upon a mother-church elsewhere. Others had a church which was given to a religious house and in which a vicar was never ordained; instead the monks enjoyed the full income of the church and merely provided a chaplain to serve the cure. It is remarkable how numerous were the dependent chapels around such mother-churches as Hunmanby and Pocklington, and how frequent the impoverished churches which belonged to such houses as Bridlington Priory. Even when dependent chapels were raised to the status of separate churches, as those around Pocklington were in 1252, they often remained poorly endowed. Many of these small chapels and churches underwent no elaborate rebuilding in the Middle Ages, and often they were patched and restored piecemeal for centuries after. The resultant charm of a modest church like Burton Fleming, spared a modern restoration or rebuilding, is one of the pleasures of the East Riding landscape.

SELECT BIBLIOGRAPHY

Beresford, M. W., and Hurst, J. G., *Deserted Medieval Villages* (1971), especially pp. 76–181.

Brooks, F. W., *Domesday Book and the East Riding* (E.Y.L.H.S. 21) (1966).

The Chartulary of Bridlington Priory, ed. W. T. Lancaster (1912).

Chronicum de Melsa, ed. E. A. Bond (Rolls Series), i–iii (1866–8).

Cox, J. C., 'The Annals of Meaux Abbey', *Transaction of the East Riding Antiquarian Society*, i (1893), pp. 5–32.

Darby, H. C., and Maxwell, I., *The Domesday Geography of Northern England* (1962).

Palmer, J., 'Landforms, Settlement and Drainage in the Vale of York', in *Geography as Human Ecology*, ed. S. R. Eyre and G. R. J. Jones (1966).

Pevsner, N., *Yorkshire: York & the East Riding* (1972).

Platt, C., *The Monastic Grange in Medieval England* (1969).

Sheppard, June A., *The Drainage of the Hull Valley* (E.Y.L.H.S. 8) (1958).

Sheppard, June A., *The Drainage of the Marshlands of South Holderness and the Vale of York* (E.Y.L.H.S. 20) (1966).

Sheppard, June A., 'Field Systems of Yorkshire', in A. R. H. Baker and R. A. Butlin, eds., *Studies of Field Systems in the British Isles* (1973).

G

Sheppard, June A., 'Medieval village planning in northern England: some evidence from Yorkshire', *Journal of Historical Geography*, ii (no. 1) (1976), pp. 3–20.

Smith, A. H., *The Place-names of the East Riding of Yorkshire* (1937).

V.C.H., *Yorkshire East Riding*, II (1974) and III (1976).

V.C.H., *Yorkshire,* II (1912) (earthworks and Domesday Book) and III (1913) (religious houses).

Yorkshire Inquisitions, i–iv (Y.A.S.R.S. xii, xxiii, xxxi, xxxvii).

5. The later Middle Ages

Contraction of settlement.   Secular and religious buildings

Contraction of settlement

BY THE END of the thirteenth century reclamation and drainage of woodland, waste and marsh, with the attendant growth of old villages and the planting of new hamlets and farmsteads, had extended man's influence into most corners of the riding. But however extensive his settlement may have been, his use of the countryside was as yet hardly intensive in terms of the nineteenth- and twentieth-century exploitation of the land. There was still a wildness which awaited a more thorough 'improvement' of fields, meadows and pastures. The shaping of the landscape had, however, reached a climax from which in many areas there was soon to be a temporary retreat.

Localised improvement doubtless continued after 1300 and throughout the fourteenth and fifteenth centuries. In many villages the ability to raise royal taxes was apparently unaffected by the Black Death and later plagues, and in 1377 the Poll Tax was paid by numerous thriving communities which had escaped or recovered from the pestilence. When we read, too, the description of the manor of Cottingham in 1408, with its park, woods, open-field arable land, meadows, pastures, mills and numerous tenants, we can see little obvious sign of decline from the palmy days when the manor was surveyed in the thirteenth century. Localised prosperity was nevertheless set against a background of widespread decay and regression in the fourteenth and

99

fifteenth centuries. The exact nature of that regression and its effects upon the landscape are not easy to determine, but some of its signs—such as empty house-sites and abandoned villages—are still plain to see in the countryside today.

The reasons for the turning of the tide of early medieval colonisation are not yet well understood. An undoubted worsening of the climate must have played a part, reducing the attractiveness of some settlement sites, inducing disease, lowering the yields of crops and stock. The continuing rise in the relative sea-level, already noted in the later thirteenth century, forced further withdrawals from the low-lying land bordering the Humber and the Ouse in Holderness and the Vale of York. The very growth of population and the colonisation of new territory which had proceeded so rapidly in the twelfth and thirteenth centuries had also, it seems, led settlers into marginal lands that could not sustain permanent cultivation. Only in a later age, when improved technical resources and methods of husbandry became available, were the most exposed parts of the high Wolds and the wettest areas of the marshlands to be finally tamed.

A half-century of decline had already passed before the Black Death swept through Yorkshire in the summer of 1349. Perhaps a third of the population died. About half of the incumbents of churches in the archdeaconry of the East Riding were smitten, and in one area—Dickering deanery on the Wolds—as many as sixty-one per cent died. Of fifty monks and lay brethren at Meaux Abbey only ten are said to have survived. So heavy a mortality inevitably resulted in some abandonment of cultivated land and decay of buildings. At Middleton on the Wolds about sixty acres were "owing to the great mortality . . . lying waste and untilled" in 1350. The value of Cottingham manor in 1349 had fallen because of the plague and the lack of tenants, and in addition widespread flooding from the Humber was reported there in 1352. At Boynton, where nine houses and their lands were already wasted by flooding from the Gypsey Race in 1327, twenty out of twenty-nine bovates of land on one estate were waste in 1352 and a windmill was in ruins. Near by at Garton on the Wolds a landowner died in August 1349 leaving much of his estate lying waste as a result, it was said, of the pestilence. And at Easton in 1353 a manor-house and six other houses were in ruins and eleven bovates were waste. Boynton, Garton and Easton were in the hard-hit deanery of Dickering, and when Parliament allowed tax relief in 1352–5 to villages unable to meet their quotas there was ample confirmation of the picture given by vacant church livings. Three Dickering villages were relieved of over two-thirds of their tax in 1354 and twenty-four of between a third and two-thirds.

Many stricken villages eventually recovered, or survived as small hamlets. More significant in terms of landscape changes were those which succumbed. Few villages were completely depopulated by the Black Death in 1349, but one that apparently *was* emptied at a stroke was Flotmanby, again in Dickering, which was relieved of the whole of its tax in 1354. A village community is not recorded there again, and earthworks still mark the sites of medieval houses near the two surviving farms. Barthorpe, near Acklam, may have been another complete Black Death depopulation. Much more common was the gradual desertion of villages which had been set on a course of slow decline by the Black Death. Later plagues, especially in the 1360s, also took their toll. It was these plague-shrunken villages that were especially susceptible to abandonment by the surviving inhabitants and prone to deliberate depopulation by their landlords. We are fortunate, however, if sufficient documentary evidence survives to indicate what happened in individual cases.

An example of probable abandonment in the later fourteenth century is provided by the hamlet of Waterhouses, beside the river Derwent in Wheldrake parish. The number of households in Wheldrake is calculated to have fallen from eighty-four in 1348 to seventy-three in 1361 and fifty-six in 1394. Part of that reduction was in Waterhouses, where one toft was certainly waste in 1361. The hamlet was apparently part of a small estate belonging to the Darel family and in 1379 the Darels sold out to Fountains Abbey, lord of the manor of Wheldrake. In the economic conditions of the time it seems that the abbey was unable, or saw no need, to re-tenant the tofts at Waterhouses.[1] There was still a lone house there in later centuries, and after the site—called Waterhouse Garths—was ploughed in 1972 much pottery of various dates was to be found on the surface. At Little (or East) Givendale, on the western edge of the Wolds, inhospitable natural conditions seem to have played a bigger part in the abandonment of the village. In 1404 and 1406 there were ruinous houses, waste tofts and uncultivated land both there and at Great (or North) Givendale, and the infertility and stoniness of the soil was commented upon at the time. Great Givendale has survived as a small hamlet, with a few banks marking out former garths, but its neighbour was deserted and close to the one remaining farm the former house-sites are clearly visible (Plate 13).

Poor land on the high Wolds, colonised in the earlier Middle Ages, may indeed have been readily abandoned in the century after the Black Death. Another comment upon its unattractiveness comes from Fordon, a shrunken hamlet lying among the dry valleys and open Wolds near Hunmanby. The date is 1597, but the evidence is clearly relevant to the earlier period. The soil was described as "very bad, barren and stony" and it could not supply the villagers' needs even when fallowed in alternate years. "Some high

[1] See June A. Sheppard, article cited on p. 70, in which the number of waste tofts in 1361 is mistakenly given as nine.

and great hills," too steep and stony to be ploughed, provided but poor common pasture, and forty acres kept for hay produced only one load to the acre. The fallow open-field land could, moreover, be grazed for only a limited period each year, otherwise grass would not grow on the thin soils. In the years of declining population such conditions must have contributed to the decay of many of the deserted and shrunken villages on the higher parts of the Wolds.

Elsewhere, especially in parts of Holderness, heavy and waterlogged soils would have been equally unattractive to surviving families who were now able to move to more favourable land in nearby villages, often left empty by plague-stricken peasants. In the south of Holderness the process of erosion as the sea-level gradually rose, already described in Chapter 4, continued during the fourteenth century. By about 1400 most of the reclaimed land beside the Humber had been lost again, and with it a string of villages and monastic granges. Further up the Humber the rising sea-level had less striking but still highly significant effects in the southern parts of the Vale of York. Not only did it prove difficult in the fourteenth and fifteenth centuries to maintain effective banks against the river, but also low-lying grounds could not be kept free of water as the water table became higher. Arable land may of necessity have been allowed to revert to pasture and marsh, often usable only in summer. The numerous deserted and shrunken villages near Howden, beside the Ouse and lower Derwent, may thus reflect the abandonment of land, much of which had been reclaimed in the twelfth and thirteenth centuries. The general situation is well illustrated by a complaint made in 1441 that freshwater floods and strong tides had so damaged the Ouse river banks west of Hemingbrough that the value of riverside lands was much reduced. Apart from the surviving isolated farm-houses and cottages, and an occasional moated site like that at Babthorpe, there is little to catch the eye now at these depopulated settlements.

The depopulation of shrunken villages, and occasionally of thriving ones too, and the reduction of others was also frequently brought about in the fifteenth and early sixteenth centuries by landlords anxious to increase their wealth by converting arable land to pasture. A falling population had reduced the demand for corn at a time when the cloth industry was increasing its demands for wool; and the shrinking rural labour force also encouraged landlords to turn to sheep farming, with its low labour costs. The acquisition of tenants' holdings was easier in villages already in decline and it was amongst the weak that most 'sheep depopulations' took place. Local circumstances appear to have made conversion to pasture a practical proposition in various parts of the riding, both on the Wolds and in some lowland districts. Much arable land in the open fields was enclosed and hedged around to contain the new flocks, and many husbandmen were evicted to make way for them.

Most of our evidence comes from a government enquiry carried out in 1517 which looked back as far as 1488 to discover cases of enclosure and depopulation. In the East Riding, however, as in some other parts of the country, the majority of enclosures seem to have taken place before 1488 and so went undetected. The enquiry nevertheless revealed cases at nearly thirty places, about ten of which are now deserted villages. There was some later sheep depopulation, too: in the 1530s, for example, Sir Robert Constable was accused of turning sheep into tenants' corn at Arras and of evictions at Kettlethorpe, both now deserted.

It is probable that enclosure for sheep farming completed the depopulation of Wharram Percy, on the Wolds, for in 1517 the lord of the manor was reported to have put down four ploughs and allowed four houses to decay. Wharram's decline had begun at least by 1354, when over sixty per cent of its tax was remitted after the Black Death. The earth-works that mark the streets and houses of the village constitute one of the finest deserted village sites in the country, and archaeological investigations, still in progress, which began twenty-five years ago have made it one of the best known. Much has been learnt about the changing landscape of a medieval Wolds village, and as a result Wharram has already served as an illustration several times in this book.

Wharram Percy lay high on the Wolds, about 500 feet above sea-level, near a group of springs in a typical steep-sided valley. Above the village site the valley is dry, but the springs feed a constant stream flowing westwards towards the Wolds escarpment. The ruins of the parish church stand in the bottom of the valley, and we have seen in Chapter 4 how the village is thought to have expanded along the hillside above. The church, two complete tofts and the twelfth-century manor-house have already been fully explored by excavation, and more recently the dig has been concerned with the valley-bottom terrace where the earliest village lay, with the probable site of a medieval water-mill and associated fishpond, and with the boundary banks of the village. Excavation of the boundaries has revealed more Romano-British evidence to add to that found in previous years, and a picture is now emerging of a medieval village superimposed upon the fields of several Romano-British farmsteads. By field-walking and collecting pottery and other objects, an attempt is now being made to study the manuring and cultivation of the village fields.

Coupled with the investigation of the medieval landscape at Wharram has been the preservation of what remains to be seen. The site has been taken into the guardianship of the Department of the Environment, the church ruins are being consolidated, and it is hoped eventually to mark out some of the excavated areas. Few deserted village sites can be

saved for posterity in this fashion. The bulldozing of earthworks to bring more and more land under the plough has
destroyed or damaged many sites in recent years, and the
cost of complete protection is high. Even such a fine site as
that at Cowlam, a few miles east of Wharram Percy, has
fallen to the bulldozer. Now there is little more than a
small Victorian church, with a splendid Norman font,
standing beside the farm buildings of Cowlam Manor to
show that a village once existed there.

Several other outstanding Wolds sites are nevertheless
still to be seen, the best being those at Argam, Towthorpe
(Fig. 6), Cottam and Swaythorpe. Argam (Plate 14) lies
above the valley of the Gypsey Race, not far from Flamborough Head, and the village earthworks are close to a
surviving stretch of the prehistoric Argam Dikes. This may
have been another village depopulated for sheep farming,
though there is little documentary evidence, and only a
shepherd lived at the site in the seventeenth century. A
rector continued to hold the church living long after
depopulation, and it was said in 1632 that he was instituted
by being presented with sods cut on the supposed site of
the church. The position of the church has not been
identified, but it was no doubt one of the buildings whose
earthworks are so clearly picked out by the low sun in the
air photograph. The extensive earthworks at Cottam
surround the shell of a red-brick nineteenth-century chapel
but, as at neighbouring Cowlam, the antiquity of the chapel
is revealed by a fine Norman font, now standing in the
mother-church at Langtoft. The depopulation of Cottam
began in the Middle Ages but it was not completed until
the eighteenth century, when the substantial residence that
still stands near by was built by the family who leased the
manor from the chapter of York Minster. All the sites so
far mentioned in this paragraph are in the northern Wolds;
further south there is a good small Wolds site at Risby,

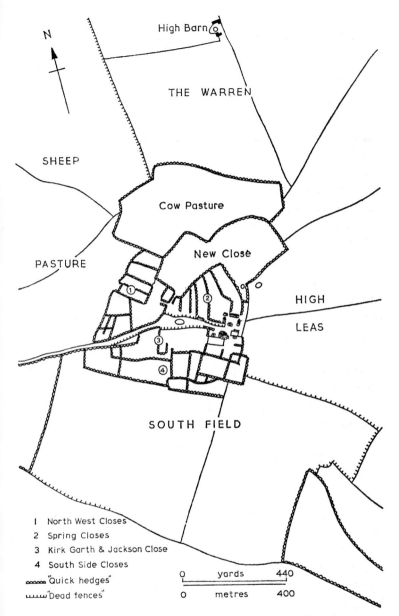

High Barn

THE WARREN

SHEEP

Cow Pasture

New Close

PASTURE

HIGH

LEAS

SOUTH FIELD

1   North West Closes
2   Spring Closes
3   Kirk Garth & Jackson Close
4   South Side Closes
〜〜〜 "Quick hedges"
ⅶⅶⅶ "Dead fences"

0	yards	440
0	metres	400

Fig. 6. The depopulated village of Towthorpe in 1772 (based on a map in Hull University Library). Hedges mark out the long empty garths of the village, but few hedges have been established on the exposed surrounding wolds. High Barn is one of two subsidiary farmsteads built on the estate.

near Walkington. One of the best lowland sites is that at Eske, in the Hull valley north-east of Beverley, where the earthworks and surviving farm-house are still surrounded by much ridge-and-furrow marking out the former open fields.

Despite twentieth-century destruction, deserted village sites remain a widespread feature of the East Riding landscape. (Not that there is *always* a great deal to see.) Less obvious but much more numerous are those shrunken villages where earthworks indicate former garths and house-sites around and among the surviving houses. Speeton, by the sea near Filey, and Grindale, a few miles inland, are two good examples. Medieval pottery has been found at both places, but the discovery of a seventeenth-century house during excavations at Grindale shows that shrinkage sometimes continued long after the later Middle Ages.

The distribution of deserted and very shrunken villages is shown in Fig. 8.[2] Some of them were certainly depopulated by one, or a combination of more than one, of the factors that have been discussed. But the landscape changes involved have in many cases yet to be explained, and peculiar local circumstances may sometimes prove to be more important than plague, poor soils, flooding, or a change to sheep farming. Detailed individual studies may in future supply some of the answers.

Secular and religious buildings

It was no doubt the landowning classes who suffered least from the changes which affected the countryside at large after 1350 and who, indeed, benefited from the opportunities to increase their personal wealth which those

---

[2] Based, with amendments, on the list given in Beresford and Hurst, *Deserted Medieval Villages*, pp. 207–9.

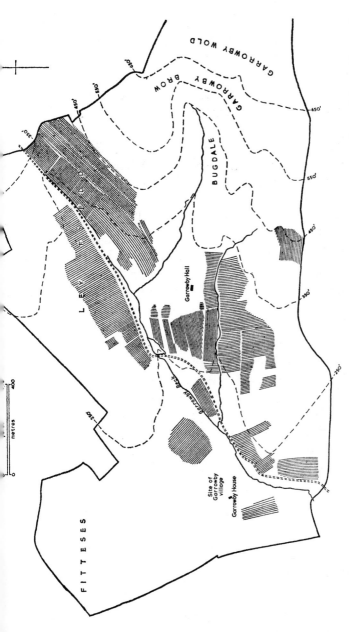

Fig. 7. Ridge-and-furrow near Garrowby deserted village. The approximate pattern of surviving ridge-and-furrow is based on a field survey (carried out by kind permission of Lord Halifax). The site of the village is still clearly visible on the ground.

changes presented. But few domestic buildings survive to show how old-established families and newcomers alike expressed their prosperity in stone or brick. Later medieval manor-houses have mostly been replaced in subsequent centuries, or reduced to mere earthworks like those of the St Quintins' house beside the church at Harpham. The house of the Constables at Flamborough is largely represented by earthworks, too, but there remains a ruined chalk tower for which licence to crenellate was given in 1351. It was a substantial manor-house in its day, incorporating a hall, various parlours, a chapel, a court-house, a mill-house and a "great barn". In Holderness manor-houses were probably more often brick-built, and a fifteenth-century brick tower with typical vaulted basement still stands at Paull Holme, beside the Humber. More impressive are the remains of Wressle Castle, in the Vale of York. It was built about 1380 for Sir Thomas Percy and originally consisted of four ranges around a central courtyard. One range survives, with its corner towers, and the fine white masonry shines splendidly beside the meadows of the river Derwent. Brick was used at this period in the Vale of York as in Holderness, and at Riccall part of a brick manor-house, including a staircase tower, still stands within the remnants of its moat. The house, which may date from the late fifteenth century, was embodied in a Victorian rebuilding when it became the vicarage house of Riccall. Still in the Vale of York, part of the Bishop of Durham's manor-house at Howden, including a vaulted stone porch, now stands neglected and vandalised.

Of other secular buildings in the countryside even less can be said. Only one farm building can confidently be dated to the Middle Ages, but that is a fine example of timber framing, so rare now in the riding. The tithe barn at Easington, in Holderness, was perhaps built in the fifteenth century, apparently by Meaux Abbey, the owner of

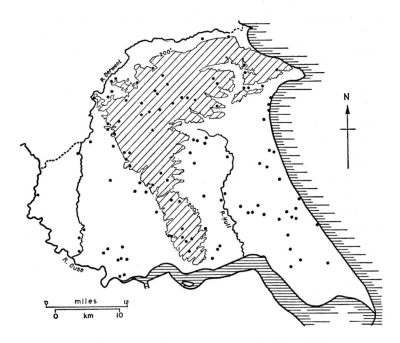

Fig. 8. Deserted medieval villages in the East Riding. Villages lost as a result of coastal changes are not shown.

Easington church. No doubt there were also more bridges being built, but little evidence survives. A small bridge over one of the headwater streams of the river Hull was, however, probably built in the mid fourteenth century. Thus "Brayceforthbrig" is recorded in 1369, replacing the "Brayceford" mentioned about 1340, and Bracey Bridge as it was later called was repaired in stone in the early fifteenth century.

Some village churches certainly suffered as a result of the impoverishment of their congregations in the fourteenth and fifteenth centuries. The churches and chapels at a number of deserted villages went the way of the abandoned peasant houses, as for instance at Argam. The chapel at Swaythorpe was still shown on a map of 1729, but it was later removed. In contrast the church at Wharram Percy survived, for it still had to serve the hamlet of Thixendale, but one of its aisles was demolished in the fifteenth century after the Black Death and the other in the early sixteenth century after enclosure for sheep farming had finally depopulated the village. The blocked arcades of the now ruined church are still a visible reminder of the fate of the village.

Many other churches were less obviously neglected and frequently they were enlarged or partially rebuilt by the more wealthy local landowners. Outstanding examples are Cottingham (Plate 16), where a new chancel was built in the 1380s, and Skirlaugh. The latter is a rare example of a wholly Perpendicular village church, put up in his native village by Bishop Skirlaw of Durham in 1401. Often it was the church tower which was added to an existing building or rebuilt in more splendid fashion. At Harpham, for example, Joan St Quintin had licence to build the tower in 1374, and there are other fine examples at Beeford, Preston, Hemingbrough, Sancton and elsewhere, as well as in the towns. The spire at Hemingbrough, 189 feet high including the low tower, was built about 1420–50 and reflects the ownership of the church by the wealthy priory at Durham.

As for the monasteries, some of their buildings were further enlarged and elaborated in the later Middle Ages. The glory of several monastic churches was completed by Perpendicular work which is still to be seen at Beverley, notably in the magnificent west front, at Bridlington, again at the west end, and at Howden, in the grand crossing tower. Those three, were, of course, in towns, and they survived the Dissolution to serve as parish churches. In the countryside there were no survivors among the monastic churches, and few anywhere among the conventual buildings of the monasteries. At Howden, however, there is the late-fourteenth-century chapter house, at Bridlington the gatehouse, known as the Bayle, for which licence to fortify was granted in 1388, and at Watton the fifteenth-century prior's lodging (Plate 18). Especially impressive is the prior's lodging, a big building of brick with corner turrets, embellished with a fine two-storeyed stone oriel window.

SELECT BIBLIOGRAPHY

Allison, K. J., *Deserted Villages* (1970).
Beresford, M. W., 'The Lost Villages of Yorkshire', 1–4, *Y.A.J.*, xxxvii (1951), pp. 474–91; xxxviii (1952–4), pp. 44–70, 215–40, 280–309.
Beresford, M. W., and Hurst, J. G., *Deserted Medieval Villages* (1971).
Pevsner, N., *Yorkshire: York & the East Riding* (1972).

6. Old and improved landscapes, 1500–1730

The old order.   Agricultural improvement.   Parks.
Medieval houses in decay.   New buildings

BEFORE THE END of the fifteenth century the downward trend of population had been reversed, and in the centuries that followed the East Riding, like most parts of England, experienced a new land-hunger, a demand for foodstuffs from towns near and far, and a call for materials needed for home industries and for shipment abroad. The marks of localised wasting were soon removed from the landscape. The sites of numerous deserted villages were, it is true, never resettled but often their abandoned fields were brought back into use by the inhabitants of nearby villages. The older gentry and a rising class of yeomen farmers, many of them taking over the lands of dissolved monastic houses, embarked upon improvements which were eventually to transform the countryside. Within the two centuries or so covered by this chapter the improvements were, however, mostly of a gradual kind, modifying rather than replacing traditional methods. The medieval pattern of open arable fields and common pastures and meadows still dominated the landscape in many parts of the riding, and it is this old order, with its important regional variations, which must first be considered.

The old order
Medieval colonisation and reclamation had, as we have seen, created around many East Riding villages large tracts

of arable land which were typical of the open fields found in much of lowland England. Individual farmers held small strips of land which lay intermixed with those of their neighbours, the strips grouped into furlongs and the furlongs into two or three fields. Hedgerows, as well as roads and streams, might divide the fields from each other or from adjoining commons and meadows. But within the fields there were no hedges, few dividing banks or ditches: the fields were truly 'open', and after crops had been harvested or while a field was rested as fallow the land was used in common by the inhabitants' animals. This is a familiar generalised picture but one which fits the East Riding well enough. Our farmers might call their furlongs 'falls' or 'flats', they might embody local customs in their open-field bylaws, but the landscape of their fields was not essentially different from that to be seen elsewhere.

It was on the Wolds that local conditions of soil and topography had in the Middle Ages encouraged the most extensive development of open-field farming. There the fields, each frequently hundreds of acres in extent, often covered most if not all of the territory belonging to a village. Many Wolds villages also had common pastures and sheepwalks, sometimes in the steep-sided dry valleys which could not be ploughed, sometimes on the least hospitable ground like the "high and great hills" that were described at Fordon in 1597. Other villages forsook such pastures and took all their land into the open fields. This situation is well illustrated at Fimber, Fridaythorpe and Wetwang (Fig. 9), where even the dry valleys seem to have been ploughed.

Detailed 'strip-maps' of the open fields, like that of South Cave drawn in 1759 (Plate 21), confirm that valley sides or the Wolds escarpment were indeed often ploughed. Similarly, ridge-and-furrow, which preserves the pattern of open-field strips to the present day, sometimes runs down

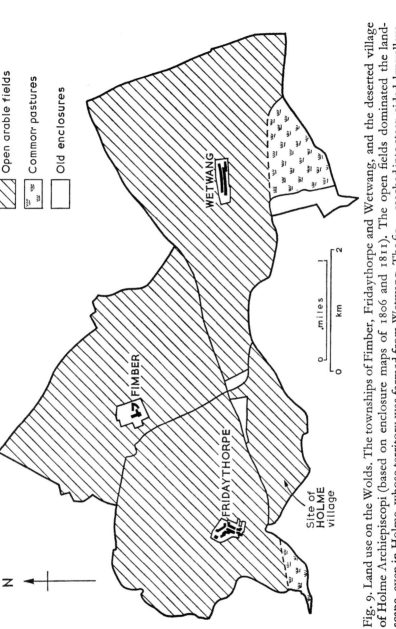

Fig. 9. Land use on the Wolds. The townships of Fimber, Fridaythorpe and Wetwang, and the deserted village of Holme Archiepiscopi (based on enclosure maps of 1806 and 1811). The open fields dominated the landscape, even in Holme, whose territory was farmed from Wetwang. The fields reached into steep-sided dry valleys, like that forming the western boundary of Fridaythorpe.

Legend:

- ▨ Open arable fields
- 〜 Common pastures
- ☐ Old enclosures

comparatively steep slopes, as in the dry valley north of the church at Great Givendale. Other slopes were steep enough to call for lengthwise ploughing, producing terraces or lynchets. Flights of lynchets may still be seen on the Wolds escarpment near Folkton, Great Givendale, Little Givendale, Londesborough and Nunburnholme, and in dry valleys at Croom (near Sledmere) (Plate 9) and Bishop Burton. Furlongs at South Cave in 1759 called *Shelves* and *Racksettles* suggest that the strips there, too, were stepped up the escarpment, and the name Ledge Field is still given to the lynchets at Bishop Burton. At Garrowby much of the open-field pattern is preserved in ridge-and-furrow in the modern parkland and pastures (Fig. 7), and again some of it lies on the Wolds escarpment. The scarp slope at Garrowby was not, however, so steep as to require individual lynchets. Instead, groups of strips were separated by high banks to produce a similar terraced effect.

The predominantly arable aspect of the Wolds was varied not only by the permanent stretches of grass and gorse of the commons but also in some townships by the practice of allowing areas of 'outfield' to go back to pasture for periods of several years. The open fields were normally cultivated in a two- or three-course rotation and so were fallowed every second or third year. But on the poorest Wolds soils only an 'infield' near the village could sustain such a rotation, while an 'outfield' was broken up much less regularly. The infield-outfield system is known to have been used at Bishop Wilton, for example, in 1611, and there is evidence of it in the early eighteenth century at places like Kilham, Wetwang and Fimber. In the two last-mentioned townships it helps to explain how pasturage was provided in such all-embracing open fields.

The land which had belonged to deserted villages was sometimes kept under grass, especially in those cases where depopulation had been carried out to enlarge a landlord's sheep pastures. In 1621, for example, one deserted village gave its name to 'a sheep pasture called Swaythorpe', used by the flocks of Sir Henry Griffith of Burton Agnes, and in 1540 Jane Constable had a flock of 400 sheep in what had formerly been the open fields of Caythorpe. Again, in 1599 the whole of Fowthorpe field—nearly 400 acres—was used as meadow and pasture. The landlords of deserted villages on the Wolds often, it seems, saw no need to divide the estates into small hedged closes. A ring-fence sufficed to contain the animals. The adjoining grounds of two deserted settlements, Battleburn and Eastburn, lay in 1698 "open for sheep walks . . . not divided by fences or ditches". It might be expected that such ring-fences would even today show signs of their long existence, and this indeed proves to be so at Bartindale, near Hunmanby. The long curving line of the hedge-banks around the territory of the deserted village contrasts with the straight and regular shape of the much more recent fields within the boundary. The old hedge, moreover, contains six or eight species of shrubs and trees, the recent hedges only one, thus emphasising the longer life of the ring-fence.[1]

Bartindale was not subdivided into closes until 1809, for it is an example of a deserted village whose lands were added to the open fields of a neighbouring village, in this case Hunmanby. The lands of Holme Archiepiscopi similarly became part of the open fields of Wetwang, those of Tranby were used by Hessle, and those of Southorpe by Hornsea. Cases are also known where two or more farmers remained after the general depopulation of a village and continued to cultivate the land by the old common-field husbandry. At Arras, for example, there were still two occupied farm-houses about 1620 and still three open fields; not until the second half of the seventeenth century did one farm absorb the other, and even then there was no im-

[1] *History from the Farm*, ed. W. G. Hoskins (1970), p. 81.

mediate enclosure into compact fields. The much-shrunken villages of Riplingham and Wauldby provide similar examples of the old order slow to give way to a new landscape.

One other feature of the Wolds landscape, in deserted and living villages alike, which emerges in these centuries is the rabbit warren. If poor soils and rough terrain made cultivation difficult, then the most profitable course might be to stock the ground with rabbits and manage them for their fur and their meat. Open-field land and common pasture were both taken into the warrens, which were often surrounded by low sod walls or palings. Warrens on the Wolds were recorded in the seventeenth century at places like Arras, Gardham and Hunsley, and they became increasingly popular in the eighteenth century: altogether nearly thirty have been noted. With their boundary marks and warreners' houses, and their swarming and troublesome 'conies', warrens had a prominent place in the Wolds countryside. In a later age of improvement they were to be erased almost without trace.

Little old woodland remained on the higher Wolds, and in the early eighteenth century much of the countryside was like that near Wetwang, "open, scarce a bush or tree . . . for several miles". The creation of plantations was still in the future. But some woodland did survive to diversify the landscape of the Wolds escarpment at places like Millington and Settrington, the latter having 235 acres of woods in 1600. Other woodland remnants were to be found on the lower Wolds slopes to the east, for example at Walkington. The Bishop of Durham's woods at Walkington illustrate the wasting of Royalist and Church property during the Commonwealth, which must have had at least a temporary effect on the landscape at many places in the riding. The woods were described in 1662 as "in these late disordered and rebellious times much destroyed".

The generally low-lying and often ill-drained country of the Vale of York had been less favourable for the development of extensive open-field arable land. The open fields of most townships were far smaller than those on the Wolds, and they lay for the most part on the relatively drier ground of the slight swellings and gentle ridges that broke up the lower tracts. Only rarely were the swellings as marked as Holme Hill, on and around which were the open fields of Holme upon Spalding Moor (Fig. 10), or the ridges as prominent as the York and Escrick moraines, which accommodated the fields of Dunnington, Heslington, Wheldrake and Escrick (Fig. 11). Often, as at North Duffield, the open fields took advantage of only the slightest of hummocks.

Everywhere in the Vale the open fields were dwarfed by large areas of closes or by unimproved commons. The assarting and enclosure of waste and marsh had, from the early Middle Ages onwards, created a pattern of irregular closes which stretched beyond the open fields into the furthest corners of many townships. The closes varied greatly not only in shape and size, but also in land-use and in ownership. Meadow and pasture were probably more common than tillage, and amongst the many closes belonging to individual farmers there were some that were in shared ownership. Escrick and Deighton (Fig. 11) well illustrate the prominent place of such enclosures in the landscape of the area between the rivers Ouse and Derwent. Even at the heart of the wettest section of the Vale, in Holme upon Spalding Moor, there were extensive assarts around the margins of the parish, worked from isolated farmsteads like that at Hasholme or small hamlets like Bursea (Fig. 10). This, indeed, was another of the characteristic features of the Vale landscape which was in such sharp contrast to the Wolds, where few isolated houses were to be seen outside the nucleated open-field villages.

Plate 18 Watton Priory. This was a double house for nuns and canons, founded about 1150. Part of the surviving buildings dates from the fourteenth century, but most striking is the fifteenth-century prior's hall, shown here. It is mainly built of brick but has a fine stone oriel.

Plate 19 Settrington manor-house in 1600. The Tudor house shown here has been demolished and its gardens and orchard have gone. A new house, built about 1790, stands south of the old one.

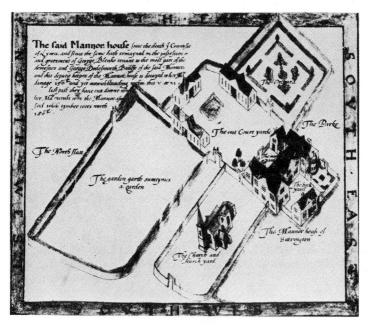

Plate 20 Burton Constable. The main, east, front of the Constable family mansion in Holderness. The centre block is thought to have been built about 1570 and the wings about 1610. The house still had an essentially medieval arrangement of great hall, screens passage, and entrance at the end of the front; only about 1750 was the entrance moved and the façade made symmetrical.

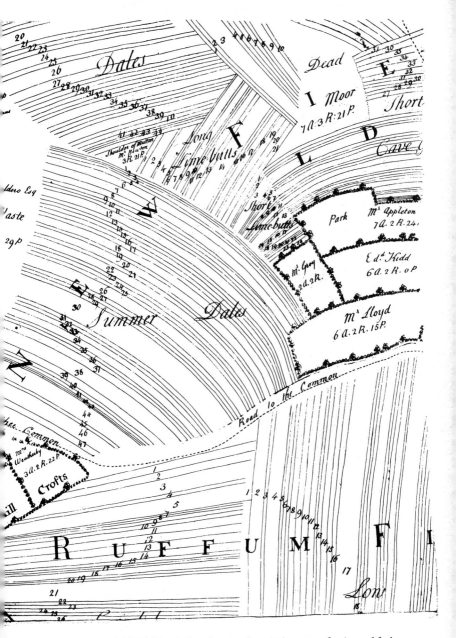

Plate 21 Part of the open fields of South Cave in 1759. A typical pattern of strips and furlongs, with a few hedged closes. Enclosure here took place in 1787.

Plate 22 The area around the hamlet of Thirtleby, in Holderness. Thirtleby was early enclosed but the date is not known. This kind of countryside, so common in Holderness, contrasts strongly with the parliamentary enclosure landscape of the Wolds. There are many streams, narrow winding

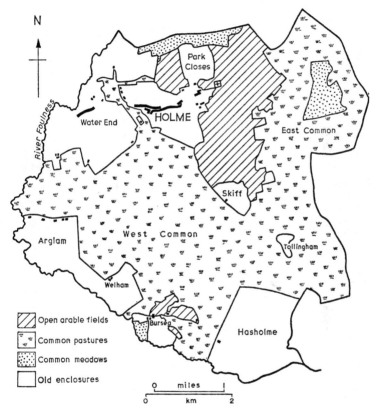

Fig. 10. Land-use in the Vale of York. The parish of Holme upon Spalding Moor (based on the enclosure map of 1774). The open fields, centred on Church Hill, are hemmed in by vast commons on the low-lying ground. Beyond are early enclosures around outlying farms and hamlets, one of which had its own embryo open fields.

Most townships in the Vale of York could count one or more houses standing alone among the assarted closes.

An equally striking feature of the countryside of the Vale of York was the survival of immense common pastures, unimproved or at best partially drained and cleared. Some, like the commons of Escrick and Skipwith, still carried a good deal of scrubby woodland; others, like Wallingfen, were open and marshy; and in sandy areas, like those to the east of Holme upon Spalding Moor, the commons were occupied by dry heathland and furze. By far the greatest in extent was the vast area of waste stretching for some ten miles northwards from Broomfleet, near the Humber, towards Holme and Market Weighton; within it were Holme Moor, alone covering about 7,000 acres, and Wallingfen, of some 5,000 acres. All over the southern part of the Vale were other commons, each covering hundreds of acres. Between Ouse and Derwent two areas of common pastures were outstanding: in the north were the commons centred upon Tilmire which extended into Heslington, Fulford, Deighton, Wheldrake, Dunnington and Elvington; and in the south was the waste that was shared by Skipwith, Riccall, Osgodby, Cliffe and the Duffields. Poor and often seasonal pasture, together with peat and turf, were all that the wetter commons provided. On the sandy soils, however, a few Vale commons, like those at Barmby Moor and Holme upon Spalding Moor, were used in the seventeenth and eighteenth centuries for the planting of rabbit warrens similar to those on the Wolds.

On the other side of the Wolds, extensive open fields were established in many villages in Holderness, especially on the better-drained areas of boulder clay. But alongside the many streams which threaded their way through the claylands there were many areas of meadow, pasture and ill-drained carr-land. Even on the boulder clay there were large common pastures that stood much in need of

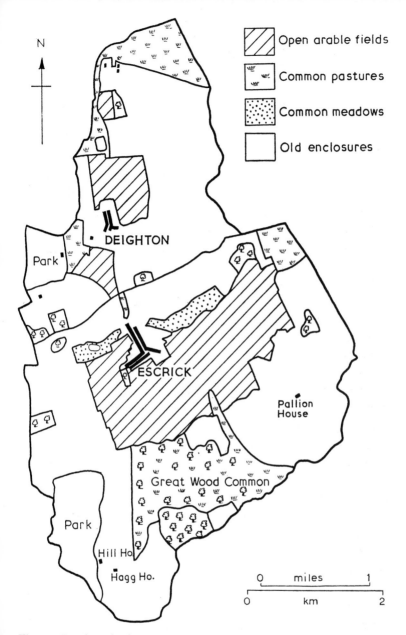

Fig. 11. Land use in the country between the rivers Ouse and Derwent. The townships of Deighton and Escrick (based on maps of about 1600 and 1619, in private possession). The limited areas of open-field land are surrounded by a great expanse of early assarts taken from woodland and waste. There are several isolated farmsteads.

123

improvement. One such was Brandesburton Moor, "a rough uncultivated spot, full of whins and water and hills". Though much of the pasture was used in common, old enclosed areas were also frequently found in Holderness and the landscape there was as varied as that of the Vale of York. The townships of Brigham, Foston on the Wolds (a complete misnomer, this), North Frodingham and Beeford well illustrate the variety of the Holderness countryside around the upper Hull valley (Fig. 12).

In the Hull valley it was the unimproved carr-lands that dominated the scene (Fig. 13). Of one such carr, covering 550 acres at Brandesburton, it was said in 1743 that "above three parts of it is nothing but bogs upon which no cattle ever goes and in a wet summer at least 9 parts in 10 lies under water". In such waterlogged conditions only limited summer pasture and hay were to be had, along with reeds and peat, fish and fowl. The carrs were, indeed, the haunt of numerous wildfowl, and at Leconfield in 1570 the villagers' animals had even been excluded from the riverside carrs because they disturbed the breeding of the wild swans so prized by the Earl of Northumberland. Lower in the Hull valley, towards the Humber, conditions were generally better as the result of well-maintained drains and river banks; meadow and pasture were more common than unimproved carr-land in the areas around the town of Hull, though such rough tracts as Myton Carr nevertheless survived into the eighteenth century.

Agricultural improvement

Although the changes made to the old order during the sixteenth and seventeenth centuries were often gradual and small in scale, they nevertheless played their part in altering the face of the countryside. Some of these changes were provoked by the inflexibility of the open-field system, which

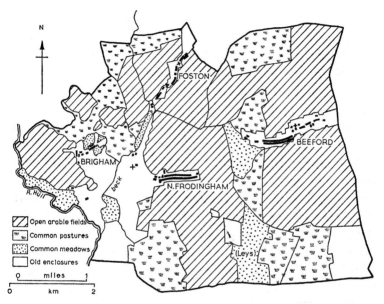

Fig. 12. Land-use in Holderness and the Hull valley. The townships of Beeford, Brigham, Foston and North Frodingham (based on enclosure maps of 1767, 1768, 1776 and 1808). Showing the typically varied landscape of these areas. Besides large open fields there were also extensive common pastures and meadows. The old enclosures in the south-east corner of Beeford were the site of Moor Grange, which had belonged to Meaux Abbey.

called for strict adherence to a communal routine and provided little scope for individual initiative. In particular a rotation based on two or three open fields involved a large area of fallow each year and prevented a more intensive use of the arable land. At the same time a regular open-field rotation prevented any increase in the area under pasture, which alone would have enabled more stock, especially cattle, to be kept.

One answer to these problems was the subdivision of the open fields so that a smaller area lay fallow each year. At Flamborough in 1572, for example, there were four fields, only one of which lay fallow, a usage already described as following "ancient custom". At Speeton three fields in the seventeenth century were replaced by at least four in the eighteenth, and Bempton, Flixton, Folkton and Staxton all had either four or five fields in the late sixteenth and seventeenth centuries. These examples from one corner of the riding can be matched from other areas too, especially on the Wolds and in the Vale of York. By a similar process the practice of sowing different crops in a single field was introduced into some of the predominantly two-field villages of Holderness.

The subdivision of fields by itself produced a more varied landscape in the open-field parts of the riding, and another improvement had a similar result. The problem of insufficient grazing land was frequently solved by the laying down to grass of one or more sections of the open fields for a period of years, before returning them to tillage. It was a practice reminiscent of the older infield-outfield system, but the new 'leys' were by no means limited to the poorer land in a township. Great Kelk, in Holderness, provides a good example of what was to become a widespread improvement. About 1680 there were still only two open fields at Kelk, "part whereof are yearly ploughed, and other part being meadow is usually mowed by the respective

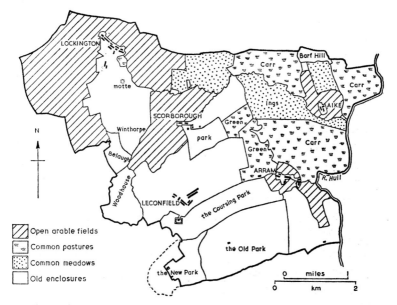

Fig. 13. Land-use on the lower Wolds slopes and in the Hull valley.
The parishes of Leconfield (with Arram), Lockington (with Aike) and
Scorborough (based on maps of 1616 and 1767, at Petworth House,
and on the enclosure map of Lockington of 1771). The mixture of
surviving open fields, early enclosures, and separate farms like Belaugh
and Woodhouse was typical of the Wolds slopes. Meadows and carrs
occupied much of the valley bottom.

owners thereof, and other part thereof is some years laid down and cast for pasture". At Hunmanby, too, leys greatly modified the appearance of the open fields. Parts of the fields were laid down for pasture in 1672, and the arrangement was confirmed in 1673 for twenty-one years and again in 1693. In the 1680s and 1690s, moreover, other open-field land in the township was set aside as horse pasture, and again the practice was continued in the next century.

The open-field landscape was also being modified by a change which gave some opportunity for individual initiative. Proprietors who were able, by purchase or exchange, to bring their scattered strips together in compact groups sometimes succeeded in hedging them round and removing them entirely from the open-field routine. At South Cave in 1759 there were several consolidated but still unenclosed flats in the fields east of the village, three of them belonging to Leuyns Boldero, the lord of East Hall manor; and Boldero had also hedged around a group of strips to produce a distinctive long and narrow ten-acre close. There can be no better illustration of this process of piecemeal enclosure than the holding of over 150 acres which John Grimston bought at Great Kelk in 1719. It consisted of fifteen scattered closes which a previous owner had enclosed from the fields, each made up of a handful of strips (Fig. 14).[2] When the surrounding open fields were finally enclosed more than 100 years later they were replaced by straight-sided rectangular closes, very different from the long curving closes of the old Grimston holding. This contrasting field pattern can still be seen at Kelk, and in several of the narrow closes ridge-and-furrow still marks out the individual strips.

More significant in its effect upon the landscape than

[2] For a map of the whole township see V.C.H., *Yorkshire East Riding*, II, p. 178.

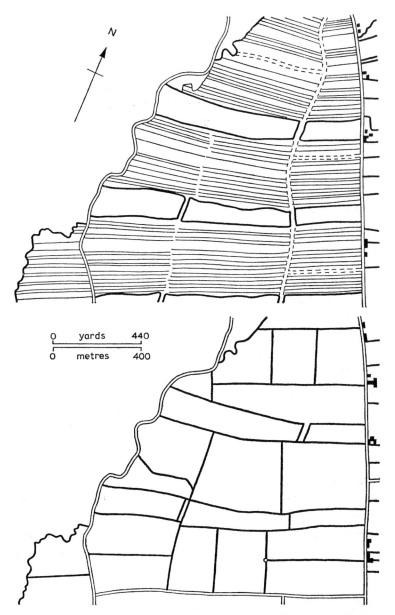

Fig. 14. Piecemeal enclosure at Great Kelk. Part of the open fields in 1789 (top), with some of the closes of the Grimston holding, and the same area after final enclosure in 1849 (based on a map in Humberside County Record Office and the Ordnance Survey map of 1854). Showing the contrasting patterns of piecemeal and parliamentary enclosure.

piecemeal enclosure was the larger-scale enclosure of open fields and commons by agreement between all the land-owners in a village; by this means the appearance of many townships was radically changed in the seventeenth and early eighteenth centuries. Frequently such enclosures by agreement were concerned with only a part of the open fields and other common lands in a village. At Sewerby, for example, some 250 acres of open-field land were enclosed about 1650, and at Settrington some of the common meadows and pastures were enclosed in 1668, in each case leaving much to be dealt with later on. Such enclosures became increasingly common around 1700, and the case of Burton Agnes, together with its four hamlets, shows how greatly the landscape was being altered. On five occasions—about 1702 and in 1719, 1722, 1723 and 1758—hedged or ditched closes replaced some of the open-field, meadow and pasture lands in the parish, by the agreement of all the freeholders. But the open fields of Burton Agnes itself still remained to be enclosed in the nineteenth century.

It was undoubtedly the landscapes of the more low-lying parts of the riding, rather than those of the Wolds, which were affected by enclosure by agreement in these centuries. There were many such cases in Holderness and the Hull valley, including an early example at Skerne (1596), others in the southern part of the Vale of York, like Gribthorpe (before 1613), and many more in the northern part of the Vale and in the Jurassic hills, including Howsham (during the seventeenth century). Where townships stretched from the lower ground up to the Wolds it was, moreover, the lower ground that was early enclosed: Leavening, Burton Agnes and Reighton, in a variety of situations, all illustrate this contrast. It was seemingly the heavier and better-watered soils, which could readily be used for meadow and pasture, that attracted this type of early improvement. A map of Howsham, which shows the land use of each new close in 1705, provides an excellent illustration, for most of the township was under grass.[3]

As with piecemeal enclosure, the early enclosures by agreement have left their mark on the modern landscape. Closes were commonly created by hedging round furlongs or other groups of strips, and the new fields were thus in many cases long and narrow. Sometimes they preserved the reversed-S shape which open-field farmers had produced by beginning to turn their plough-teams before reaching the end of the strips (Fig. 15).

Widespread enclosure by agreement has ensured a greater variety of landscape in some parts of the riding than on the Wolds, where enclosure was mostly carried out at a later period by parliamentary commissioners, with their preference for larger fields and straighter boundaries, a topic to be discussed in Chapter 7. In Holderness, for example, townships wholly or partially enclosed by agreement are interspersed with others enclosed by Act of Parliament, and field patterns are correspondingly varied (Plate 22). In the Jurassic hills large areas similarly bear the imprint of the more intimate methods of the early improvers. Sinuous fields, winding lanes and narrow roadside verges all make a striking contrast with the landscape of the Wolds.

The improvers were also turning their attention to such areas of woodland as had survived into the sixteenth century. At Settrington, for example, nearly 1,600 trees were felled in the 1590s in the woods on the Wolds escarpment; nearly 1,000 more were left, but it was suggested in 1600 that the denuded 'haggs' and 'springs' should not be replanted but used instead as pasture. In the Vale of York over 300 acres of woods were sold in 1636 at Seaton Ross and clearance no doubt began soon afterwards. The same thing was happening in neighbouring Holme on Spalding

---

[3] Harris, *The Rural Landscape of the East Riding of Yorkshire, 1700–1850,* Fig. 28, p. 76.

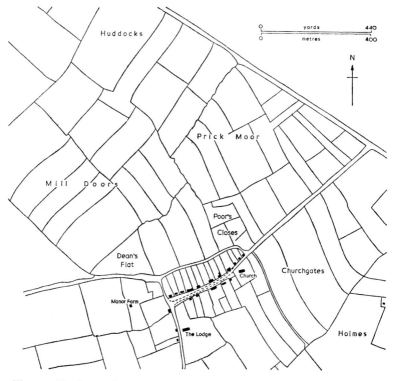

Fig. 15. Enclosure by agreement at Allerthorpe. Part of the township (based on the Ordnance Survey map of 1855), showing the pattern of long narrow closes, some with a reversed-S shape, which follows the outline of former open-field furlongs and strips. Allerthorpe was enclosed by agreement in 1640.

Moor. The medieval woods there included an area known as Bulmer which still contained eighty acres in 1586. By 1620 it had been converted to arable and pasture, and in 1661 it was described as formerly woodland but then in several closes. Other woods and pastures in Holme were similarly improved, while some of the medieval assarts were being subdivided: by 1697, for example, the former Arnest pasture had been split up into seven or eight closes. Irregularly-shaped fields in the north-west of Holme still preserve the pattern of these changes. In the area between the Ouse and Derwent much timber was being used from the woods of Escrick, Deighton and Wheldrake in the late sixteenth and earlier seventeenth centuries.

Improvements to the drainage of the low-lying parts of the riding were few in the period 1500–1650 and no drastic changes were made to the landscape of such areas as the Hull valley carr-lands or Wallingfen, in the Vale of York. A regular system of maintenance for existing drains and banks had, it is true, been developed by the commissioners of sewers in the sixteenth century, but it was only after about 1660 that vigorous attempts were made to provide new works. Some additional drains were dug and windmills made their appearance alongside the river Hull to lift water into the river. The administration of the Vale of York drainage was separated from that of the Hull valley in 1676, but only limited improvements were made before 1730.

Of greater interest for their effect upon the landscape were the attempts that were made to reclaim land from the Humber, both in south Holderness and in the Vale of York. Along the Humber shore in Holderness the earlier inroads by the sea were coming to an end in the sixteenth century. The sea-banks were still occasionally broken, as at Saltaugh in 1554 when a storm made "three great breaks" in the bank and a new sea dike further inland was called for.

Natural accretion, nevertheless, was beginning to establish new mud flats and sand banks along the shore. By about 1560 'sunk sand' was visible at low water and a century later part of it was ready for reclamation. Land gained from the bed of the sea and tidal rivers belongs to the Crown, and it was under a Crown lease of 1669 that about twenty acres were embanked; by 1684 the name Sunk Island was in use. It was William Gylby, the son of the first lessee, who pushed out the banks to enclose a substantial area of valuable grazing ground. When he died in 1744 the island covered 1,560 acres; it had been divided into farms and several houses had been built, together with a chapel. Not until the end of the century was there to be further reclamation and a detailed map of 1797 shows the island much as it had been in the early 1700s (Fig. 19). The shape of the island is still clearly preserved by the line of a roadway and by field boundaries and drainage ditches. Other boundaries suggest that the outline of the island at a slightly earlier stage may be recognised, too.

In the Vale of York similar gains were made in the bend of the river between Broomfleet and Brough. In 1690 it was found that ground had been "left derelict" by a change in the deep-water channel of the Humber, and about 900 acres beyond the old river bank were leased by the Crown for grazing. A fresh lease in 1706 gave the right to embank the land against renewed encroachment by the river. The reclaimed areas included the 'New Groves', or 'Growths', at Broomfleet, and tracts of mud and silt which long retained the names of Ellerker, Brantingham and South Cave 'Sands' (Fig. 16). When those townships were enclosed later in the eighteenth century they were found to extend as far as "the New Bank". The reclamation which took place soon after 1706 was consolidated by later improvements, but the New Bank was no doubt substantially that shown on the first Ordnance Survey map in 1850. Parts of the

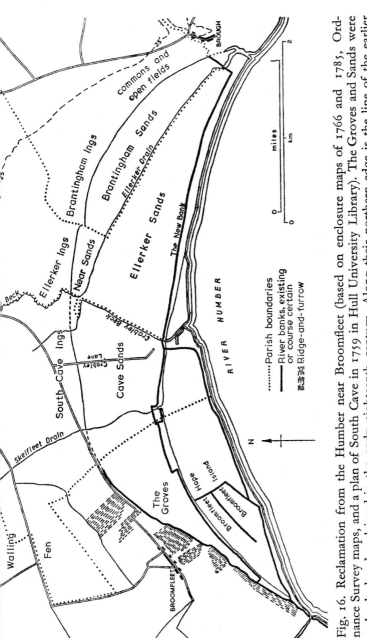

Fig. 16. Reclamation from the Humber near Broomfleet (based on enclosure maps of 1766 and 1785, Ordnance Survey maps, and a plan of South Cave in 1759 in Hull University Library). The Groves and Sands were embanked and reclaimed in the early eighteenth century. Along their northern edge is the line of the earlier river bank, and near Broomfleet village the bank itself survives. Broomfleet Hope and Island were not reclaimed until the late nineteenth century onwards. As ridge-and-furrow still shows, the open fields of Broomfleet lay close behind the old bank.

earlier river bank, probably on a line established in the Middle Ages, can still be seen near Broomfleet village, now far-removed from the Humber. Surviving ridge-and-furrow shows that Broomfleet's open fields had stretched right up to it. The line of other parts of the early bank can still be traced by changes in the ground level, as, for example, where Crabley Lane crosses the line of the medieval bank.

Parks

The place of deer parks in the landscape also underwent a change during these centuries, for after being well maintained in the Tudor period some at least were later put to agricultural uses. The number of sixteenth-century parks in the riding is quite uncertain. Saxton's map of 1577 shows only seven—at Burstwick, Burton Constable, Catton, Everingham, Leconfield, Risby and Wressle—but some of the smaller parks surviving from the Middle Ages were certainly omitted, and even one of the Earl of Northumberland's spacious parks was overlooked. It is the Earl's parks which provide the most graphic picture of the changes that were taking place.

At Leconfield in the 1530s Leland saw a park "very fair and large and meetly well wooded", with a brick tower for a hunting lodge. With the rest of the Earl of Northumberland's estates in Yorkshire, Leconfield passed to the Crown in 1537 and Henry VIII enlarged the park and divided it into three, the Old, New and Coursing Parks (Fig. 13). In 1577, after their lands had been restored to the Percy family, the last-mentioned park was described as "of great pleasure for coursing and, as it seems, devised only for that purpose". The three parks together contained about 1,300 acres and 950 deer; two had timber-built lodges, but in New Park there was a moated brick lodge "made for a house of pleasure, with houses of office and divers lodgings". At Wressle, in contrast, the park pales were decayed in 1577 around the Earl's Little Park, of twelve acres, and Great Park, covering 180 acres; there were still fifty-seven deer in Great Park, though it was considered capable of supporting over 300. At nearby Newsholme the Earl had a 500-acre park where no deer were left, and at Catton the pale of the 350-acre park was in disrepair and only twenty-four deer remained.

By 1616 the parkland landscapes had been further altered. All three parks at Leconfield had been divided into closes, convenient for stock-rearing or tillage but clearly making the chase no longer practicable; two of the lodges, however, still stood. At Wressle, Great Park was still undivided and retained its lodge, but Newsholme park was enclosed like Leconfield. The park at Catton had contained several wooded groves, but between 1577 and 1601 over 1,000 oaks there were felled. One grove was converted to an arable close and the Earl's tenant was enjoined to "set the ring of the pale and other inclosures in the said park with quickwood". By 1616 the park had been split up into a dozen closes, and the former hunting-lodge was being used by the tenant under the name of Park House. Another disemparked pleasure ground was that of the Bishop of Durham at Howden, a mile and a half around, it was said, but in 1648 described as "anciently . . . well stored with deer and very full of wood and timber, now utterly decayed".

Little trace remains of these great Tudor parks. Signs of the pale at Catton have been mentioned in an earlier chapter, for the boundary had been established early in the Middle Ages. Appropriately-named farm-houses still stand near the lodge sites at Catton, Leconfield and Newsholme, but two moats in New Park at Leconfield have recently been filled as part of the insatiable twentieth-century urge to level and plough.

Not all of the sixteenth-century parks failed to survive, for Burton Constable, where fallow and red deer were referred to in 1578, and Everingham were later enlarged and landscaped as the surrounds of great mansions. At Scorborough, too, the Hotham family's park, which was still intact in 1616 after the parks of neighbouring Leconfield had been dismembered, survives around the hall. Significantly the parks of the Earls of Northumberland shared the fate of their houses, for Catton and Leconfield manor-houses and Wressle Castle all fell into ruin during the sixteenth and seventeenth centuries.

Medieval houses in decay

By 1577, when the Northumberland estates were surveyed, there was already no trace of the manor-house in Hall Garth, near the church at Catton. But the house at Leconfield, although in some decay at that time, must still have been impressive. Within its moat and built around a great courtyard, it consisted of four ranges forming a square with sides of 108 yards. The galleries, stables and lodgings which made up three of the sides were timber-framed, but the corner towers and gatehouse were of brick, and the fourth side—"the chief mansion"—was of brick and stone. No doubt it was partly royal disfavour which brought Leconfield to ruin. Thomas Percy, the seventh Earl, had been executed in 1572 for his part in the Northern Rebellion, and Henry Percy, the ninth Earl, was heavily fined in 1606 for his papist sympathies. Subsequently materials and ornaments are said to have been taken from Leconfield to Wressle Castle. All that remains at Leconfield now is a big dry moat enclosing an impressively large area within.

Leland had described Wressle in the 1530s as "one of the most proper [houses] beyond Trent", "all of very fair and great squared stone". By 1577 it was in great decay, though all four ranges and five towers were still standing. Its neglected surroundings were still recognisably splendid. The house was moated on three sides, while on the fourth an inner gate gave access from "the basse court"; within the moat were a garden, orchard and bathing house. Around the base court were an outer gate, stables and barns, while on the south side of the castle lay gardens, orchard, bowling alleys, and fish ponds "used for pleasure". Though Algernon Percy, the tenth Earl, was one of their supporters, Parliament nevertheless ordered the destruction of the castle in 1648 to avoid the possibility of its seizure as a Royalist stronghold. Within a few years all but the south range had gone and that was occupied as a farm-house until it was accidentally burnt in 1796. The shell still stands today, but there is little sign of the ornamental grounds which graced the landscape until the mid seventeenth century.

Many other medieval manor-houses were allowed to decay, or were replaced by more fashionable houses, during these centuries. Baynard Castle at Cottingham, for example, had gone by Leland's day, and only four "mean farmers' houses" stood in the manor-house grounds. Again, the Bishop of Durham's manor-house at Howden was held in 1662 by men who had "unleaded and spoiled" it, and only a small part of it survived. The bishop also had a house called Wheel Hall beside the Ouse at Riccall; it still stood in the early sixteenth century, and the "old gate house" and the "water gate house" were mentioned in the seventeenth. Today, however, only an eighteenth-century farm-house remains beside slight traces of the old moat. Decaying medieval manor-houses clearly made their contribution to the Tudor and Stuart landscape, but it is time to consider the new houses which took their place.

New buildings

While the East Riding apparently did not experience such a widespread 'Great Rebuilding' in the sixteenth and seventeenth centuries as did other more prosperous counties, there was nevertheless a good deal of building activity by the country gentry, both old and new. In the general absence of medieval houses, it is indeed the Tudor and Stuart manor-houses which make the first notable contribution to the surviving domestic architecture in the county. The families whose growing estates and widening social aspirations made it possible and desirable for them to build new houses were of highly varied origins. Some of the old-established East Riding families rebuilt their medieval manor-houses, the Boyntons at Barmston, for example, the Creykes at Marton, and the Constables at Burton Constable. Other houses were built by old landowning families from elsewhere who moved into the riding during these centuries, like the Stricklands from Westmorland and the Osbaldestons from Lancashire. Yet other families established new country estates with wealth acquired in Hull or York, or even London: the Thompsons at Escrick had been York merchants, the Broadleys and Gees had traded at Hull, and John Legard, a younger son of an old East Riding family, bought the manor at Ganton with money made as a London haberdasher. Many of the smaller landowners of these centuries, whether of old manorial families or of newly-risen yeomen stock, must have shared the desire to rebuild, though few examples of their more modest houses survive. Such families certainly shared in the acquisition of former monastic property which the Dissolution had brought into the market. Many old estates were enlarged and many new ones created by the purchase of land that had belonged to Bridlington Priory or Meaux Abbey or one of the other religious houses which together had owned so much property in the country.

140

The great houses built in the riding in the later sixteenth century have been much altered since, but documentary and pictorial evidence helps to reveal their original appearance. These houses show that the new fashions of the time were only slowly gaining ground in Yorkshire. Medieval manor-houses characteristically had a great hall, frequently open to the roof, with a kitchen wing at one end and a bedroom and sitting-room wing at the other. The great hall and the kitchens were separated by a screens passage by which the house was entered, and the main front of the building was thus asymmetrical, with the doorway towards one end. The new sixteenth-century fashions called for a symmetrical front with a central entrance, while inside they required a number of specialised rooms instead of the all-purpose great hall. The choice of old style or new varied from house to house, and some owners in the East Riding, as elsewhere, sought to combine a conservative layout with a stylish façade.

The Strickland mansion at Boynton, built late in the century, retained the basically medieval arrangement of two-storeyed great hall, screens passage, and cross wings at each end. The house was considerably altered in the eighteenth century and its façade given a symmetrical arrangement in the process, but much of its charm still derives from the warm red Tudor brickwork with its blue diapers. Similar dark diaper-work adorns Beswick Hall, near Beverley, built about 1590. In contrast to Boynton, Heslington Hall, near York, was more fashionable. The manor of Heslington had belonged to St Leonard's Hospital, York, and after the Dissolution it was leased from the Crown by Thomas Eymms, the secretary of the Council in the North. For him the house was built in the 1560s. It is now clothed in the hard red brick of a Victorian restoration, but it is still impressive with its many mullioned and transomed windows overlooking a courtyard framed by long projecting wings. The central doorway, with its Corinthian columns, satisfied the taste for symmetry, though there was still a traditional great hall going up through two storeys.

Contrasting fashions are also to be seen in the three houses which are perhaps the brightest jewels of domestic architecture in the East Riding landscape—Burton Constable, Burton Agnes and Howsham Halls. At Burton Constable, in mid-Holderness, the old manor-house of the Constable family was rebuilt in the late sixteenth and early seventeenth centuries. The new house was still in the medieval tradition, though of magnificent proportions (Plate 20). It had a two-storeyed hall, a screens passage, kitchens in one of the wings, and a door at the end of the main front: only about 1750 was the front made symmetrical. Burton Agnes, which was probably completed in 1610, was a mixture of traditional and novel design. The same old-fashioned layout as at Burton Constable was here cleverly combined with a symmetrical front: two matching projections provided the symmetry, and the entrance (leading to the screens passage) was in the *side* of one of them, thus hiding the fact that it was not in the centre of the façade. Burton Agnes also had a fine wide gatehouse of the same date. The builder here was Sir Henry Griffith, whose family had owned Burton Agnes since the mid fourteenth century and had previously lived in the small Norman manor-house close by (Plate 29). The third of these outstanding houses, Howsham Hall, was built by Sir William Bamburgh about 1619. Its front is perfectly arranged around a decorative entrance bay, and for the first time we have a house entirely built of stone to contrast with the brick, merely trimmed with stone, of all the others that have been mentioned. Howsham had belonged to nearby Kirkham Priory and it may have been from the monastic ruins that at least some of the stone for Howsham Hall came.

Several of the smaller houses of the early and mid seventeenth century display the new-fashioned shaped and Dutch gables, though like so many other architectural innovations these were generally slow to reach the north of England. Perhaps the most attractive house incorporating such features is Knedlington Old Hall, near Howden; others include Holmes House, near South Duffield, Hornsea Old Hall and Arram Hall. Southwold Farm at North Dalton is an unusually fine example, built with much stone as well as brick and having shaped gables and mullioned windows. It was oddly placed, for it was built two miles out of the village amongst the open fields and pastures on the Wolds slopes. The house is small and may perhaps have been a hunting or shooting lodge. Willerby Hall, near Hull, dates from the later seventeenth century and has both of the new types of gable, but by that time other forms of ornamental brickwork had also made their appearance in the riding. As good as any work of this kind is the façade of Southwood Hall, Cottingham, with its pilasters and pediments and three-storeyed porch. There are pilasters, too, at the manor-house at Barmby Moor, pediments at Manor Farm, Fraisthorpe, and another tall porch at Eske Manor. It is not difficult to imagine the source of at least part of the family wealth at Eske, for the house stands isolated amidst the earthworks of the deserted village site and the ridge-and-furrow of the former open fields.

In the last twenty or thirty years of the seventeenth century East Riding builders and their patrons progressed beyond the 'Artisan Mannerism' of houses like Southwood Hall and Eske Manor to a refined classical style, perfectly expressed in Bell Hall, Naburn, built for Sir John Hewley of York in 1680. The new style may also been seen at Portington Hall, near Howden, built for the local Portington family and perhaps replacing a medieval house on the moated site near by. All over the riding houses in the new style were appearing in the earlier eighteenth century, and indeed for long after; their contribution to the Georgian transformation of the landscape will be considered in the next chapter. The rebuilding of village churches by local landlords is another matter that could safely be left to that chapter if it were not for the exceptional case of Thorganby. The delightful red-brick nave and chancel there were added to the medieval stone tower by Francis Annesley in 1710 and 1719 respectively, though in a style more reminiscent of the late seventeenth century.

The new houses of the later sixteenth and the seventeenth centuries were mostly built of the preponderant East Riding brick. Exceptions, like Howsham Hall and Southwold Farm already mentioned, are of special interest when they are found. The house that John Legard bought at Ganton in the 1580s was "new builded" of chalk, apparently a relatively humble material, though it was many years before the Legards rebuilt the house. There are, it is true, examples of later houses built of carefully-cut chalk 'ashlar'. Two chalk buildings of the seventeenth century which still survive are a dovecot near Bessingby Hall, and Low Hall at Hunmanby, the manor-house of the Stutvilles, who built up an estate at this period and often challenged the authority of the Osbaldestons at Hunmanby Hall. In the south of the riding brick was also eschewed at Hotham Hall, which was built in the late seventeenth century of the dark local Jurassic limestone—though deceptively cut in brick-sized blocks.

Of the ornamental, often formal, gardens which were no doubt laid out around the houses of the sixteenth and seventeenth centuries we know very little. An exception is Londesborough, for John Kip's drawing of the estate in the early 1700s shows in some detail the walks, terraces, lawns, orchards and avenues which surrounded the late-seventeenth-century house belonging to the Earl of

Burlington. The house has gone, however, and the overgrown grounds are sadly desolate now.

At Burton Agnes the great brick garden wall still stands, but the clipped yews within were not planted until the eighteenth century; in 1697, when Celia Fiennes stayed at the house, there was a bowling green in the forecourt and the grounds were ambiguously described as "large and capable of being made very fine".

Enough buildings survive to give an impression of the contribution that the houses of the greater and lesser gentry made to the landscape during these centuries. When we turn to the modest village houses and cottages of the time there is much less evidence. On the Wolds and in the stone belt it is likely that rubble walls of chalk or limestone were prevalent, and some form of mud walling was doubtless common, too, all over the riding. By the later seventeenth century, moreover, the use of brick had spread well down the social scale; early brickwork is to be seen, for example, in several small houses at Wheldrake. But whatever material was used for the walls, it seems that a timber framework was still a common form of construction, despite the scarcity of woodland trees in many parts of the riding. There are few timber-framed houses left today, at least to outward appearances, the most picturesque survivors being individual buildings at South Dalton, on the lower slopes of the Wolds, and at Stillingfleet and Wheldrake, in the still comparatively well-wooded country between the Ouse and the Derwent.[4] On closer examination, however, many houses and cottages are proving to have remnants of a timber framework under the brick or stone cladding that was added later on.[5] In a few cases a cruck type of frame-

[4] Barbara Hutton, 'Timber-framed houses in the Vale of York', *Medieval Archaeology*, xvii (1973), pp. 87–99.
[5] Mrs Vanessa Neave's detailed work on the vernacular houses of the riding is making this clear.

work can still be recognised, best of all in a small cottage at Octon, high on the Wolds, where brick and chalk walls hide two pairs of crucks. Until recently some crude crucks, as well as patches of mud walling, could also be seen among the eighteenth-century brickwork of a cottage at Skipsea Brough. The prevalence of such timber-framed houses, even on the Wolds, is suggested by a rare piece of evidence from Settrington in 1600. A detailed survey shows that most of the 78 houses in the village were built on crucks, and in the previous five years nearly 1,600 trees from local woods had been sold to men from three dozen villages round about.[6]

An impression of the layout of sixteenth- and seventeenth-century houses and their outbuildings is occasionally given by early estate maps, like that of Settrington accompanying the survey of 1600 or those drawn in 1616 of Catton, Leconfield, Thornton and Wressle, which belonged to the Earls of Northumberland. Other evidence is being provided by excavation on the sites of depopulated villages. At Cowlam, for example, a seventeenth-century house has been uncovered with a plan basically unchanged from the long-houses of the Middle Ages. It had, nevertheless, a separate building for a byre, as well as a barn and a walled yard.

[6] H. King and A. Harris, eds., *A Survey of the Manor of Settrington* Y.A.S.R.S. cxxvi (1962).

SELECT BIBLIOGRAPHY

De Boer, G., 'Accretion and Reclamation in the River Humber', *East Yorkshire Field Studies*, 3 (1970), pp. 15–29.
Harris, A., 'The Lost Village and the Landscape of the Yorkshire Wolds', *A.H.R.*, vi (part II) (1958), pp. 97–100.
Harris, A., *The Open Fields of East Yorkshire* (E.Y.L.H.S. 9) (1959, reprinted 1974).

Harris, A., *The Rural Landscape of the East Riding of Yorkshire, 1700–1850* (1961, 2nd edition 1969).

Harris, A., 'Some Maps of Deserted Medieval Villages in the East Riding of Yorkshire', *Geographische Zeitschrift* (1968), pp. 181–93.

Harris, A., 'The Rabbit Warrens of East Yorkshire in the Eighteenth and Nineteenth Centuries', *Y.A.J.*, xlii (1971), pp. 429–43.

Pevsner, N., *Yorkshire: York & the East Riding* (1972).

Sheppard, June A., *The Draining of the Hull Valley* (E.Y.L.H.S. 8) (1958).

Sheppard, June A., *The Draining of the Marshlands of South Holderness and the Vale of York* (E.Y.L.H.S. 20) (1966).

Sheppard, June A., 'Field Systems of Yorkshire', in A. R. H. Baker and R. A. Butlin, eds., *Studies of Field Systems in the British Isles* (1973).

V.C.H., *Yorkshire East Riding*, II (1974) and III (1976).

7. The Georgian and Victorian countryside: the land

The pattern of parliamentary enclosure. New farmsteads. Drainage and reclamation

IN MANY PARTS of the riding, and above all on the Wolds, the face of the countryside was transformed in the eighteenth and nineteenth centuries by the large-scale enclosure of remaining open fields and commons. A pattern of settlement and land-use which had slowly evolved over many centuries was overlaid, though nowhere obliterated, by a new landscape, more regular and efficient, which in its essential elements remains intact today. An observer of the Wolds scene in 1850, when enclosure was nearly complete, described it aptly if a trifle idyllically:

> The country is all enclosed, generally by thorn hedges; and plantations, everywhere grouped over its surface, add beauty to the outline, while they shelter the fields from the cutting blasts of winter and spring. Green pasture fields are occasionally intermixed with corn, or more frequently surround the spacious and comfortable homestead. Large and numerous corn ricks give an air of warmth and plenty, while the turnip fields, crowded with sheep, make up a cheerful and animated picture.

The new husbandry indeed went hand-in-hand with enclosure. The introduction of turnips and clover, sainfoin and grass seeds, made it possible to use improved rotations and methods of livestock husbandry. The old order of farming and the medieval landscape, which had long been subject to piecemeal and localised change, now finally gave way before the combined efforts of the enclosure commissioner and the improving landlord.

It was the Wolds that felt the full force of parliamentary enclosure from 1730 onwards: two out of every three acres there are estimated to have been involved. But despite the greater extent of earlier forms of enclosure in the lowlands areas, there was nevertheless much open-field and waste land still to be dealt with in Holderness and parts of the Vale of York. Moreover, in many townships a process which had been started by earlier forms of enclosure was completed by parliamentary enclosure Acts. The lowlands also witnessed during these centuries other far-reaching improvements. In the Hull valley and the Vale of York the carrs and marshes were finally drained, and along the Humber shore much new land was reclaimed from the sea.

The pattern of parliamentary enclosure

Enclosure by Act of Parliament was often a costly business because of the complicated legal procedure involved, the immense labour of the commissioners who made the award, and the difficulties that were involved in getting up hedges around the new fields. It is therefore hardly surprising that efforts to improve open-field farming without resorting to enclosure continued throughout the eighteenth century. New rotations and crops were sometimes introduced into the open fields, as at Helperthorpe and Hunmanby, and 'flatting'—the grouping of each man's strips into compact but still unenclosed blocks—was suggested, for example at Langtoft, as an alternative to an 'entire' enclosure. Wolds farmers contemplating enclosure were always mindful of the inconvenience and loss that would be involved in keeping their sheep away from the new hedges until they were established.

Only by enclosure, however, were the full benefits of the new husbandry to be enjoyed, and progress was rapid in the second half of the eighteenth century. The first East Riding enclosure Act was for Catwick, in Holderness, in 1731. Nearly fifty Acts were passed in the peak decade, the 1770s, but there was an average of more than twenty in each decade between 1760 and 1820. By 1850 there had been 162 private Acts, while several townships made use of the general enclosure Acts passed after 1800; a few other enclosures were made by agreement, sometimes confirmed by an Act. By these various means some 250 townships were affected by enclosure after 1730. The area involved was very large: it has been estimated that between 1730 and 1810 some 206,000 acres were enclosed on the Wolds, 68,000 acres in Holderness, and 44,000 acres in the Vale of York. Most of the later enclosures were in the Wolds, and about 45,000 acres were dealt with there in 1815-50. The last enclosure in the riding, as late as 1904, involved the open fields of Skipwith, in the Vale of York.[1]

The extent to which the enclosure commissioners reshaped the landscape is suggested by the overall statistics, but in the individual townships it clearly depended upon the proportion of open land that was involved. In some cases there was so little old enclosure in a township that the commissioners had virtually unlimited scope. At the adjoining Wolds villages of Wetwang and Fimber in 1806, for example, the commissioners' awards dealt with 3,207 acres and 1,840 acres respectively out of total township acreages of 3,436 and 1,927. In North Holderness

[1] A forty-acre remnant of the open fields of Waxholme survived until 1962, when the intermixed parcels were quietly consolidated.

1,002 out of a total of 1,382 acres were enclosed at Brigham in 1767, 994 out of 1,108 acres at Foston in 1780, and 886 out of 1,173 acres at Great Kelk in 1849. At the other extreme there were townships in the Vale of York where medieval assarts and later enclosures by agreement had left only small areas on which the commissioners could impose their distinctively regular landscape. At North Duffield, for example, only 1,106 acres of open fields and commons remained to be enclosed in 1814 out of the 3,417 acres in the township.

The enclosure commissioners replaced each man's scattered open-field strips and his grazing rights in the common pastures with a number of fenced closes, grouped as far as possible into compact farms. The commissioners and their surveyors worked to functional and efficient geometrical patterns. We have seen that early enclosure by agreement could produce long curving closes following the lines of open-field strips and furlongs, and it is not difficult to find examples of similar field shapes produced by parliamentary enclosure. But more characteristically the commissioners ruled their new field boundaries with little regard for the past, and the typical landscape of parliamentary enclosure is marked by a regular pattern of rectangular fields (Plate 23). The field pattern that we see today is not, of course, exactly that created at enclosure, for many of the large fields allotted by the commissioners have since been sub-divided. This is the case, for instance, in that part of Walkington shown in the aerial photograph: many smaller fields have been made from those allotted at enclosure in 1795. Sub-division has been especially important on the Wolds, where large fields, sometimes of several hundred acres, were set out at enclosure. Even so, the fields of the Wolds, often covering forty or fifty acres, are still generally larger than those of Holderness or the Vale of York. Nowadays, with the widespread destruction of hedges, the trend is back towards larger fields in many districts.

Although ditches sufficed in some especially low-lying districts and stone walls were occasionally built in the Jurassic hills, hedges were everywhere the usual means of marking out the new fields. On the Wolds chalk walls were impractical: it was said of Wetwang, for example, that "The stones upon the place moulder like lime in the winter, so that no wall fence can be made, therefore a quickset must be raised whatever it costs." Hedges were indeed expensive. They had to be 'nursed up' under the protection of underwood or posts and rails, and in the general absence of suitable local timber it was necessary to use great quantities of north European wood, imported through Hull and Bridlington. The young hedges also had to be saved from devouring animals, and the enclosure commissioners barred sheep from the fields for up to ten years. Most commonly hawthorn was used for the hedges, and today low trim thorn hedges are still one of the most widespread features of the East Riding landscape. Occasionally other species were used, such as elder in some exposed situations on the Wolds or willow in particularly wet places, for example at Wawne common in the Hull valley. More rarely mixed hedges were planted, like some of those on the former common at Holme upon Spalding Moor, use presumably being made of bushes growing near by: clearly there are exceptions to the recently propounded view that the more species a hedge contains the older it is.

East Riding hedges were rarely planted on raised banks during these centuries, though there were some exceptions, apparently where natural conditions were considered especially unfavourable to ready hedge growth. Thus there are prominent banks on several sandy areas in the Vale of York, for example on the former common at Barmby

Plate 23 The Wolds near Walkington. The typical landscape of parliamentary enclosure (Walkington was enclosed in 1795), showing wide straight roadways, regularly-shaped fields, isolated post-enclosure farmsteads, and shelter belts. Many of the fields were sub-divided in the nineteenth century. The area is dotted with old pits from which chalk was dug to lime the fields. The only notable curving lines (bottom) mark the parish boundary, following a shallow dry valley.

Plate 24 Langton. An 'estate village' built mainly of the local Jurassic stone. Many of the houses date from the earlier nineteenth century.

Plate 25 Warter Priory. The house, built in the seventeenth century but much altered and enlarged in the nineteenth, was demolished in 1972. The gardens and the parkland, with its fine mature trees, were among the most impressive in the riding.

Plate 26 Middleton on the Wolds. The church occupies a raised site overlooking the village pond. Since this picture was taken the village centre has been prettified with a garden that hides the pond from view. As in so many cases in the East Riding, a farmstead (right) survives here in the heart of the village, although most of the post-enclosure farm-houses are out in the fields.

Plate 27 Kilham. A large village, on the lower slopes of the Wolds, which from the thirteenth to the nineteenth century was a local market centre. East Street, shown here, contains a collection of eighteenth- and nineteenth-century brick and tiled houses typical of those in many East Riding villages.

Plate 28 Skidby windmill. Built in the 1820s, this is the only mill to survive in the riding complete with sails. Running up to it (left) is a long curving hedge-bank which forms the parish boundary between Skidby and Cottingham. In line, form and number of shrub species it makes an instructive contrast with the adjoining parliamentary enclosure hedges which divide the fields on either side.

Plate 29 Burton Agnes. The seigneurial landscape around the great house. The hall and its fine gatehouse (right) were built about 1600–10. The building between hall and church contains the vaulted undercroft of a Norman manor-house. The stable block in front is Victorian, and the large rectory (left) was built about 1760.

Moor; similar banks run down to the cliff edge on the exposed northern flank of Flamborough Head, where the sparse trees and shrubs are stunted by winds from the sea.

On the Wolds the hedges were often interrupted by dew ponds, constructed at or soon after enclosure and so placed as to provide water for animals in two or more adjoining fields. An improved method of making these age-old ponds is said to have been perfected by Robert Gardener of Kilham about 1775. Scores of dew ponds, with their perfect saucer shape and surrounding bank, are still to be seen, some still wet but many dry now that their seal has been broken. A good surviving example on Beverley's Westwood may be the "new watering pond" which John Gardener made for the corporation in 1784.

In some parts of the Wolds small pits were once as common as dew ponds. Following enclosure the thin leached soils of the area were treated for acidity by the spreading of chalk dug out from below the top-soil, though modern opinion doubts the need for the practice. At the southern end of the Wolds the surface was pockmarked with such pits, often two or more to a field. Many have since been ploughed out and are now only shallow depressions, but others remain, filled with water or scrub (Plate 23).

Woodland, whether functional or purely ornamental, was an important element in the post-enclosure landscape, especially on the Wolds. Shelter-belts were invaluable around upland farmsteads and alongside exposed fields; coverts were provided for foxes and game-birds; and timber was the only crop that steep valley sides could be made to yield. Some Wolds plantations may have been intended to give shelter for sheep, like that near Heslerton laid out in the form of a cross and offering protection against winds from any quarter. Close by were two earlier sheep 'bields' formed by embankments, one circular and the other of the more usual cross shape; both have since been ploughed down. While much new woodland was being created, there were nevertheless also cases of woodland clearance in the post-enclosure period. At Walkington, for example, the large woods which had existed for centuries at the east and west ends of the parish were almost entirely felled during the half century after enclosure in 1795.

Parliamentary enclosure finally disposed of the open fields, but subsequent cultivation has not everywhere obliterated the ridge-and-furrow that preserves the form and shape of the old open-field strips. Although the predominantly arable husbandry of the Wolds has resulted in the levelling of much ridge-and-furrow, some survives in many townships, often where pasture fields have been retained near village or farmstead. It is also occasionally to be seen where former open-field land now lies within a park, as at Bessingby, near Bridlington. More than one golf course near Hull is patterned with ridge-and-furrow. At Springhead, for example, golfers tread the former open fields of Wolfreton, enclosed as early as the sixteenth century. Ridge-and-furrow is useful in reconstructing past landscapes, but it must be treated with caution. When they truly represent 'fossilised' open-field strips, the ridges are several yards wide, often high-backed and sometimes in a reversed-S shape.[2] But ploughing in more modern times has occasionally produced another, much narrower and smaller, form of ridge-and-furrow. In the nineteenth century, moreover, some of the heavy soils of the riding, such as the warps near the river Ouse, were 'gripped' or drained by the digging of furrows, the excavated soil being thrown on to the ground between them. Gripping may, however, generally be recognised by the sharply grooved furrows and the comparative flatness of the in-

[2] See above p. 131.

tervening ground. A good example may be seen in a field at the crossroads near Sunk Island church.

A few traces also remain of the many common wastes and pastures that were enclosed in these centuries. While the commons themselves have been replaced by regular fields, the outgangs or drove roads that provided access from the villages have sometimes been preserved. There are particularly good examples of wide grassy outgangs at Breighton and Heslington. There are still traces, too, of the long trackway used by the inhabitants of Skidby to reach their common carrs and meadows, which lay four miles away beside the river Hull and formed a detached part of the parish. The wider parts, known as Carr Lane, were enclosed along with the common in 1788. Where the trackway crosses the township of Bentley (in Rowley parish), however, it survives as an overgrown sunken way between raised banks, and is known as Jilly Lane. This trackway dates back to the Middle Ages, for in the early sixteenth century Skidby was making an already customary payment to the lord of Bentley manor for the use of it (Fig. 23).

Remnants of the extensive common pasture at Barmby Moor also survived after enclosure in 1783. Two projecting arms of the common which formerly pushed into the heart of the village now form, in effect, 'village greens': it was a very different origin from that of most greens. Occasionally, true village greens which had been created centuries before were dismembered by the enclosure commissioners. At Harlthorpe, for example, the small green was enclosed in 1838 and divided into gardens and paddocks, and as a result the few remaining houses of the village now stand well back from the road.

As characteristic as any features of the landscape of parliamentary enclosure are the wide straight roads laid out by the commissioners. Roads crossing open fields and commons frequently had no precisely-defined course, but varied with the season to avoid ruts and mud. At enclosure these roads were confined by the hedges of adjacent fields, though leeway was still afforded to travellers on their wide verges: most of the commissioners' roads were forty feet wide from hedge to hedge, only the central twenty feet being made up. Even so, there were complaints that busy roads became virtually impassable after enclosure had fixed their courses. Townships on the Wolds and in the Jurassic stone belt used local materials for road repair, and many of the small quarries allotted for the purpose at enclosure can still be traced; elsewhere, gravel and cobbles were brought from the coast in large quantities.

The enclosure commissioners took the opportunity to straighten many roads, while others were realigned to benefit the owners of nearby property.[3] Old roads were frequently stopped up and entirely new ones laid out as part of the rationalisation of the landscape that enclosure made possible. Indeed, road diversions in the period 1750–1850 affected dozens of places in the riding. One piece of countryside which may serve to illustrate this theme is a five-mile stretch of the valley of the Gypsey Race, on the northern Wolds, where enclosure took place at various dates between 1769 and 1840 (Fig. 17). A major change here was the shifting of the east–west road along the valley bottom from a course close to the Race to one further north, probably to avoid the seasonal flooding of the stream. The channel of the Race was also straightened and several minor road diversions made, apparently in 1776, when the Wold Newton commissioners certainly did their share. Further changes were made in 1839, during the enclosure of Foxholes.

Within the newly-enclosed landscape there were fundamental alterations in land-use which contributed to the

[3] See pp. 186, 191.

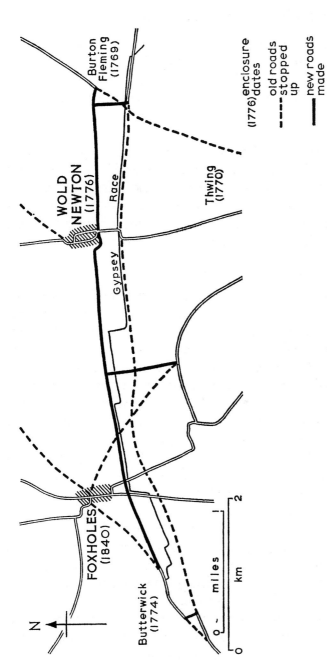

Fig. 17. Roads around Foxholes and Wold Newton (based on Jefferys' Map of Yorkshire of 1772, enclosure and tithe award maps, and the Foxholes highway diversion order of 1839). Showing changes made in the period 1770–1840 during the enclosure of a group of townships in the valley of the Gypsey Race.

changing scene. On the Wolds the conversion of old pasture to tillage was especially striking: not only were the commons enclosed and ploughed, but land which individual proprietors had thought fit only for rabbits was, with improved husbandry, also put to the plough. Many of the old warrens were thus broken up, especially in the first half of the nineteenth century. By 1812 it was estimated that two-thirds of the Wolds were under tillage, and the trend continued for most of the century. Contemporaries sometimes spoke of a "rage for ploughing" which impoverished the poorer soils, for there was a temptation to take too many corn crops in the early years. The practice widely adopted, however, was the four-course rotation of turnips, barley, seeds (grass or clover), and wheat, though there were many variations on it to suit different soils. Sheep were still essential and were folded in large numbers for their manure, but winter-fed store cattle also became a feature of the Wolds husbandry during the nineteenth century.

The Holderness husbandry was less spectacularly improved than that of the Wolds. Despite the major drainage works that took place, of which we must say more later on, it was really only with the popularisation of tile drainage after the mid nineteenth century that many of the heavier soils could be successfully cultivated. In 1812 only a third of the land in most parts of Holderness was said to be tilled, but the proportion was steadily increasing. Holderness, however, maintained its old variety of land-use. There continued to be much grassland, and cattle were far more numerous than on the Wolds. Around Hull market-gardening was also beginning to develop about 1800, though it was to be many years before it became a conspicuous feature of the landscape. In the Vale of York, areas with heavy soils had much in common with Holderness, but there were many districts with light soils which more readily benefited from the new husbandry. Marling was widespread in the sandy districts, making use of the Keuper Marl that lay not far below the surface; many old pits still dot the fields in the area south of Market Weighton, for example.

A final word may be given to woodlands, for, despite the open character of much of the East Riding even today, one of the most significant aspects of the 'spirit of improvement' that followed parliamentary enclosure was the planting of trees. All over the Wolds plantations of Scotch pine, spruce, larch, beech and ash were established and many individual trees were planted in the quickset hedges, where the ash was a particular favourite. On some estates large acreages of woodland were involved at such places as Sledmere on the higher Wolds, at Boynton in the valley of the Gypsey Race, at Kilnwick Percy, Wintringham and Welton on the escarpment, and at Neswick and Bishop Burton on the lower eastern slopes. By 1905 there were 870 acres of woodland at Sledmere, 470 acres at Londesborough, 350 acres at Wintringham, and 300 acres at Bishop Burton. On the lower slopes of the Wolds, and in Holderness and the Vale of York, oak and elm are much more common in the hedgerows. Large-scale planting was rare in Holderness, though Rise, Burton Constable and Winestead were noteworthy exceptions. In the Vale there was much planting on the light soils near Houghton, at Holme upon Spalding Moor, at Melbourne, and around Laxton, near the river Ouse. Houghton woods contained 690 acres in 1905, and there were 590 acres at Holme. Other woodlands in the Vale of York were the successors of older woods, like those at Escrick, Kexby, Scoreby and Wheldrake. Escrick had 530 acres in 1905, the others over 200 acres each.

New farmsteads

Parliamentary enclosure was followed by a proliferation of one of the most common features of the East Riding landscape, the isolated farm-house standing in the midst of its fields. It has already been seen that some isolated houses were built during the medieval colonisation of parts of the Vale of York and Holderness, and more had appeared in townships where early enclosure was achieved by agreement, again mostly in the more low-lying districts. Even there, however, most farm-houses were still to be found in the villages, while on the Wolds it was rare indeed for them to stand anywhere else. So long as a man's lands lay scattered in the open fields, and while he enjoyed common rights in various meadows and pastures in a township, then the village was the most convenient location for his house and farm buildings. The creation of compact farms by the enclosure commissioners, however, encouraged a break with tradition. Water supply was still of paramount importance, but, provided that a well could be sunk and a cattle pond constructed, a central situation in the freshly enclosed fields was usually chosen for the new farmstead.

Individual farmers may have been disinclined to make such a move, and some landlords doubtless also preferred to retain old village farm-houses until they could no longer be economically repaired. Other farmsteads remained in the village because their newly-enclosed lands were close at hand, or because the farms were so laid out by the commissioners as to pivot upon the old farmyards. The latter situation is well-illustrated at Wold Newton, where enclosure took place in 1776. By 1818 three isolated farm-houses had been built in the parish, and two more had been added by 1850; but six of the new enclosure allotments extended right into the village and continued to be farmed from there. One or more farmsteads still give an authentic 'working' quality to the streets of most East Riding villages. And many of them, in their cramped surroundings, retain older buildings which on more spacious isolated sites would have long since been replaced.

Some of the new isolated farm-houses were built soon after enclosure, a few apparently even before the commissioners finally made their award. Haverfield House, Welwick, for example, is said to have been built in 1779, eight years after enclosure, but Riston Grange, Long Riston, was erected in 1773—after the Act was passed in 1771 but before the award in 1778. Similarly, Tibthorpe House and the nearby Manor House were both put up in 1795 after the passing of the Act but still before the making of the award in 1796. Other houses were built later on, when large farms were subdivided or as poorer land was improved and more intensively farmed. At Eastburn, for example, the whole territory of the deserted village formed a single farm, with its farmstead at the village site. Part of the farm was used as a rabbit warren, but when that was divided into fields in 1849 a new farmstead was built to work them. Little Wauldby Farm was similarly built in the eastern part of Wauldby shortly before 1835, and Sancton Hill Farm was newly constructed on the Wolds escarpment in 1854. Fewer new farms were erected later in the century, but examples are to be found, like Avenue and Manor Farms at North Cliffe, the latter dated 1885. The pattern of scattered farmsteads thus evolved gradually from the mid eighteenth century onwards.

The lonely houses and ranges of farm buildings which became such a characteristic feature of the landscape were frequently built of new materials and to new designs. In 1794 Isaac Leatham could still write of "some few" mud-walled buildings and many built of chalk on the Wolds,

L

often with thatched roofs, though he saw "an equal quantity" of buildings constructed of more solid materials, bricks and pantiles. The older materials were still very apparent to Strickland in 1812, but bricks steadily gained ground and thatch was described by Charles Howard in 1835 as "properly abolished". Chalk is still frequently to be seen in farm buildings on the Wolds, but the houses are almost all of brick; even some of the chalk farm buildings have footings, quoins and eaves courses of brick, as on the Birdsall estate and at Speeton. Only in the Jurassic belt did the local stone continue to be widely used, sometimes for the facing of whole new farmsteads, like Home Farm at Birdsall, which was rebuilt in 1868. Pantiles were not replaced as a roofing material until the middle of the nineteenth century, for slate was still "too expensive for common use" in 1835. But the old buildings at Eastburn were rebuilt in brick and slate in 1851, and slate was used at Sancton Hill and Birdsall Home Farm. A little later there was a wholesale rebuilding of farm-houses and farm buildings on the Warter Priory estate, including Blanch Farm in 1873, by which date slate was a much more common material. Also in the later nineteenth century the local brown brick was sometimes supplanted by exotic yellow or grey: Avenue and Manor Farms, North Cliffe, for example, are of grey brick.

Most of the Georgian farm-houses were plain and unfussy in appearance, a virtue extolled by Strickland in 1812: "What indeed", he wrote, "can be so absurd and devoid of taste as a Gothicised farm-house or castellated cottage?" Occasionally, especially on the larger estates, some ornamentation might be introduced, like the big central pediments on the fronts of several farm-houses at Escrick, belonging to Lord Wenlock. Castle Farm at North Cave, also built in the late eighteenth century, was formerly crenellated, intended as an eye-catcher from Hotham Hall, and

Gothic features were to become increasingly common in Victorian farm-houses. It was not only the brand-new farm-houses which expressed new fashions, for many older houses were wholly or partially rebuilt during the nineteenth century. Sometimes a new house on a grander scale or in more fashionable style was built beside its more humble predecessor, and both still stand as a visual reminder of growing fortunes and pretensions: examples may be seen at High Field and Garton Field Farms, Garton on the Wolds, and at Woodhouse Farm, Eppleworth.

To say that Georgian farmsteads were built to new designs is perhaps less accurate than to suggest that for the first time farm buildings were built to any coordinated design at all. Pre-enclosure farm buildings had usually been rebuilt and extended in a haphazard way, and many such old-fashioned farmsteads lingered on through the nineteenth century, some indeed down to the present day. Such were the buildings that Howard found at Wauldby, a much shrunken Wolds hamlet, in 1835: they were large and numerous, but "old, ill-constructed, and have been erected at different periods, with a view of supplying the present want, but without any attention to regularity of plan or regard to general convenience". The farm-house of Ridgemont, at Burstwick, in Holderness, had only recently been built and was described by Howard as excellent, but the farm buildings suffered from the same faults as those at Wauldby. They formed, nevertheless, "a little town of useful buildings" and well illustrate the complexity of even some of the older, unplanned, farmsteads. They afforded every convenience for keeping a large number of cattle: threshing and straw-cutting machinery on a large scale, horse mills, carpenter's and smith's shops, and various sheds for carriages and implements.

The regularly planned farmsteads which began to appear in the East Riding countryside in the late eighteenth century were similar to those being built in many parts of lowland England. The buildings lay around a square fold-yard, sheltered by the barn and stables to the north, flanked by cattle houses to east and west, open to the south save for a wall; often there was still a dovecot—a common sight even today on East Riding farms—though losses of crops were by now beginning to outweigh the value of meat and manure from the pigeons. The farm-house itself frequently stood close by to the south or west. Marshall and Leatham had seen such farmsteads before 1800, and in the 1830s Howard described them as "usually found on all the well-managed estates" in the riding. Larger farmsteads might have two foldyards, like Sancton Hill Farm, erected in 1854, or Cold Harbour Farm at Bishop Burton, built to replace an older set of buildings in the later nineteenth century. But the same basic layout was followed, with occasional modification, for almost all new farmsteads in Wolds and lowlands alike.

The larger Wold farms might also boast one or more subsidiary farmsteads, often placed on the higher and more remote parts of the estate. Such farmsteads usually comprised a small foldyard, a barn and a cottage, and frequently they took the name High Barn or Wold Barn. A good example is High Barn at Sewerby, which consists of a single range containing cottage, barn and stable. The 1,000-acre Burdale farm had two of these smaller units, situated on the higher land north and south of the valley in which the main farmstead lay.

Farm design normally involved the arrangement of traditional buildings in a regular and convenient layout. In one respect, however, technological change resulted in the introduction of a new building on many East Riding farms during this period. After the invention of the threshing machine in the 1780s, and the harnessing of horse power to drive it, sheds were built beside many barns to accommodate horse-wheels. Leatham saw few threshing machines in 1794, but less than twenty years later Strickland found that they were "becoming now very general on the considerable farms throughout the district". Numerous wheelhouses can be identified on the Ordnance Survey maps of the 1850s, and surviving buildings are mostly of late-eighteenth or early nineteenth-century date. Power from the wheel was also used for turnip-chopping, straw-cutting, oat-rolling, cake-crushing, and so forth, and the wheelhouse thus became an integral and lasting part of many cattle-rearing farmsteads. Most surviving wheelhouses are single-storeyed, sometimes square but more often six- or seven-sided. Though it is clear from map evidence that they were once common on the Wolds, it is in the Vale of York and in Holderness that they are now most frequently to be seen.

In the mid nineteenth century horse power for threshing was replaced by steam on some farms in the riding, but there is little sign that the development was as widespread here as in some other parts of the country. 'Factory farms', with their chimneys and engine houses, were few. Enholmes, near Patrington, was built with a steam-engine house in 1849, and so was Sancton Hill Farm in 1854. Soon after it was built Enholmes was described as a model farm, laid out "on the most improved plan", the land managed and beasts fattened "on a new principle". This latter was probably a reference to the feeding of cattle in numerous closed boxes, for Enholmes had no traditional open fold-yard at all. Such a departure from tradition was rare. More often, improved cattle accommodation was provided by roofing-in the foldyard: Home Farm, at Birdsall, for example, was rebuilt in 1868 with covered yards, and most of the farmsteads on the Birdsall estate had one of their yards partially or wholly covered-in during the years 1899–1902.

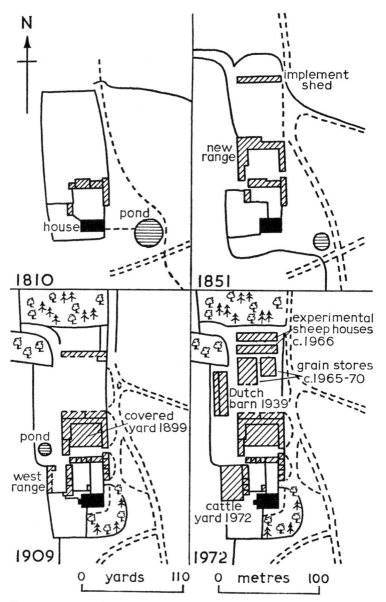

Fig. 18. Aldro Farm, Birdsall. Showing the changing landscape of a typical large Wolds farmstead in the nineteenth and twentieth centuries.

One of the Birdsall farmsteads, Aldro, well illustrates the changing landscape around a typical Wolds farmhouse (see Fig. 18).[4] The township was enclosed in the 1690s, and a map of 1772 shows that there were already five isolated farmsteads there; one of them was Aldro, which had probably been built since 1766 when a sheep pasture called 'Alrow' was added to the estate. As a map of 1810 shows more clearly, the early buildings stood around a foldyard, and near by lay the cattle pond. By 1851 a larger range had been added, enclosing a second yard, with a separate implement shed. The new buildings included a barn and granary, no doubt reflecting a change from pasture to arable farming as more high wold ground was broken up. A smaller west range had been added and the pond moved to a more convenient position by 1891, and in 1899 the main yard was covered in. During the later nineteenth century, too, shelter belts and plantations were established, and some ornamental planting was done near the house. Many of the features of the Victorian farmstead may still be seen at Aldro, though there were to be striking additions in the twentieth century.

Drainage and reclamation

The eighteenth and nineteenth centuries saw the long drawn out but ultimately successful drainage of the water-logged lands in the Hull valley, the Vale of York and the Vale of Pickering, as well as the reclamation of further substantial areas of new land alongside the Humber. When the threat of flooding had been finally removed from the low grounds, there emerged a landscape of rich new farmland, of narrow dikes and wide 'agricultural drains', of banks, sluices and humble brick bridges. Equally distinctive, but more bleak, are the windswept expanses of reclaimed land,

[4] Based on plans in Popham, 'Farm Buildings' (see bibliography).

a landscape planned to the smallest detail and unrelieved by any relict features of an older more natural countryside.

The carr-land of the Hull valley was still subject every winter to extensive and deep flooding in the mid eighteenth century, and even the better-drained siltland at the southern end of the valley was not entirely safe from Humber floodwater. Major drainage works were not attempted until 1763, when a large area on the eastern side of the valley was removed from jurisdiction of the old Court of Sewers to that of a new body, the Holderness Drainage. During the next few years a large drain was constructed, discharging into the river immediately to the north of the Old Town at Hull; this is the drain now known as the Foredyke Stream. The limited success of this scheme inspired attempts to improve conditions on the west side of the river. A joint enclosure and drainage Act was passed in 1766 for Cottingham, and the drain known as Setting Dike constructed; the Beverley and Skidby Drain was dug under an Act of 1785, and better drains in Hessle constructed under one of 1792.

Only the southern part of the Hull valley benefited from these schemes, and the carrs further north remained in their old state for some years more. For the whole western side of the valley the crucial step was the passing of the Beverley and Barmston Drainage Act in 1798. Under it the most impressive of the agricultural drains was made, passing in long straight strides down the valley for some fifteen miles, from Hempholme in the north to a junction with the river in the suburbs of Hull. A further improvement under the Act was the diversion of water draining from north Holderness away from the river Hull to an outfall into the sea at Barmston. Though conditions in the northern carrs were much improved by the Beverley and Barmston Drainage, many areas remained waterlogged or subject to seasonal flooding.

On the east bank of the river a major improvement was made under an Act of 1832 which authorised a new drain to be constructed, discharging into the Humber at Marfleet. The drain was designed to take the water only from low-lying carrs, while the old main drain dug in the 1760s was henceforth reserved for the 'upland' water draining into the Hull valley from Holderness. This separation of function enabled the two drains to operate efficiently and, with other improvements, reduced flooding to a brief winter season. Efforts to further improve conditions on the other bank of the river included the erection of a steam pump at Arram in 1868, to raise water from the Beverley and Barmston Drain into the river. Then, in 1880-2, the Hull was dredged and its banks heightened, so increasing its capacity to complement the work of the drains, and further steam pumps were installed at Hempholme and Dunswell.

One of the best vantage points from which to appreciate the drained landscape of the valley is beside the river at Hempholme. The surrounding arable fields, lying markedly lower than the high-banked course of the river, are criss-crossed by dozens of small ditches and drains, while the great Beverley and Barmston Drain, culverted under the river, strikes out towards the south. Little brick bridges carry paths and farm roads over the drains, and here and there a sluice regulates the flow of water. Close to a lock once used by boats on their way up to Driffield stand the derelict pumping station and attendant's house. In the background, on slightly rising ground, the farms of the old hamlet of Hempholme, approached by a winding lane from the valley margin at Brandesburton, remind us that even in the early Middle Ages there were colonists making a living here among the undrained marshes and carrs.

In the Vale of York local piecemeal improvements

continued to be made during these centuries, but more concerted efforts were needed to deal with the two greatest problems, namely the drainage of Wallingfen and Bishopsoil commons. These extensive carrs were waterlogged or flooded for several months of the year, and Wallingfen still even contained several permanent meres. The draining of the commons necessarily went hand in hand with their enclosure, for many villages and hamlets had summer grazing rights there. Bishopsoil, amounting to nearly 4,000 acres, was enclosed under an Act of 1767 and two new main drains constructed: Bishopsoil Near Drain, which enters the Ouse near Skelton, and Far Drain, some ten miles long, which reaches the river near Faxfleet. The enclosure of Wallingfen, containing some 5,000 acres, took place in 1781, allotments to the interested townships producing, as in the case of Bishopsoil, a complex pattern of boundaries which was simplified by changes made in the nineteenth century. The drainage of Wallingfen was effected by the cutting of the Market Weighton Canal in the 1770s and 1780s (see Chapter 8). Though the carrs were considerably improved as a result, the dual-purpose waterway was naturally less effective as a drain on account of the high water level required for navigation. The canal served, moreover, as the outlet for the river Foulness, or Foulney, which collected water from a large area in the heart of the Vale. It was not until well into the present century, after the demise of the navigation, that the drainage of this area could be substantially improved.

Other districts of the Vale of York where serious flooding continued in the eighteenth and nineteenth centuries were the valleys of the river Derwent and its chief tributary, Pocklington Beck. The construction of the Pocklington Canal had little effect on the low grounds around it, for it was kept quite separate from the local drainage channels. Similarly the Derwent Navigation could not be blamed for the age-old flooding of the riverside meadows in the southern part of the Derwent valley. Indeed, the neglect of the river after the navigation declined in the later nineteenth century increased the frequency of flooding. It was again only in the twentieth century that the Derwent and Pocklington Beck were effectively dredged and embanked. Nevertheless, as the traveller crossing the Derwent at Bubwith Bridge plainly sees, the valley floor is still occasionally flooded after winter rains.

In the upper reaches of the river Derwent and along the river Hertford, in the Vale of Pickering, a substantial area of the riverside land awaited adequate drainage in the eightenth century. The "low grounds" were reckoned at almost 6,000 areas in 1773, most of them described as "fenny and of small value". They stretched from Muston in the east to Norton, attaining their greatest extent in the parishes of Folkton and Willerby. Their draining was carried out under a single Act, passed in 1800, and long stretches of both rivers now flow in straight embanked courses across the former carrs, showing scant regard for the old boundary between the East and North Ridings, which followed the sinuous natural courses of these rivers. Improvements continued, and one sad consequence of work done in the 1960s was the demolition of the high-backed stone bridge of 1731 which carried the road over the Derwent at Yedingham.

Along the shore of the Humber the deposition of sand and silt and subsequent reclamation of new land, which began in the late seventeenth century, brought considerable changes to the landscape. A little to the west of Sunk Island, which we have already seen emerging from the river, were extensive sand banks called Cherry Cobb. They were first named in 1684, and by 1723 they could be described as dry at low water and "never all covered but with a high spring tide". The sands were separated from the shore by the much reduced waters of the North Channel (Fig. 19). A Crown claim to them as growing from the bed of the estuary was consequently disputed by the Constable family, claiming them as growths on the foreshore which the family owned. William Constable eventually secured a court verdict in his favour in 1763, and he it was who embanked Cherry Cobb against the sea about 1770.

On Sunk Island itself further reclamation beyond the limits of the early-eighteenth-century island began at the turn of the century and continued throughout the 1800s. To the existing embanked area of 1,560 acres another 2,730 acres were added in 1798–1800. The limits of this new ground were indicated on a map of 1797, and they correspond with the dike now known as the Humber Delve (Fig. 19). From that time the reclaimed land virtually ceased to be an island, for the remnant of the North Channel dividing it from the mainland rapidly became warped up. This new phase of reclamation was followed by the building of eight more farm-houses, together with a new chapel standing just outside the older sea bank.

The reclamation of the island was completed by the embanking of 400 acres on the south side in 1810 or 1811, and by successive extensions to the eastern side which added 1,200 acres in 1826, 700 acres in 1850, and 350 acres in 1897. By similar stages the old North Channel, increasingly choked with silt, was also embanked. When the last sluice, New Clough, was built as part of the work of 1897, boats were finally denied access to Patrington Haven, whose commercial life had been gradually declining since 1800. The 'island's' links with the mainland were improved by the turnpiking of the road from Ottringham to Sunk Island church under an Act of 1836, and in 1850 the trust was also given responsibility for the road from Patrington Haven and for that leading on

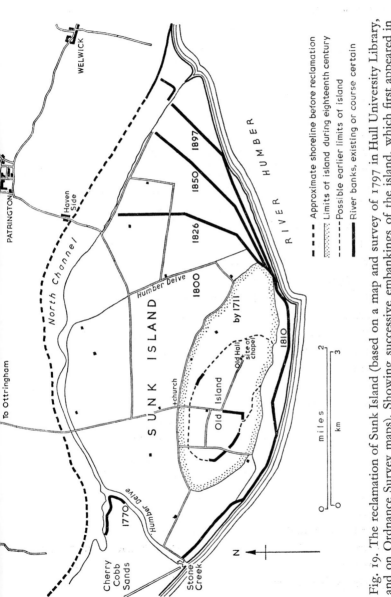

Fig. 19. The reclamation of Sunk Island (based on a map and survey of 1797 in Hull University Library, and on Ordnance Survey maps). Showing successive embankings of the island, which first appeared in the Humber in the late seventeenth century. As the island was reclaimed and North Channel silted up, so the hitherto flourishing trade of Patrington Haven was gradually extinguished.

to Stone Creek. Provision was also made for the building of wharves at Stone Creek, though little trade ever seems to have been attracted to this spot.

The reclamation of Cherry Cobb Sands and Sunk Island had one harmful consequence—a worsening of flooding in several low-lying valleys along the southern margin of Holderness. Not only was the North Channel progressively silted up, thereby reducing its ability to carry off drainage water from Holderness, but also the newly-won lands constituted a barrier to mainland streams draining towards the Humber. The problem was eventually solved by the cutting of new channels for these streams. The Thorngumbald Drain was dug in 1766, emptying into the Humber west of Cherry Cobb instead of into the North Channel as its predecessor had done. It was not until 1802, however, that the old Keyingham Fleet was given a new outlet, in this case straight across Cherry Cobb to Stone Creek. Further east no such drastic step was needed to deal with the Winestead Fleet, which still discharges into the former North Channel, itself now no more than an agricultural drain. The new drains are prominent features of the countryside, especially where their wide deep cuts converge on the 'clows' or sluices at Stone Creek.

The bleak landscape of Sunk Island is like that of no other part of the riding. The large arable fields are mostly divided by deep dikes, for there are few hedgerows and those mostly in the centre of the Old Island, while trees are to be seen only around some of the farmsteads and near the church. The field pattern is as regular as any conceived by enclosure commissioners elsewhere in the riding. To the south the horizon is formed by the modern river bank, with ships regularly passing in the background. Of the old river banks which surrounded the island in its early stages there are still modest traces here and there, as well as the much more obvious northern bank, which now carries the road running from East Bank Farm past the church and on towards Stone Creek Farm. A stretch of the bank built around the area reclaimed in 1798–1800 similarly carries the roadway north and south of Channel Farm. The remnant of Fisherman's Channel near by is still a surprisingly large area of water at the heart of the reclaimed lands.

Sunk Island's buildings are not the least distinctive part of its landscape. Most of the farmsteads and cottages were either built or rebuilt in the mid nineteenth century; nearly all are of dark-red brick with slate roofs, and many are decorated with pointed arches over the door-ways and windows. Many, too, bear a crown, the initials of Victoria and Albert, and a date in the 'fifties or 'sixties. A wheelhouse was once a feature of several of the sets of farm buildings, and at least one of them, at Shrubbery Farm, has survived. Of the earlier farm-houses few survived the mid-century rebuilding, a notable exception being Stone Creek Farm. Like the early farm-houses, the chapel built at the turn of the century has also been replaced; the new red-brick church built in 1877 on the same isolated site strikes a fittingly harsh note in these wind-swept surroundings.

Further up the Humber, at Broomfleet, the work of reclamation carried out in the early eighteenth century was not resumed until the middle of the nineteenth century. An area of sand there had grown up to high water mark by 1820, and in 1846 it was reported that 130 acres had been embanked. The new island was, however, washed away soon afterwards, probably as a result of a change in the deep-water channel of the river. Accretion nevertheless began once more and by 1866 six acres had been enclosed with banks. By 1870 Broomfleet Island had grown to sixty acres, and by the end of the century Broomfleet Hope, the channel separating the island from the mainland, was so warped up that it was dry at low water. The final reclamation of 1907 linked the island to the shore and increased the area of the new land to some 600 acres. A single farm-house stands within the big new river bank, and much of the redundant bank along the earlier shore-line has been levelled.

In the low-lying district bordering the river Ouse the landscape has been largely shaped by the long process of drainage; but in one locality, around the villages of Yokefleet and Blacktoft, the final pattern of banks and dikes also owes something to the practice of warping. Perhaps from the late eighteenth century onwards the fields here were enriched by the deposition of silt or 'warp', which was carried up the Humber and Ouse in large quantities by the incoming tide, much of it derived from the crumbling cliffs of Holderness. Special drains were dug to admit the tidal waters to riverside fields, and both the drains and the fields were contained within high banks designed to hold a considerable depth of water. When warping was completed the water was returned to the river at low tide. The three chief drains concerned were the Yokefleet, Blacktoft and Scalby Warping Drains, running up to three miles inland. Warping was last carried out about 1950, but both before and after that date many of the obsolete field banks were levelled; some good examples remain, however, including several north-east of Metham Hall near the Yokefleet drain. The warping drains themselves, with their substantial sluices opening into the river, now serve like their neighbours for the mundane removal of land water; but the wide, deep and high-banked Yokefleet drain nevertheless still evokes memories of an inrushing warp-laden torrent.[5]

[5] The especially impressive stretch of the drain between the village and the Ouse was being affected by new river works in 1974.

The Georgian and Victorian countryside: the land

SELECT BIBLIOGRAPHY

De Boer, G., 'Accretion and Reclamation in the River Humber', *East Yorkshire Field Studies*, 3 (1970), pp. 15–29.

Harris, A., *The Rural Landscape of the East Riding of Yorkshire, 1700–1850* (1961, 2nd edition 1969).

Harris, A., 'The Rabbit Warrens of East Yorkshire in the Eighteenth and Nineteenth Centuries', *Y.A.J.*, xlii (1971), pp. 429–43.

Neave, Vanessa, *Handlist of East Riding Enclosure Awards* (1971).

Playne, Elizabeth, and De Boer, G., eds., *Lonsdale Documents*, Surtees Society (forthcoming).

Popham, J. H., 'Farm Buildings: Function and Form', unpublished thesis, Diploma in Conservation Studies, University of York (1973).

Sheppard, June A., *The Draining of the Hull Valley* (E.Y.L.H.S. 8) (1958).

Sheppard, June A., *The Draining of the Marshlands of South Holderness and the Vale of York* (E.Y.L.H.S. 20) (1966).

Sheppard, T., *The Lost Towns of the Yorkshire Coast* (1912).

V.C.H., Yorkshire East Riding, II (1974) and III (1976).

Wilkinson, Olga, *The Agricultural Revolution in the East Riding of Yorkshire* (E.Y.L.H.S. 5) (1964).

M

8. The Georgian and Victorian countryside: the village

Country houses and parks. Estate villages.
The fabric of the village

Country houses and parks

THE AGRICULTURAL IMPROVEMENTS which did so much to reshape the East Riding landscape after 1730 also provided the means for many of the landed gentry to create handsome houses for themselves. Some older manor-houses were 'remodelled', but dozens of new houses, great and small, were also put up during the eighteenth and nineteenth centuries; frequently they were in their turn altered, enlarged or completely rebuilt as Georgian and Victorian fashions changed, and a great variety of architectural styles is consequently represented among them. Of greater importance for the landscape than the houses themselves are the settings with which they were enhanced, ranging from the modest gardens of the smaller houses to the parkland, lakes and plantations that surrounded some of the larger mansions. A few parks survived from earlier centuries, like that at Burton Constable, where there are said to have been deer until about 1720. That park was later much enlarged and 'landscaped'; many others were completely new. Beyond their own grounds, moreover, the wealthier squires refashioned whole villages, frequently beautifying old churches or providing new ones, and building chapels, schools and other public buildings.

178

Increasingly during these centuries the ancient dynasties of the East Riding were joined by men from Hull, the West Riding or even further afield, whose wealth derived from trade or the professions. The desire to build and empark was common to most of them, old and new alike. Newly-risen mercantile families like the Sykeses, Broadleys, Denisons and Watts vied with such old-established land-lords as the Constables, Grimstons, St Quintins and Hildyards. None of them built palatial houses to compare with the grandest Georgian houses elsewhere, and even the splendour of Burton Constable was founded on that of the Elizabethan house. Indeed, some of the most charming houses in the riding, as well as the general run, belong to the category of the small compact 'villa' which became so popular in England during the eighteenth century.

Most of the East Riding's country houses followed the classical styles which dominated the Georgian Age. One exception is Buckton Hall, a prominent feature in the bare landscape on the windswept northern flank of Flamborough Head, where it stands in splendid isolation less than a mile from the cliff-top. Built in 1744–5, perhaps to the old-fashioned taste of the elderly squire John Robinson, Buckton was still in the Baroque style, with its heavy rustication and contrasting chalk and freestone façade. But the harmonious Palladian style of classical architecture soon came to the fore. That great exponent of Palladianism the Earl of Burlington had his seat here, at Londesborough, and he and his Bridlington-born protégé William Kent may have had a hand in the designs of several houses in the riding. Londesborough Hall itself was demolished in 1819, but the neglected parkland with its flaking stone ornaments and ageing trees still recalls the splendid surrounds of the Burlington house, as shown in one of Kip's drawings. Among the architects who contributed classical buildings to the East Riding landscape was John Carr of York

(d. 1807), whose work included Everingham Hall in 1757–64 and extensions at Escrick. The more notable classical houses in the riding also include Sledmere House and Houghton, South Dalton and Scampston Halls.

The parks at Sledmere and Scampston well illustrate the 'natural landscape' which was being carefully created in the later eighteenth century by men like 'Capability' Brown. Indeed, to stand among the urns and statues beside the noble house at Sledmere and to enjoy the sweeping vista of grassland and trees is, for many people, to see the 'lordly landscape' at its best. The grounds at Scampston, complete with a Palladian bridge, were Brown's work, and he may have had a share in the emparking at Howsham and Rise. Less well-known landscape gardeners employed in the riding included Thomas White, who did plans for several parks, among them Houghton and Burton Constable in 1768.

John Carr also contributed to the Gothic Revival of the late eighteenth century, and Grimston Garth, built in 1781–6, is a charming example of his work in this style. It lies quite close to the sea, hidden among the trees in one of the few landscaped parks along the Holderness coast. The house is triangular in plan, with round corner towers and battlements, and a big Gothic gatehouse, added later, stands starkly alone some distance from it. Another castellated Gothic house is Cave Castle, at South Cave, built in 1804 for the Barnards, a family with a Hull mercantile background. The grounds had been landscaped a little earlier by William Emes, a gardener better known in midland and southern counties, and here again a matching gateway was added later. Burton Constable Hall also has its Gothic lodge.

Alongside these Palladian and Gothic houses others appeared in the early nineteenth century in the fashion of the Greek Revival. Outstanding perhaps is White Hall at

180

Winestead, built in 1814–15 for Arthur Maister, a member of a prominent merchant family of Hull. The Maisters built their first house at Winestead after they had acquired an estate there in 1699, but their principal residence was probably Maister House, in High Street, Hull, until White Hall was built. Other Greek Revival houses are Rise Hall and Kilnwick Percy Hall; both have giant porticoes, and Kilnwick also has a charming lodge in the same style. In quaint contrast to White Hall is Wood Hall, Ellerby, built for Arthur Maister's brother Henry in 1820 in an Italian style, though probably also designed by the architect of the Winestead house, Charles Mountain of Hull.

Finally, there are the large Victorian houses, usually in some form of the Gothic style, often fanciful and sometimes overbearing. The most noteworthy include Anthony Salvin's Moreby Hall of 1818–31, along with Thicket Priory, Brantingham Thorpe, Ganton Hall and Garrowby Hall. Warter Priory must be mentioned, too, even though it has recently been demolished. The extensions made there in the 1880s and 1890s for C. H. Wilson, the Hull ship-owner, produced "a big bleak French house", standing in one of the finest parks in the East Riding (Plate 25). The parkland here, as at Ganton, Garrowby and Londes-borough, takes full advantage of the slopes of the Wolds escarpment, and contains many splendid mature trees and plantations. Of the many smaller Victorian houses, a good example in a completely different setting is Yokefleet Hall (1870), with its matching Tudor lodges and stables, standing in a small park close behind the flood bank of the river Ouse.

Country houses and parks are, of course, scattered all over the riding, though the larger parks are less common on the high Wolds. In one area, on the lower Wolds slopes west of Hull, an especially rich landscape was created during these centuries. It was here that many of the more wealthy townsmen began in the early eighteenth century to build country retreats, which soon came to replace their principal town houses. The typically bare Wolds landscape was gradually transformed by tree planting and emparking, and from their houses many of the new country gentry looked over sloping gardens to the shining waters of the Humber. By 1796 North Ferriby and Welton could be described as "full of handsome buildings belonging to several wealthy merchants of Hull". The full charm of this landscape is suggested by the sale particulars of the Melton Hill estate, near Welton, which was on the market in 1822: "the mansion house stands in a delightful lawn of nearly a hundred acres, well sheltered with plantations and tastefully ornamented with shrubberies and groups of forest trees, and together with the pleasure grounds commands an extensive and enchanting view scarcely equalled in any part of the kingdom". The 'lawn' at Melton Hill was one of many small and medium-sized parks to which that word was applied lying in the parishes around the southern end of the Wolds, from Cottingham in the east to Brantingham.

The neighbouring villages of Welton and Melton may be taken as representative of all the villages in this area. Enclosure awards in 1752, 1773 and 1775 enabled several roads to be diverted and provided the framework within which building and planting could proceed. The Welton House and Melton Hill estates belonged in 1748 to James Shaw of Hull, but they subsequently passed by marriage to Joseph Williamson, a prominent merchant in the Swedish iron trade at Hull, and it is especially to the Williamsons that the two villages owe their present character. Joseph Williamson built Melton Hill House about 1780 and his brother Thomas rebuilt Welton House, and together they were responsible for much tree-planting. Melton Hill House has been demolished, but its East Lodge—a charming early-nineteenth-century classical building—still stands, though spoilt by unsympathetic restoration. Welton House has gone too, but before its demolition it had been twice remodelled by other owners with Hull origins, by the Raikes family about 1820 and the Harrison-Broadleys about 1890. The Raikes family mausoleum, dated 1818, still stands among the plantations at the head of Welton Dale. The break-up of the Harrison-Broadley estate opened the way for the development of the villages in the twentieth century, but among the surviving mansions at Welton are the Grange, the Manor and the Hall, all built or remodelled in the eighteenth or early nineteenth centuries.

Other houses in the area built or enlarged by Hull men include Sir Henry Etherington's Ferriby House (about 1760), with its fine stables, Joseph Sykes's West Ella Hall, and the recorder Robert Osborne's Braffords Hall. Several more survive at Hessle, Kirk Ella and elsewhere. Nevertheless, the leafy landscape and spacious living of the whole district have been subjected to many changes in the present century.

Estate villages

In many East Riding villages the replacement of open fields and commons by hedged closes, the laying-out of well-defined roadways, and the building of new isolated farmsteads completed the transformation of the old landscape. Minor alterations would later be made, but parliamentary enclosure was the all-important agent of change. There were other villages, however, where enclosure set in train a series of changes which all played as great a part as the enclosure itself in shaping the new landscape. They were mostly places with a wealthy, powerful and ambitious leading landowner. To such men 'improvement' meant not only hedged fields, rebuilt farmsteads and new crops, but also enlarged manor-houses, landscaped grounds, expanded parks, and often the diversion of roads and the removal of unsightly houses and cottages. The medieval village was sometimes changed beyond recognition. In its place was created the orderly 'estate village', lying outside the park at a seemly distance from the big house. In other cases the changes were less drastic but certain characteristic features of the estate village are nevertheless plain to see. Some of the most picturesque villages in the riding are of this kind, outstanding among them being Sledmere, Settrington, Escrick, Sewerby and Howsham.

The village of Escrick amply illustrates the wide-ranging changes which could be made by improving squires, in this case the Thompsons, whose family fortunes had been made in nearby York. They enclosed open fields and commons, diverted roads, created parkland, replanned the village, and rebuilt not only their own and the tenants' houses but also the parish church. Today Escrick bears little resemblance to the medieval village which stood astride the Escrick moraine (Fig. 20). Although it was enclosure which triggered-off the long sequence of changes to the old landscape, there was no enclosure Act of the customary kind and no award by a group of commissioners. The lord of the manor, Bielby Thompson, did indeed secure an Act of Parliament in 1781, but its aims were not limited to enclosure: rather, it authorised the "many considerable improvements" which he intended to make around his manor-house.

The house itself had already been considerably changed and enlarged. The building erected by Henry Thompson about 1680-90 had been refronted and raised a storey, perhaps in 1758, and in 1763 the well-known York architect John Carr had been employed to design additions to it. Carr's work included a range which more than doubled the length of the main front of the house, as well as a large stable block. Such a splendid seat must have seemed worthy of a more spacious setting.

Plate 30 Stamford Bridge water-mill. One of the largest of the riding's water-powered mills, it was closed only in 1964 and has since been converted to a restaurant. Part of the present building, visible at the right of the picture, dates from the eighteenth century, but the main block was built in the nineteenth. One of the two water-wheels survives.

Plate 31 Great Driffield. The head of the Driffield Canal, which was opened in 1770. The building on the right was a steam corn-mill. The crane dates from 1858. Recently the warehouses on the left have been converted into maisonettes.

Plate 32 Newport about 1890. The village was established after the enclosure of near
Wallingfen and the opening of the Market Weighton Canal between 1776 and 1784. Bric
works boosted trade on the canal and encouraged the further growth of the village.

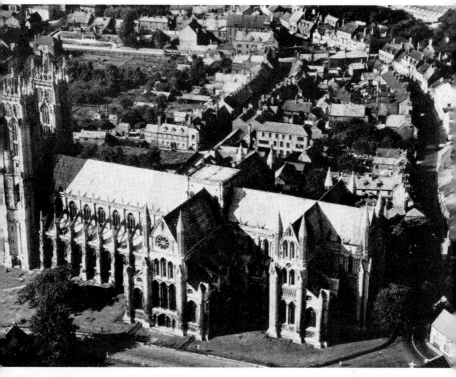

Plate 33 Beverley Minster from the south. The eastern half of the church was built in the early thirteenth century, the nave in the fourteenth century, and the west front in the first half of the fifteenth century. At the top of the picture is the small triangular Wednesday Market, which may be the remnant of a larger market-place lying between the curving Highgate and Eastgate.

Plate 34 Beverley. Saturday Market, with St Mary's church in the foreground. Showing encroachments on the market-place, perhaps including the whole block of houses in front of the church. The curving streets to either side of the picture are Walkergate and Lairgate. Since this photograph was taken a new road has been driven in from the left, carrying through-traffic across the market-place and destroying its enclosed character.

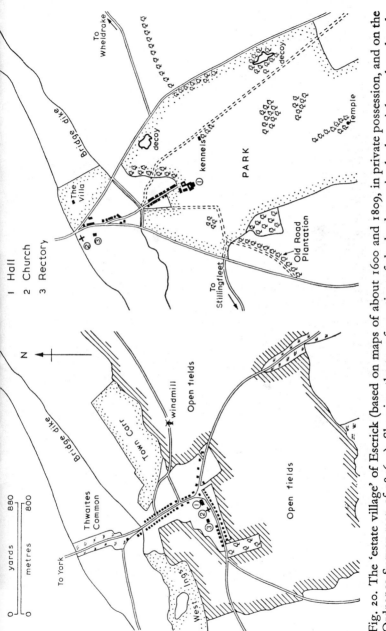

Fig. 20. The 'estate village' of Escrick (based on maps of about 1600 and 1809, in private possession, and on the Ordnance Survey map of 1846–7). Showing the transformation of the landscape in the late eighteenth and early nineteenth centuries. Roads made by 1809 but later replaced are shown by broken lines.

In plan the medieval village of Escrick was 'L'-shaped, with the shorter arm lying along the top of the ridge and the other running down to Bridge dike, and so on towards York. A seventeenth-century map of the township shows the hall, church and rectory all standing in the angle formed by the two streets. By 1809, when a new map was drawn, the "considerable improvements" mentioned in 1781 had been duly made. The open fields, the great common wood, and the town meadows had all been enclosed, and the church and the rectory house had been rebuilt north of the village, beyond Bridge dike. Twenty-six of the village houses, moreover, had been removed. Houses still stood at both ends of the 'L', but now separated by the new parkland around the hall. The severing of the village streets made it desirable for new roads to be made, and the Thompsons did in fact lay out a bypass on each side of the village, beginning at Bridge dike and running at a respectful distance from the hall. Old Road Plantation marks the course of part of one of these roads.

Even these far-reaching alterations were not the end of the story. By 1847 the nine houses at the south-western end of the village which had survived the earlier demolitions had been removed, new roads bypassing the village at a greater distance had been made by P. B. Thompson, created Baron Wenlock in 1839, and the park had been extended to some 450 acres. The hall was also much enlarged in the 1840s, and both church and rectory house were again rebuilt. Bielby Thompson's new church had been a modest brick building in the Classical style. Its replacement of 1857 was a "more seemly and commodious building of stone", in fact one of the most ambitious Victorian Gothic churches put up in the East Riding. The grand new rectory house was built in 1848, reflecting an uncommonly wealthy living. Later changes have included the remodelling of many of the village houses in the early 1900s, and the building by the third Baron Wenlock of almshouses in 1904 and a large village institute in 1908. An elaborate fountain, erected in 1897 to commemorate the queen's diamond jubilee, completes the picture of one of the riding's most impressive estate villages. Escrick's character has as yet survived the conversion of the village into a dormitory for York, partly, no doubt, because the Escrick Park Estate has itself survived, and partly because the hall has remained intact as a private school.

Another estate village, Settrington, lying below the Wolds escarpment in the extreme north-west of the riding, experienced wholesale changes in its landscape around 1800, with the final enclosure of the open fields and commons playing a prominent part in the events. Our knowledge of Settrington before enclosure is richer for three fine plans, one of the whole parish, another of the village, and a third of the church and manor-house, all drawn to accompany a detailed survey made in 1600.[1] The village then as now had two distinct parts (Fig. 21). The first was centred upon two rows of houses facing one another across a village street, down the middle of which flowed Settrington beck. Behind the garths of these houses lay two back lanes. A water-mill stood on the beck, and south of the mill there were a dozen houses around the approach to the church and manor-house. The second part of the village, at right-angles to the first, lay around a green, which was continued westwards as a drove-way or outgang leading to common meadows and pastures on low ground near the river Derwent. Almost surrounding the village were its three open arable fields, while to the east were the meadows, pastures and woods which occupied the escarpment and the high wold above.

Enclosure of the low-lying meadows and pastures was

[1] The survey is published, together with the parish plan, in H. King and A. Harris, *A Survey of the Manor of Settrington* (Y.A.S.R.S. cxxvi) (1962).

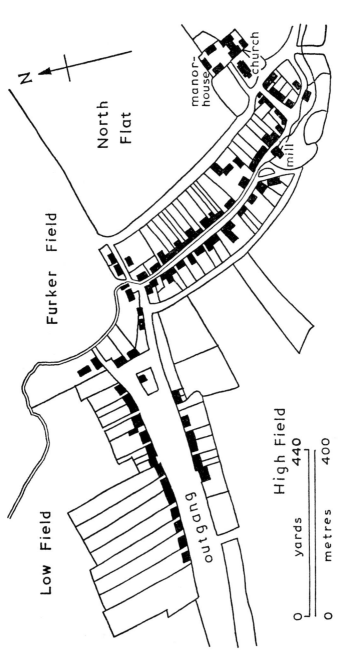

Fig. 21. Settrington in 1600 (based on a copy in the Geography Department, Hull University, of a plan in private possession). Many changes were made to the village two centuries later, when the fields and the outgang were enclosed. Some houses were removed, while many others were rebuilt in a more spacious setting. The manor-house was rebuilt at the same time.

achieved by an agreement made in 1668, and at an unknown date part of the open-field land was enclosed in the same manner. But when enclosure was completed in 1799, under an Act passed two years earlier, there were still nearly 2,000 acres in the open fields and wold pastures to be dealt with. The prime mover in the enclosure was no doubt Sir Mark Sykes of Sledmere, who had aquired the manor of Settrington in 1795 by marrying Henrietta, heir to the Masterman family. In one respect the layout of the village was directly affected by enclosure. The broad outgang was reduced to a roadway of normal width and most of the houses standing on its south side were removed. A prominent bank in the new closes marks the edge of the former outgang, and a couple of isolated houses still stand there, too.

While the enclosure was in progress Sir Mark Sykes and his wife were also rebuilding both the manor-house and the village. The water-mill was apparently rebuilt before their marriage, for it bears the date 1790, but the new manor-house seems to date from about 1795. Certainly by the time the enclosure map was drawn in 1799 the old H-shaped house, depicted on the plan of 1600 with its courtyards and gardens, had gone (Plate 19). The new stone-built house still stands near by, but its appearance has been greatly changed by renovation following a fire in 1963. When the new house was built, space was made for its gardens by the removal of all the houses at the south end of the village, around the approach to the church. As a result the village street now stops short at the water-mill, and access to the church is provided by one of the back lanes.

The rebuilding of the old timber-framed village houses in the local Jurassic limestone is said to have been the work of Henrietta Sykes, who died in 1813, and one of the new houses is dated 1796 and another 1801. Many of them have big distinctive lintels over the doorways and windows. The rebuilding has produced a great contrast in the appearance of the two parts of the village. Beside the former outgang the rebuilt houses remain in their old positions, cheek by jowl with one another, and all fronting directly on to the roadway. But in the main street only a few houses stand, as of old, close together by the stream; the rest, mostly in nearly identical semi-detached pairs, are set well back in large gardens. This part of Settrington now has the spacious air of a planned estate village, one of the best of its kind in the riding.

The changes at Sledmere, Howsham and Sewerby have been described elsewhere,[2] and all admirably illustrate the activities of improving landlords. The Sykes family had begun to change the appearance of Sledmere even before enclosure took place in 1776. Part of the village was removed to open up a view from the hall over the new parkland and plantations, but the mere that gave the place its name remained, with groups of houses lying to its east and west. It was probably the rebuilding of the hall, started in 1751, which prompted these initial improvements, but it was the enclosure of Sledmere which allowed Sir Christopher Sykes to carry the changes further. The rest of the village was demolished and rebuilt outside the park; roads were stopped up; the mere was drained and the park enlarged; and in the 1780s the hall itself was extended and embellished. The church was not involved in these alterations and, although rebuilt in 1897-8, still stands in the park close to the hall. The estate housing also includes some late Victorian work, whose hard red brick and Gothic gables give variety to the architecture of the village.

The changes at Howsham were probably made about 1770 by Nathaniel Cholmley, whose fine Jacobean hall

---

[2] Sledmere and Howsham in Harris, *The Rural Landscape of the East Riding, 1700–1850*, pp. 73–7; Sewerby in V.C.H., *Yorkshire East Riding,* II, pp. 93–4.

occupied restricted grounds between the village and the river Derwent. The extension of these grounds involved the removal of all the houses lying along the west side of the village street. The resulting 'one-sided' village is unusual in plan but of attractive appearance, the cottages of warm brown Jurassic stone looking across a wide grass verge to the trees and parkland beyond the street.

The creation of a parkland landscape at Sewerby, close to the cliffs of Flamborough Head, and at the nearby hamlet of Marton is of interest for the way in which the enclosure commissioners provided the framework within which the work was done. There is evidence to suggest that as early as 1714 ten houses had been demolished to improve the surrounds of Sewerby House, but no further changes were made until the early nineteenth century. Before enclosure in 1811 a roadway across the open fields and meadows ran close to John Greame's house at Sewerby and to Ralph Creyke's at Marton. The commissioners replaced that road by another lying further away from the two manor-houses, and by 1850 all the land to the east of this new road had been converted to parkland and plantations. The Greames also demolished about a dozen houses at the head of the village street at Sewerby, apparently replacing them with a terrace of cottages behind the street front. Sewerby House had been considerably altered just before enclosure, and by 1850 the house had been enlarged and numerous buildings erected in the grounds, among them a striking gatehouse facing down the village street. Additional ornaments to the park were a Norman-style church (1848) and an attractive Gothic school (1849), built to the designs of G. G. (later Sir Gilbert) Scott.

There are no doubt other examples, Birdsall among them, of villages where radical changes have helped to mould the landscape in the eighteenth and nineteenth centuries. In other cases the changes were smaller in scale, like those carried out at the hamlet of Woodhall, in Hemingbrough parish. There, in the 1830s, the manor-house was enlarged and its grounds improved, two or three houses were demolished, and a road was diverted. Enough has been said to show how extensively a village could be changed by an energetic squire, but it would be misleading to leave the subject of estate villages without making it plain that not all of them have witnessed the bending of roads, the shifting of churches, and the extension of parks over former house-sites. Changes were often restricted to the rebuilding of houses and cottages, and sometimes of the church, too. Scampston, Bishop Burton, North Cliffe, Warter and Langton (Plate 24) are all improved estate villages of this kind. An especially charming example is West Ella, where the Victorian Gothic houses were built, probably about 1860, by the Sykes family of West Ella Hall. The rough-cast and whitewashed houses, with their slate roofs, have distinctive gabled dormers and porches, as well as decorative hoodmoulds and bargeboards.

The fabric of the village

Country houses and showpiece estate villages tell only part of the story of rural building in these centuries. The average East Riding village is a far cry from Escrick or Sledmere. It is the rebuilding of older farm-houses and cottages, and the constant infilling with new ones, from the early eighteenth century onwards which accounts for most of the surviving domestic buildings in the riding. The activities of church builders and restorers left their mark on many villages, too, and it was above all in the nineteenth century that dozens of schools and nonconformist chapels were added to the village scene.

Villages which were dominated by a single landowner were not all refashioned on the picturesque lines of some that have been described. But all of them were characterised by a compactness of layout and a sparsity of cottages which marked them out as 'close' villages. Already in the eighteenth century and increasingly in the nineteenth it was the practice of such landlords to restrict the numbers of labourers in order to avoid the likelihood of a heavy burden on the poor-rates; as a result old cottages were sometimes demolished and no room was found for new ones. The reduced labour force of the 'close' village was frequently supplemented by individuals and gangs who travelled from neighbouring 'open' villages. The latter were characterised by a multiplicity of proprietors, an abundance of cottages, and a large number of poor, and it was in such independent communities that nonconformity received an especial welcome. Although villages of both types were to be found all over the riding, 'close' parishes were especially common on the Wolds—about forty per cent of the total, at one estimation. The dominance of individual proprietors over Wolds villages had been fostered by several developments, including widespread depopulation in earlier centuries. Much of the Wolds was, moreover, a 'new country', where improving landlords during the period of parliamentary enclosure were able to restrict cottage building and maintain the small size of so many villages.

It seems likely that the restrictive activities of dominant landlords may sometimes explain the partial depopulation of villages which has produced empty house-sites at many places on the Wolds. Thus at Speeton, which was certainly a 'close' village, the depopulation which we have noticed in earlier centuries was continued in the late eighteenth and nineteenth centuries. The enclosure commissioners' map of 1772 shows several houses there which had gone by 1850. At Kirby Grindalythe, too, there are extensive earthworks marking the sites of houses that still stood when a map was drawn in 1755. The shrinkage of villages is, indeed, a constant theme in the landscape history of parts of the riding.

The contrasting characters of 'close' and 'open' villages may be illustrated by Boynton and Burton Fleming, both lying in the valley of the Gypsey Race on the northern Wolds. So dominant was the lord of the manor at Boynton that at enclosure in 1783 all but eight acres of the entire parish belonged to Sir George Strickland. The visitor to Boynton now climbs the valley side into the village, for the old road close to the Race was diverted in 1768 to enlarge the Stricklands' park and secure their privacy. The village is small and trim, and many of the houses are white-washed; there has never been a nonconformist chapel here, or a public house. Only about twenty families lived in Boynton in the eighteenth century, and in the nineteenth the population was usually little more than a hundred. In 1868, when one cottage for each 100 acres was thought sufficient, most of the labourers worked in the Stricklands' woods and stables, and it was said that the tenant farmers "have to get their labourers from a distance". Sir George Strickland was also a landowner at Burton Fleming, but that manor had been divided between heiresses in the seventeenth century and there were other substantial proprietors there as well as the lords of the manor. At enclosure in 1769 five men were each allotted 400 acres or more, and four others got over 100 acres. It was a large and 'open' village, with forty families in the 1700s and a population rising from about 240 in 1801 to as many as 574 in 1851. Dissenters were numerous and there were three Methodist chapels by the mid century, as well as two public houses. Today Burton Fleming is a large and sprawling village which contains a great variety of small houses and cottages of the eighteenth century and later.

Brick became the almost universal material for house and cottage building in the eighteenth century, ousting the traditional timber frames and mud walls, though lime-stone long continued to be used in the Jurassic hills. Some mud and thatch cottages nevertheless survived into the twentieth century, for example at Watton, in the Hull valley, though they are all but extinct now. In the first half of the eighteenth century houses often still followed a traditional plan in which the door opened on to a central chimney stack, with one room on either side and others above, sometimes in the roof; surviving examples of this plan are widespread, particularly in the Vale of York. A variant of this plan is the central stack house with three rooms on a floor, often comprising a 'house', kitchen and parlour, this being the typical arrangement in the larger pre-enclosure farm-house, as evidenced by probate inventories and in the field. By the mid-eighteenth century a change had begun to take place by which the central stack plan was gradually usurped by the house with a stack at each end and, in the two-storeyed examples, a central staircase. The more substantial farm-house would have a third bay, with its own stack, serving below as a back kitchen, with separate access to a first-floor bedroom for the farm men who lived in. In the nineteenth century most village houses and cottages were being built to new standardised patterns which showed few regional characteristics.[3]

The motley collection of brick and pantiled houses which make up so many East Riding villages are thus overwhelmingly eighteenth- and nineteenth-century in date. Only rarely do they possess the old-world charm of the products of the 'Great Rebuilding' which had taken place in many parts of the south and the Midlands between about 1560 and 1640; villages like Kilham (Plate 27) have, rather, a plain and unambiguously rural appearance, only latterly beginning to be spoilt by fashionable 'restorations' and embellishments.

[3] Mrs Vanessa Neave has kindly provided much of this paragraph.

The constant need to repair and restore, and the occasional failure to do so, altered the appearance of many village churches during these centuries. The changes were not always as drastic as at Lowthorpe, near Great Driffield, where in the eighteenth century the imposing medieval collegiate chancel was abandoned as a roofless shell; the tower was, however, heightened in brick, and in the nineteenth century the nave was rebuilt. If piecemeal restoration was commonplace, extensive rebuilding was rare before 1800. There are only four completely new Georgian churches in the riding, the small and utilitarian brick buildings at Barlby, East Cottingwith, Seaton Ross and Wressle, and three others, at Boynton, Everingham and Wheldrake, where a new brick nave with apse or chancel was added to a medieval tower. By contrast the nineteenth century in the East Riding saw an abundance of ruthless restoration and rebuilding, as well as the provision of some new churches, like the tiny attractive building at Kexby, where a separate parish was created in 1853. The biggest and most showy of the rebuilt churches were probably Escrick, which we have already met with, and South Dalton, of 1858-61, whose tall slender spire is one of the great landmarks of the Wolds.

A special mention must be made of the younger Sir Tatton Sykes of Sledmere (1826-1913), who spent more than any other East Riding landowner in beautifying the churches on his estates. Ten were restored, five completely rebuilt, and two newly founded. Sir Tatton, like his father, employed the best architects: Pearson, Street, Temple Moore and Hodgson Fowler. It is Street's work which makes the greatest impression, with its wide variety of plan and composition, but Moore was responsible for Sledmere itself (1897-8), a building which has evoked such differing expert comment as "perhaps one of the loveliest churches of England" and "patently dull". The elder Sir Tatton (d. 1863) was commemorated in 1865 by another widely visible Wolds landmark, the 120-foot high tower put up near Sledmere by "those who loved him as a friend and honoured him as a landlord".

Parsonages had their place in the Georgian and Victorian landscape, too, for although many humble houses remained on the poorer livings some incumbents lived in great comfort. The grander houses include the mid eighteenth-century vicarage at Hunmanby, the slightly earlier rectory at Rowley, and Goodmanham rectory of 1823-4, all three now put to other uses. A rash of rebuilding in the second half of the nineteenth century introduced many red-brick Gothic parsonages, none of greater interest than Riccall (1869), which incorporates the remains of the medieval manor-house.

The only surviving Roman Catholic church of note outside the towns is that built in 1836-9 beside their hall at Everingham for the Constable-Maxwell family. Of great size, Italian in appearance, and with striking decoration, it has been described as "an alien and magnificent piece of architecture". But nonconformist chapels, mostly Wesleyan or Primitive Methodist, form part of the village scene all over the riding. Their numbers may be illustrated from one area in the north-east of the Wolds where only eight villages out of some forty never had a chapel; altogether about fifty chapels were built in the area, half of them in the period 1800-25, though in many cases it is a later rebuilding which survives today. Mostly the buildings are plain brick boxes, but some of the larger villages, like Nafferton and Flamborough, have chapels with ornate fronts of stone or polychromatic brick which are much more typical of the towns.

Few of the village schools that existed in 1850 were held in buildings erected for the purpose, but new schools and new buildings proliferated in the second half of the century. Altogether 146 schools were started in the riding during that time, nearly fifty of them in the 1850s and about sixty in the 1870s. Many have since been enlarged, rebuilt or replaced, and like the chapels they now not infrequently stand empty or converted to other uses. There is little space to mention the other buildings that some villages acquired, whether by benevolence or self-help: the handful of alms-houses, like those at Heslington (1795) or South Dalton (1873); the occasional reading rooms; and in the larger villages, such as South Cave and Nafferton, the halls of friendly and temperance societies.

SELECT BIBLIOGRAPHY

Bamford, T. W., *The Evolution of Rural Education, 1850–1964, Three Studies in the East Riding of Yorkshire* (1965).

Georgian Society for East Yorkshire, *Transactions, passim.* See especially R. A. Alec-Smith, 'A Review of the Villages of Welton and Melton', *Transactions* for 1958–61, pp. 67–81.

Holderness, B. A., 'Open and Close Parishes in England in the Eighteenth and Nineteenth Centuries', *A.H.R.*, xx (part II), pp. 126–39.

Long, E. T., 'Churches of a Victorian Squire', *Country Life*, 26 September 1968 (Sir Tatton Sykes).

Pevsner, N., *Yorkshire: York & the East Riding* (1972).

V.C.H., *Yorkshire East Riding,* II (1974) and III (1976).

Ward, J. T., *East Yorkshire Landed Estates in the Nineteenth Century* (E.Y.L.H.S. 23) (1967).

9. Industry and communications

Industry.   Roads.   Rivers and canals.   Railways

HULL APART, the East Riding can boast few areas of concentrated industry and its truly industrial landscapes are of only small extent. Industry intrudes most obviously into the rural landscape of the riding in the form of quarries and brickworks, and indeed the various extractive industries make up a strong group. Less intrusive but contributing an essential element to the landscape of many villages and towns are those industries which served the riding's farmers, providing goods and materials or processing agricultural products. Some of these traditional industries, and all of the exotic light industries introduced to provide twentieth-century employment, have responded to improved transport facilities.

Industry

The only durable stone for building found in the riding is the limestone of the Jurassic belt, and it has been worked since the Middle Ages in many scattered quarries. Stone from Brough and Ellerker was used about the staiths and sewers of Hull, for example, in the fourteenth and fifteenth centuries, and some of the stone used for Beverley Minster came from Newbald. Along the Jurassic belt itself many houses, boundary walls and churches are built of the local stone, and it was carried several miles over the Wolds to villages like Bishop Burton and Walkington. In appearance the limestone varies from the dull buff or grey of the Oolite in the south to the rich brown of the Lias in some areas further north: there is a marked contrast, for example, between the stone-built villages of Newbald and Howsham. In the extreme north of the riding a few buildings are constructed of Jurassic stone brought across from the North York Moors, and stone from Filey Brigg has been used in the sea walls at Filey, in Bridlington's piers, and for parkland features at Hunmanby and Rudston.

Far more numerous than the disused quarries of the Jurassic belt are the chalk pits of the Wolds. They provided a poor stone for building, rubble for roadways, and the raw material for whiting manufacture, and many of them contained kilns to burn lime, especially for agricultural use. Small overgrown pits, many of which served the needs of a single village, still dot the Wolds. There are relatively few larger quarries and only a handful that are still worked. One large active quarry, however, is that at Ruston Parva, where a lime-kiln was mentioned as early as 1723 and where lime-burning ended only about 1930. Also still worked is Burnby quarry, near Pocklington, whose white scar is visible from far across the Vale of York. Disused lime-kilns may still be seen at Wharram le Street, where the quarry has become a nature reserve, and at Eppleworth and Little Weighton.

The manufacture of whiting, for use in paint and many other products, has largely died out in the riding, but one active works remains as a prominent landmark beside Beverley's Westwood common. Equally conspicuous is a disused whiting works next to a large quarry at Middleton on the Wolds, and chalk 'flour' is still produced in an adjoining building. By far the most extensive chalk quarry in the riding, however, is the half-mile-long crater at Melton which supplies a cement works beside the Hull–Selby railway line (Plate 41). Other conspicuous disused quarries overlook the river Humber near Hessle; they provided stone for Hull in the Middle Ages and produced lime and whiting into the present century.

Sand and gravel workings are generally features of the lowland parts of the riding. Small village pits have doubtless been used from the Middle Ages onwards, but eighteenth- and nineteenth-century road improvements, together with the growing demands of the building industry, led to the opening up of larger workings. Active or disused and flooded pits scar the Holderness landscape around Brandes-burton, at Kelsey Hill (near Burstwick), and on several small 'hills' near Gransmoor, Kelk and Brigham, for example. The workings at Kelsey Hill are not entirely recent, for much material was removed thence for the construction of the Hull to Withernsea railway line in the 1850s. Pits in the Vale of York include those at Allerthorpe and Stamford Bridge, while valley gravels on the Wolds support the still active workings at Garton Slack (near Garton on the Wolds), where many prehistoric and later sites are being carefully excavated in advance of the bulldozers.

Clay suitable for brick-making occurs in many parts of Holderness and the Vale of York, as well as on the lower slopes of the Wolds. Brick-making has a long history in the riding, for there was a town 'tilery' at Hull from about 1300 until the fifteenth century, and Beverley also had its medi-eval brickyard. By the seventeenth century brick-kilns were beginning to appear in country villages, too—one at Rudston in 1618, for example—and they became more widespread in the eighteenth century, when they were mentioned at such places as Flamborough, Hunmanby and Kilham. By 1850 there were at least eighty brickyards in the riding, many of them serving a single village or large estate. The grass-grown hollows of shallow clay workings are usually all that we can expect to find at the smaller sites, but at Garton on the Wolds, where the Sykes family had a brickyard from at least 1812 until 1914, there is still a kiln and a row of former workmen's cottages. Brick-making on a larger scale continued into the present century all over the riding, from Filey to the suburbs of Hull and from Catton to Patrington. There are still—for the moment—large active brickworks at Newport and Broomfleet, and smaller ones at Hemingbrough and Escrick, all in the Vale of York. For the rest, flooded clay-pits, derelict wind-pumps and crumbling kilns are all that remain.

If the extractive industries have extensively pitted the East Riding landscape, those concerned with the processing of foodstuffs have left dozens of scattered buildings upon its surface. Corn-milling was perhaps the most basic of these processes and even after many earlier mills had fallen by the wayside there were still some sixty water-mills, more than 150 windmills and a handful of new steam-mills at work in 1850. Water-mills, once to be found even on the uncertain streams of the high Wolds or on the sluggish becks of Holderness and the Vale of York, have in modern times been concentrated around the margins of the Wolds: on the streams flowing down the escarpment to the north and west, and on those flowing eastwards towards the river Hull and the sea. Many of the typically small and plain buildings still stand, derelict or converted to other uses, together with their long-neglected races and dams. A few were more ornate, like the Gothic gem at Howsham which has become a total ruin in recent years. And a few were larger, like those which still dominate the riverside scene at Stamford Bridge (Plate 30) and Sutton upon Derwent: the one a restaurant now, displaying a water-wheel to its customers, the other a dangerous shell which yet contains both its wheels. Two smaller mills are still at work, powered by electricity, together with Bell Mills near Driffield, with electricity and a turbine. The towering factory of the new Bell Mills, rising above the meadows beside the river Hull, is a conspicuous part of the twentieth-century landscape.

Only stumps remain of most of the riding's windmills. They decrease in number year by year, but a few—like that on the skyline above Beverley—may be sufficiently picturesque to escape demolition for some time yet. The mill at Skidby alone retains its sails and stands resplendent as a reminder of a once common feature of the East Riding countryside (Plate 28). Of the steam-mills built in the nineteenth century a good example is the small disused building, with its tall chimney, standing beside a windmill stump at Seaton Ross. The larger Station Mills at Nafferton, built about 1860 and rebuilt in 1878, have been enlarged and modernised and still produce flour.

Maltings and breweries, too, were once common features of the market towns and villages of the East Riding. The smaller ones, long since disused, have practically all gone, but a few of the larger buildings survive: there are former maltings, for example, at Driffield, Cliffe (near Hemingbrough) and Nafferton. The Nafferton building, rising high above the pond near the centre of the village, was rebuilt in 1840, and part of it was a water-powered corn mill. At Market Weighton the combined malting and brewery still stands behind the main street, its long malting floors and pointed kilns recalling the traditional methods by which barley was malted. The modern malting industry is represented in the riding by a huge undistinguished factory at Knapton, standing isolated below the northern escarpment of the Wolds, and by another at Sewerby, on Flamborough Head.

The seed-crushing industry, producing edible oils from imported linseed and cotton seed, with cattle cake as a by-product, was largely concentrated in Hull. A few mills were, however, built elsewhere in the riding, at points accessible from Hull for the supply of raw materials. A picturesque building still standing beside the river at Hull Bridge, near Beverley, for example, is part of a former seed- and bone-crushing mill. And a handsome factory near the Canal Head at Driffield, rebuilt in 1888 after a fire had destroyed the original mill of 1862, is another relic of the industry. Away from Hull, only at Barlby is seed-crushing still carried on, in what is virtually an industrial suburb of the West Riding town of Selby, on the opposite bank of the river Ouse. Flour-milling was established at Barlby in 1905 and seed-crushing in 1909; now, mills and estates of workers' houses line the main road for a mile north of Selby Bridge, with riverside wharves on the one hand and railway sidings on the other.

More exotic industries had only a small place in the riding, but a few water-mills were used for paper-making in the eighteenth and early nineteenth centuries and several others for cloth manufacture. Most noteworthy for cloth were mills at Boynton and Wansford. The former was built about 1770 by the Stricklands to provide work for unemployed farm workers; it went out of use after some thirty or forty years, but later became the estate saw-mill and is still standing, isolated among the woodland near Boynton Hall. The much larger building at Wansford was built about 1790, chiefly for the manufacture of carpeting, but ceased operation after about thirty-five years. There is now no sign of the building but for an outline of parched grass, in a dry summer, between the river Hull and the Driffield Canal. Still standing, however, are some of the small terraced cottages put up near by for workers at the factory.

Light industry in various forms, often quite unconnected with the traditional industries of the area, has been introduced all over the riding in the twentieth century. Isolated factories or small industrial estates are often prominent in the present-day landscape: a plastics factory greets the visitor to Stamford Bridge, aircraft, cement and smelting works stand beside the rail approach to Hull, and at Bridlington the holiday-maker who arrives by train sees the industrial estate long before he smells the sea.

Roads

The complex pattern of roads in any district is the result of many centuries of gradual development, and reference has been made in previous chapters to the place of roads in the evolving landscape of the East Riding. It has been suggested, for example, that a few roadways, like Wold Gate, may have originated as prehistoric tracks. Others were laid out during the Roman occupation, though the Roman road system in the riding has still not been completely worked out. During the Middle Ages a network of roads grew up around the ports and market towns, and a few bridges were built, though even these longer-distance routeways were only haphazardly repaired and improved. The maze of local roads and paths connecting village with village varied in form, as we have seen, from one part of the riding to another. Many minor roads, and some more prominent ones, were given their precise modern alignment only during the enclosures of the eighteenth and nineteenth centuries. And during those same centuries many roads were diverted or realigned by 'improving' or self-seeking landlords. All over the riding much remains to be discovered about these various ways in which roads have been built into the landscape.

From the eighteenth century onwards more systematic attempts were made to improve road communications, and many of the changes brought about have contributed in a small way to the present-day landscape; in a few cases the impact has been more emphatic. The formation of turnpike trusts to improve individual roads began in the East Riding in 1744, and some fifteen trusts were established between then and 1836. Most of them were continued until the 1870s or 1880s. The turnpike network naturally centred upon Beverley and Hull, easing the way for market traffic, early commuters, and travellers alike. The longest turnpike roads, providing links with the rest of Yorkshire, led to York (1764-5) and to Selby (1793).

Practically all of the trusts were set up to deal with existing roads, by improving their surfaces, erecting toll-houses at the bars, and setting up milestones. The turnpike contribution to the modern landscape is thus generally small, especially since none of the toll-houses appears to have survived, as many have done in other parts of the country. A pair of picturesque cottages at White Cross, on the Beverley–Bridlington road, is often said to have been a toll-house, but there was in fact no bar at that point. That most of the toll-houses were demolished soon after the trusts were wound up is suggested by sale notices for the disposal of turnpike property, which stipulate that houses were to be taken down and the materials promptly removed.

Many milestones have, in contrast, survived, their pattern varying from trust to trust: the mounting block variety on the York–Beverley road, for example, and simple slabs with iron plates on the road from Market Weighton to Selby. Milestones on the White Cross to Bridlington road are of special interest, for the trust established in 1767 was not renewed when its term expired twenty-one years later. In all probability the trust could not cope with the coast erosion which eventually, in the earlier nineteenth century, washed away several miles of the road between Barmston and Wilsthorpe. The first milestone out of Bridlington now stands incongruously in a quiet road of the resort. In two areas of the riding, around Hunmanby and Warter, there are other milestones which were not the work of the turnpike trusts. They seem to have been erected in the late eighteenth or early nineteenth centuries, perhaps by such local gentle-men as the Osbaldestons of Hunmanby Hall or the Penningtons of Warter Priory.

Only rarely did turnpike trusts in the East Riding con-

struct completely new roads. The most noteworthy example
is the road running directly eastwards from Hull to Hedon,
which replaced a circuitous route through the villages of
Bilton and Preston. The five-mile long road was completed
at great expense in 1833. In many places, however, it is
likely that the trusts created short stretches of new road
when old roadways were diverted and straightened. Some
trusts were, moreover, set up soon after the enclosure of
adjoining parishes, and the turnpike trustees started virtually from scratch with the new roads laid out by the enclosure commissioners. The restriction of roads to forty-foot
wide strips across former common land sometimes made
them virtually impassable in bad weather, and one cam-
paigner for a turnpike trust at Pocklington could point to
the bad state of the road, "rendered much worse by the late
enclosures".

It would be wrong to suppose that all road surfaces were
immediately or enduringly improved by the turnpike trusts.
The Beverley to Kexby Bridge turnpike, for example, was
still far from perfect in 1813–14, fifty years after the trust
was formed. In Pocklington parish it was said to be much
rutted, and "the road in the township of Catton, except 120
yards covered with stones, is very bad and much cut up.
The township of Newton is all bad and Barmby Moor is
considerably worse". Nevertheless, the general state of the
turnpike roads must have been greatly improved by the
filling in of holes, the spreading of a layer of stones, and the
'barrelling' or cambering of the surface to facilitate drainage.
More effective, no doubt, was the work done after about
1820, when the technique of J. L. McAdam, involving a
carefully consolidated surface of fragmented stones, was
being used in the East Riding.

There are naturally few opportunities to observe at first
hand the kind of causeways and road surfaces that were
constructed by the turnpike trusts. One chance is, however,

probably afforded at Riplingham, on the Wolds west of Hull, where a prominent causeway near the site of this much shrunken village is thought to have been a coach road. The turnpike road from Kirk Ella to Newport (1774) ran this way, as milestones still testify, and thus the trustees may have constructed the causeway. It ran through the then unenclosed open fields of the village. Enclosure took place in 1803, however, and the road was apparently realigned by the enclosure commissioners, perhaps to take it a little further away from the front of Riplingham House. The causeway stands about a foot high and is some twelve feet wide; excavation showed that it consisted of a ten-inch-thick layer of chalk rubble, finished with a cambered surface of flints and pebbles, and a potsherd suggested a late-eighteenth-century date.[1] It is probably typical of the kind of roadway that was being made at that period.

The turnpike roads made use of several existing bridges, like that over the Derwent at Kexby. Their repair was not, however, the responsibility of the new trusts and they continued to be maintained by the county. Between Market Weighton and Selby two new bridges were built at about the time that the road was turnpiked, both replacing ancient ferries. The stone bridge over the Derwent at Bubwith was erected in 1793 and the timber one to carry the road over the Ouse into the West Riding in 1792. Both bridges were built and maintained by private companies, taking tolls; the Bubwith bridge was freed of toll when taken over by the county council in 1936, but Selby Bridge—rebuilt, again in timber, in 1969—is a toll bridge still. Another private toll bridge, in this case on a road that was never turnpiked, was built over the Derwent in 1804 to replace Loftsome ferry, between Selby and Howden. The bridge has since been replaced but the remains of its timber structure still stand in the river. It was also in 1804 that a new bridge was

[1] *Y.A.J.*, xli, pp. 608 sqq.

built over the river Hull at Tickton, on the Beverley to White Cross turnpike, by the Driffield navigation trustees; it survived until a successor was built by the county council in 1913.

The improved roads and increased traffic of the eighteenth and nineteenth centuries led to the opening of a number of inns, thus adding to the country landscape the detail of an often isolated building. Not all have survived as inns, though the houses still stand: such are the New Inn at Bentley, on the Beverley–Hessle road, and the New Inn at Ruston Parva, between Driffield and Bridlington. Another isolated inn, in existence in the early nineteenth century, accounts for the large three-storeyed house with a façade of chalk ashlar which stands high on the Wolds on the Driffield–Scarborough road near Ganton. The inn is said to have served a former coach road which ran along the valley bottom at right-angles to the present road. No doubt there were other such roads which for some reason failed to survive as part of the modern long-distance network. There are clues to another at Garton on the Wolds, where Coach Road plantation is shown on the 1855 Ordnance Survey map beside a green lane that runs along the parish boundary. It is thought to have been part of an abandoned road between Pocklington and Driffield.

In the 1890s, after the abolition of the turnpike trusts, the maintenance of main roads became the responsibility of the new county council. The more prosaic straightenings and diversions since carried out more forcefully take the attention of the traveller than any of the achievements of the turnpike era. Many of the changes date from the 1920s and 1930s, when the Selby–Hull trunk road, for example, was extensively improved, complete with several village bypasses and an ugly new Loftsome Bridge over the Derwent. Hull's road links with the West Riding and the South were further improved in 1929 by the bridging of the river Ouse at Booth, near Howden; the 700-foot long Boothferry Bridge has become a great landmark on the main road into the riding. Other improvements were those made to the Hull–Bridlington road. The erosion of the coast road, already mentioned, had thrown an intolerable burden upon the village roads in Barmston, Fraisthorpe and Carnaby. Consequently, in 1924, a new road called Kingsway was built to carry holiday traffic for the last few miles into Bridlington. Since the Second World War the pace of road improvement has quickened and mention will be made in the final chapter of several dramatic additions to the riding's landscape.

Rivers and canals

Although navigation and trade on the Ouse take us back to Roman times and on the Hull to the early Middle Ages, it is hardly practicable to discuss the riding's navigable rivers separately from its more modern canals: all form part of an interrelated system of waterways. Moreover, in terms of landscape it is only from the eighteenth century onwards that the natural courses of the rivers have been significantly altered in the interest of navigation. In the Middle Ages sailors and boatmen struggled against the natural obstacles thrown up by the Ouse and the Hull, but it was neighbouring landowners and farmers who were largely responsible for the draining and embanking which created the landscape of the river valleys. The contribution of the later waterways engineer to the landscape was common to river and canal alike.

The great artery of trade formed by the rivers Humber and Ouse could hardly be excluded from a discussion of the East Riding landscape simply because (with some insignificant exceptions) it everywhere constituted the riding's boundary with Linclonshire and the West Riding. Until the day of the engineer the Ouse was a tidal river up to and well beyond York, but the advantage of the free motive power of the tides was offset by several drawbacks. The pattern of ebb and flow was, for example, a complex one, and many tides were needed to carry vessels up to York. The speed of the tidal flow was in itself a hazard, especially in such a winding course as that of the Ouse. The long-drawn-out ebb tide was, moreover, too weak to scour the river bed and keep a navigable channel open, and banks and shoals consequently posed a considerable problem. Modest attempts at dredging began in the sixteenth century, but it was not until 1757 that a more daring attempt was made to improve the Ouse.

It was in that year that a dam or weir was built at Naburn, with a lock beside it on the East Riding bank capable of admitting small coastal vessels. The weir was successful in raising the level of the river upstream, but by holding back the tide it only increased the deposition of silt on the downstream side. The 'improvements' of 1757 were of doubtful value, but with them was begun the creation of a complex and fascinating piece of riverside landscape. The first addition, in 1823–4, was an imposing but hardly beautiful building standing close to the lock: this was a banqueting house, extravagantly put up by the trustees (drawn from York corporation) who managed the navigation. Then, in 1888, a steamship lock was built alongside the no longer adequate lock of 1757. The assemblage was completed by a toll-house, lock-keepers' houses, and cranes. From about 1815 until its demolition in 1958 a water-mill standing on the island between the main stream and the lock cut gave further variety to a busy landscape. Though the banqueting house is now disused, and York's trade is no longer what it was, the scene at Naburn remains spick and trim.

Alterations to the riverside landscape further downstream have nothing of the picturesque quality of the work done at Naburn, and they may be briefly dismissed. A timber jetty built on the East Riding bank at Blacktoft in 1875 for ships to ride out unfavourable tides on their way to or from Goole, in the West Riding, is still to be seen at low water. More extensive works were put in hand in the 1880s, however, to improve the shipping channel in the lower Ouse and to avoid groundings. Several miles of training walls were built, largely of slag from the blast furnaces of Teesside, to direct the tides into a narrower and more regular channel and so increase their scouring effect. The especially sharp bend in the river at Swinefleet was also moderated at that time by the cutting of a new channel on the East Riding side. The training walls, lengthened and improved, still line the banks of the busy seaway up to Goole and Selby.

The unimproved river Hull posed similar problems to those encountered on the Ouse, though the Hull was, of course, an altogether more modest waterway. Nevertheless, its lowest reach before the Humber was joined served as the harbour of the town of Hull; it carried the trade of Beverley from at least the fourteenth century, and indeed still does; and it served the market town of Driffield in its heyday, as well as the adjoining countryside. A description of the river in its upper reaches, written in 1641, vividly recalls the natural condition of the river: " They . . . say that one that is not very skilful in the way may very well come to leave his boat behind him, there are so many stakes sunken down, and here and there shallows." Effective improvement did not come until the eighteenth century.

In the case of Beverley Beck, a three-quarter-mile-long stream leading from the river Hull to the town, it was indeed as late as 1803 that a lock was built to raise the water level and to keep out tide-borne silt. Since then continual improvement has given the beck every appearance of a canal rather than a stream, and it now crosses the Beverley and Barmston Drain by a simple aqueduct—the only one needed on the East Riding waterways. Improvements higher up the river Hull came earlier. The Hull and one of its headwater streams, Frodingham Beck, were dredged and a five-mile-long canal was dug from the beck up to the town of Driffield, complete with three locks. The new navigation was opened in 1770. Later improvements included the conversion of Snakeholme lock, on the canal, into a staircase pair, and the building of a lock on the river itself, at Hempholme.

The Driffield navigation had an active life, providing the countryside with coal, bricks and other materials, transporting agricultural produce, and serving mills and factories in several villages, as well as at Driffield. Regular traffic to Driffield ended in the 1950s and the canal soon became derelict, though today a host of sailing boats using the reach below Brigham bring a bustle to an otherwise quiet scene. The navigation's most striking contribution to the landscape, however, is the canal head at Driffield, with its warehouses built in the 1780s and 1790s, a former steam corn-mill, and two cranes dating from the mid nineteenth century (Plate 31).

Less obvious today are the remains of another 'agricultural' canal, a mere three miles long, leading from the river Hull to the village of Leven and possibly opened in 1804. In recent years its entrance lock from the river has been sealed and one of the warehouses beside its crumbling wharves demolished.

The third navigable river in the riding is the Derwent, which rises high on the North York Moors and for many miles forms the boundary between the North and East Ridings before flowing southwards through the Vale of York to join the Ouse near Barmby on the Marsh. Its improvement began under an Act of 1702, and work done by about 1720 included the construction of a lock at Elvington. Four more locks were added later, together with two picturesque drawbridges at Wheldrake and Cottingwith (sadly removed during modern drainage works), and several swing bridges and lock-keepers' houses. Though villages close to the river all had their landing-places, most of the Derwent's trade was with the North Riding town of Malton. After being sold to the North Eastern Railway Co. in 1855 the navigation was neglected, and it slowly declined until trade finally came to an end in the 1930s. The several lock cuts are the navigation's most obvious memorials, four of them designed to bypass weirs associated with water-mills. The lock at Elvington was reconstructed in 1972 for the use of pleasure craft, but upstream the river remains in a state of peaceful neglect.

The Derwent supported one canal, which left the river at East Cottingwith and wound its way for nearly ten miles across the Vale towards Pocklington. Opened in 1818, the Pocklington Canal had nine locks, but it stopped about a mile short of the town. At the canal head, within a few hundred yards of the main road from York to Hull, are to be seen disused wharves, a warehouse, a lock and lock-keeper's cottage, the former Pocklington Canal Inn, and the ruins of a saw-mill; demolished buildings included a terrace of workmen's cottages. One other noteworthy feature of the Pocklington Canal is the set of brick bridges carrying minor roads over it; steeply humped and with widely splayed side walls they add a somewhat bizarre note to the flat scenery. Sale to the York & North Midland Railway (later the North Eastern) in 1848 was followed, as in the case of the Derwent navigation, by a gradual running down of the canal and it was finally closed in the 1930s. The rebuilding of the first lock in 1972 gives promise of the canal's eventual restoration.

The last of the East Riding's canals was an offshoot of neither the Hull nor the Derwent but opened directly into the Humber. From its starting point between Faxfleet and

Broomfleet, the Market Weighton Canal ran directly northwards for more than nine miles, ending in this case two
miles short of its name-town. Expensive extra locks would
have been needed to see both this and the Pocklington
Canal to their hoped-for destinations. Unlike the other
canals, this was a dual-purpose waterway, designed to drain
Wallingfen as well as to carry goods. It fully satisfied neither
landowners nor navigators, however, the former wanting
a lower water level than was desirable for navigation. The
various sections of the canal were opened between 1776 and
1784. There were four locks, including a tidal one near the
Humber, and modest works at the two branching canal
heads. Parts of the upper reaches of the canal have now been
drained and the picturesque qualities of the Driffield and
Pocklington canals are absent. The Market Weighton Canal
has, however, an important place in our landscape history
because of the growth of a commercial 'canal village' at
Newport.

To some extent the Market Weighton Canal, like the
other waterways, carried such goods as coal, lime and
manure, groceries, and corn: a typical rural and domestic
trade. But the development of brickworks beside the canal
soon came to provide the dominant cargoes, and in good
years bricks and tiles were carried by the million. It was
close to these brickworks that the village of Newport grew
up. At first three adjoining groups of houses were separately known as New Gilberdyke (in Gilberdyke township),
Newport (a township created at the enclosure of Wallingfen
in 1781), and New Village (an extra-parochial district, also
created in 1781); eventually, however, the whole came to
be called Newport. Dates on surviving houses show that
building was already under way in the 1780s, and the
population reached 277 in 1801 (excluding New Gilberdyke)
and 777 in 1851. By the 1850s there were several brickyards,
with their extensive clay-pits, as well as a chicory kiln, a

wind corn-mill, and a flax-mill, while beside the turnpike road from Hull there were Wesleyan and Primitive Methodist chapels (Plate 32).

Conflict between navigation and drainage interests, and neglect by the York & North Midland Railway which acquired the navigation in 1847, hastened the canal's decline, though its commercial life did not finally end until the 1950s. Newport now derives little benefit from either brickyards or canal, and traffic pouring along the main road towards Hull ignores it completely. It is, nevertheless, still recognisably the one substantial new settlement in the riding created by the development of industry and communications in the eighteenth and nineteenth centuries. Only the seaside resort of Withernsea, a product of the railways, has any claim to a place in the same category.

Railways

The movement of goods to and from the factories and docks of Hull, the servicing of country markets and agricultural communities, and the carriage of holiday-makers to the seaside resorts together ensured that a railway network of some considerable interest would emerge in the East Riding. From 1840, when the Hull–Selby line provided the first link with the West Riding, until the opening of the Driffield to Market Weighton line in 1890, nearly a dozen lines were built. In the flat country on either side of the Wolds their impact upon the landscape was hardly dramatic. Several substantial iron bridges, lifting or swinging, were nevertheless needed to carry lines over the Ouse and the Derwent, and the wide valley of the latter river at Stamford Bridge called for a lengthy viaduct of fifteen brick arches with a central iron span. Only where lines were forced to cross the Wolds were larger engineering works necessary. Most of these lines have been closed, but several tunnels, a few

Plate 35 Hedon. An aerial view of the medieval 'new town', looking south-west towards the Humber. The market-place lies to the right of St Augustine's church. The main streets run down to Hedon Haven, the natural stream that led to the Humber. Running parallel to the streets is the first of the possible man-made havens (arrowed).

Plate 36 Kingston upon Hull. A view from the south, with the Humber in the foreground and the river Hull on the right. The walls of the medieval Old Town roughly followed the inner edges of the docks (left) and gardens (middle), the latter on the site of the town's first artificial dock. In recent years, since this picture was taken, the Old Town and the redundant docks have seen much demolition and some rebuilding. A new highway, designed to connect the modern docks east of Hull with the nascent Humber Bridge and motorway to the west, will strike across the middle of the Old Town.

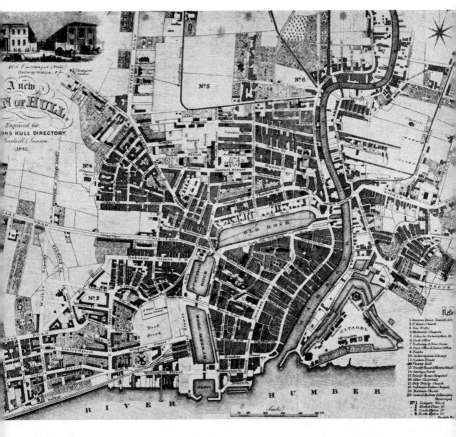

Plate 37 Kingston upon Hull in 1842. The medieval defences around the Old Town have been replaced by three docks, completed between 1778 and 1829. The southernmost tip of the Old Town was reclaimed from the Humber, partly with material excavated from the nearby dock. The first extra-mural suburb was begun north of the Old Town in the 1770s.

Plate 38 Bridlington. An aerial view of the 'Quay', looking north-west. The older streets lie close to the harbour. Immediately behind the sea front are several imposing terraces of lodging-houses, built in the second half of the nineteenth century, while further inland there are rows of more modest resort housing. Christ Church (1841), top left, stands beside the main road leading to the 'Old Town', a mile inland.

bridges and some considerable cuttings and embankments still show which way they ran.

The first of the cross-Wolds lines to involve large-scale works was that from Malton to Driffield, opened in 1853. The Bridlington–Filey line of 1847, at the low seaward end of the Wolds, had hardly been a test of strength. In the ascent of the Wolds escarpment great quantities of stone were needed to make a firm foundation for the Malton–Driffield line in the valley between North Grimston and Wharram Percy, while below the escarpment a deep cutting was required in the Jurassic stone near Settrington. But the greatest task on this line was the construction of a tunnel 1,734 yards long through the chalk between Wharram Percy and Burdale, nearly 700 feet above sea-level. The now blocked entrance at the southern end of the tunnel is still a prominent landmark. Two other lines required works on a smaller scale. The Market Weighton to Beverley line, opened in 1865, followed a valley route through the Wolds (the so-called Market Weighton Gap) and needed only some lengthy cuttings and embankments. And, not far to the north, the Market Weighton to Driffield route of 1890 was only a little more testing, though a deep cutting was necessary at Enthorpe.

Greater scars were, however, inflicted upon the Wolds landscape by the engineers of the Hull and Barnsley line in 1880–5. The North Eastern Railway already occupied both the Humber bank around the southern end of the Wolds and the Market Weighton Gap. When a new competitor was proposed in order to break the N.E.R. monopoly of railways and docks at Hull it was thus inevitable that a difficult route would be followed. Running into the Wolds escarpment from the west, the line occupied long cuttings and two short tunnels in a winding steep-sided valley near North Cave. At Weedley it plunged through a 2,116-yards-long tunnel, emerging into deeply-incised cuttings at Little

Weighton whose steep chalk walls remain bare and white today. Though the cuttings are hardly visible from nearby roads, several airshafts are prominent in the fields above the tunnel. Few of the bridges built along this line are still standing. A notable exception is the high five-arched brick viaduct which carried the line over a road near Eppleworth, an evocative piece of railway architecture whose present uselessness no doubt dooms it to eventual demolition (Plate 40).

The Hull and Barnsley, like most of the 'uneconomic' railways of the East Riding, has been closed and its tracks lifted. Of the nineteenth-century railway network, all that remain are the Hull–Selby line, with its branch line to Doncaster, the Selby–York line, in the extreme west of the riding, and the 'seaside line' from Hull to Bridlington, Filey and beyond. For the rest, the grass-grown lines await their fate, to be reclaimed for agriculture, utilised as routes for new roads, or preserved for walkers and naturalists.

Whether still open to traffic or converted to other uses, most of the riding's railway stations and crossing-houses still stand. Many of them, designed in what has been aptly described as a domestic Georgian style, are plain and unassuming. A few village stations, such as Nafferton and Stamford Bridge, are embellished with stone porticoes, but they are exceptional, and even such town stations as Market Weighton and Beverley are merely larger in scale rather than notably more elaborate. Most of these stations were designed in the office of George Hudson's architect G. T. Andrews, and it was Andrews who was responsible for the altogether more imposing Paragon Station in Hull, opened in 1848, and the adjoining hotel. Despite considerable alteration, a good deal is left of Paragon's Italian Renaissance façades. A few of Hull's suburban stations were also more showy, like the surviving Tudor Gothic building at Stepney (1853), designed by a local architect. At the other extreme are the little wooden stations of the Derwent Valley Light Railway, which was opened in 1912 to serve the villages south-east of York; goods are still carried on about four miles of the line, but the rest of the track has been lifted and most of the stations are put to other uses now.

Though much of the riding's early railway mileage was controlled by George Hudson, the landscape bears a more personal mark of his audacious career. When a rival line was planned from York to Hull in 1845 its route was blocked by Hudson's purchase of the 12,000-acre Londesborough estate, near Market Weighton. Two years later he built his own line from York to Market Weighton, complete with a private station approached from Londesborough Hall by an existing mile-and-a-half-long avenue of trees. Hudson's fall came soon after. Now the former station house stands alone in the fields, bereft of its line, and most of the fine old trees have been replaced by young saplings.

Now that the remains of many of the riding's railways are gradually being removed from the landscape it is clear that the 'permanent way' is not as indelible as was once supposed. More than one fearful landowner had successfully resisted the intrusion of the railroad upon their estates. The course of the Hull–Selby line was modified to meet such opposition, and Sir George Strickland prevented Hudson from building lines from York to Bridlington and from Driffield to Hornsea. But when Strickland insisted that a railway would be "totally destructive" to his home at Boynton and enlisted the help of his neighbour to stop "the nuisance .. entering our valley", he may well have ensured that the narrow valley of the Gypsey Race should remain even now one of the most picturesque corners of the riding.

SELECT BIBLIOGRAPHY

Allison, K. J., *East Riding Water-mills* (E.Y.L.H.S. 26) (1970, reprinted 1975).

Duckham, B. F., *The Yorkshire Ouse* (1967).

Duckham, B. F., *The Inland Waterways of East Yorkshire, 1700–1900* (E.Y.L.H.S. 29) (1972).

Hadfield, C., *The Canals of Yorkshire and North-East England* (2 vols. 1972–3).

Hoole, K., ed., *The Hull and Barnsley Railway*, I (1973).

MacMahon, K. A., *The Beginnings of the East Yorkshire Railways* (E.Y.L.H.S. 3) (1953, revised by B. F. Duckham 1974).

MacMahon, K. A., *Roads and Turnpike Trusts in Eastern Yorkshire* (E.Y.L.H.S. 18) (1964).

Watts, H. D., 'The Industrial Geography of East Yorkshire', unpublished M.A. thesis, University of Hull (1964).

10. Town landscapes

Market towns. Beverley. Medieval new towns.
Kingston upon Hull. Seaside resorts

THE ONLY REALLY large town in the riding is the sprawling city of Kingston upon Hull, a county in itself from 1440 and for long one of England's leading ports. Its population was over 286,000 in 1971. Hull was one of those many planted towns that were created in England during the centuries of medieval prosperity when growing trade needed new outlets. So was Hedon, which faded after its early flowering and had a mere 2,600 inhabitants in 1971. Other 'new towns' in the riding were Ravenserod, now submerged beneath the sea, Brough and Skipsea Brough. The last two, one on the river Humber and the other beside a large Holderness mere, were unsuccessful plantations and the landscape was little affected by their brief enjoyment of borough status. Brough is best known for its Roman settlement and Skipsea Brough for its castle earthworks, though in the present century an aircraft factory has made Brough into a small industrial outlier of Hull.

Of the dozens of places which held markets and fairs in the Middle Ages, only a handful passed beyond the arbitrary division between villages and towns. There was probably little to distinguish the landscape of most market villages, though some of them may have been reshaped for the better accommodation of market-place or fairground. Kilham, North Duffield and South Cave have already been mentioned in this connection (see Chapter 4). Several towns, however, did grow naturally from village beginnings, but few attained either much size or the privileges of a borough. The only possible pre-Conquest boroughs in the riding were Bridlington and Pocklington. Both were said to have a few burgesses in 1086, but in the absence of any later medieval evidence of borough status it has been suggested that the Domesday 'burgesses' may have been specially privileged tenants put in to reclaim these two great manors after William's wasting.[1]

Beverley is clearly outstanding among the riding's organic towns, though it is a special case, for it has always been much more than a market town. At the height of its medieval prosperity it stood high among the towns of England. As the county town of the East Riding, and still a significant local market and industrial centre, it had a population of some 17,000 in 1971. Apart from Hull only Bridlington was larger. Other market centres which by virtue of their advantageous siting grew into small towns included Great Driffield, Pocklington, Market Weighton and Howden. Driffield, with a population of about 7,900 in 1971, is by far the largest of the four, nearly twice the size of Pocklington and three times that of the others.

Bridlington was the earliest of the riding's watering-places, developing in the later eighteenth century beside a little harbour which had served the medieval market town, itself standing well back from the sea. The popular seaside resort of 1971 had a population of nearly 27,000. The more fashionable resort of Filey, which grew only to 5,300 inhabitants in 1971, and the late-starters Hornsea (7,000) and Withernsea (6,000) never achieved the commercial success of Bridlington.

These dozen towns represent, Hull apart, a relatively small urban contribution to the make-up of the riding in

[1] F. W. Brooks, *Domesday Book and the East Riding* (E.Y.L.H.S. 21) (1966), p. 25.

terms of area and population. The variety of their origins and subsequent fortunes is nevertheless reflected in their varied landscapes, and all of them deserve to be explored in more or less detail.

Market towns

Great Driffield, the self-styled 'Capital of the Wolds', is the largest of the riding's market towns and the only one to have ever been an industrial centre of much significance. Even today its townscape has a special flavour . The town's situation, beside the river Hull and between the Wolds and the lowlands of Holderness, enabled it to serve a wide and varied area. In the Middle Ages it was Little Driffield, a village a mile to the west, which had the chartered fairs, and these survived into the nineteenth century. Little Driffield church is also the reputed burial place of Aldfrith, king of Northumbria, who died in A.D. 705, but neither this dubious claim nor the existence of the fairs gives any reasonable support to the notion that Little Driffield was in early times the more eminent of the two places.

By the eighteenth century, and perhaps much earlier, Great Driffield had secured for itself a Thursday market (held by prescription, not by charter). And when a map was drawn in 1742, at the enclosure of its open fields, it was a large and populous town. The oft-repeated assertion that the opening of the Driffield Canal in 1770 brought about the rise of Great Driffield and the fall of Kilham clearly exaggerates the role of the canal: Driffield was already flourishing and Kilham's market and fairs were already in decline long before the canal was cut.

The modern plan of the town differs only slightly from that shown on the map of 1742. The street plan was dictated largely by the course of Driffield Beck, flowing southwards towards the river Hull. The two chief streets lay on either side of the beck, roughly parallel to it, and several back lanes lay behind them. Connecting these streets with each other and with the beck were more than a dozen small lanes, and houses were widely spread over the whole network of streets. One change since 1742 has been a modest extension to the southern end of the town, around the canal head and the railway station that was opened in 1846. The new transport facilities increased Driffield's ability to supply the needs and process the produce of the surrounding countryside, and it was in the nineteenth century that the town enjoyed its industrial boom. As a result its population increased from about 1,300 in 1801 to 4,000 in 1851 and 5,700 in 1901.

It is likely that the oldest part of the town is that lying around the church, with its tall and showy Perpendicular tower. A manor-house may have stood near by in the Middle Ages, on the west bank of the beck, where a recreation ground on the site of Hall Garth still contains prominent earthworks. But the most unexpected feature of the townscape is the motte of a small medieval castle, standing opposite the manor site on the other side of the beck. The motte and what remains of its bailey are now partly surrounded by houses and are only here and there to be glimpsed from the streets.

The medieval contribution to Driffield's landscape is, however, small and the overwhelming impression is of a thriving Georgian and Victorian country town. The main street is lined by larger houses, shops and public buildings, but in the back lanes and side streets there are many terraces and courts of workers' cottages. Industrial remains are still numerous, too, especially near the beck; the former corn mills, breweries and maltings, and the warehouses and cranes at the canal head (Plate 31), remind us that even as late as the 1890s it could be said that Driffield "presents, with its array of lofty chimneys, at least the semblance of a manufacturing town".

Pocklington, standing in the Vale of York near the foot of the Wolds escarpment, in many ways mirrors Driffield as a market centre and minor industrial town. But it was never to the same degree the focal point of a large hinterland, and York itself is only twelve miles away. Nor was Pocklington so well served by land and water communications, though it, too, had its canal, opened in 1818 but ending a mile from the town to save the expense of extra locks. Pocklington consequently did not enjoy the same prosperity as Driffield in the nineteenth century. It was larger, in fact, at the start, with 1,500 inhabitants in 1801, but it grew only to 2,500 in 1851 and was even a little smaller by the end of the century.

The town plan affords some comparisons with Driffield, for the main street and back lanes run parallel with Pocklington Beck and are connected by a host of side streets. The greatest contrast in the townscape is provided by the market-place. At Great Driffield, where the markets developed at a late stage, there is no spacious market-place at all. At Pocklington, however, the thirteenth-century grants of several fairs and a market are reflected in a market-place which extends across the heart of the town and was even larger before encroachments were made upon it. If there is another contrast between the two places it is in the less workaday atmosphere of Pocklington, for which the grammar school, founded in 1514, is perhaps mainly responsible.

Only six miles from Pocklington, and in a similar situation at the foot of the Wolds, is the smaller and less complex town of Market Weighton. The railway and a road leading to it from the main street are the only significant additions to the layout shown on a plan of 1776. Market Weighton had grown up on either side of another small stream draining from the Wolds, but by the eighteenth century its houses were mainly concentrated along the east–west road from

P

York to Beverley which formed both High Street and Market Place in the centre of the town. This main road was turnpiked in 1764 and has emerged in the twentieth century as one of the chief trunk roads leading to Hull. Formerly it crept down the steep Wolds escarpment into High Street, but now, widened and 'improved', it pours traffic into the town past a pit for runaways at the foot of the hill. Like Driffield, Market Weighton still has no immediate prospect of a bypass that might help to preserve both its townscape and its inhabitants.

The market-place in the main street widens at its western end into a triangular space, on which several encroaching buildings now stand. It also seems likely that a projecting row of houses and shops in front of the church is an encroachment on the market-place. Another notable feature of the town plan, though it is being gradually destroyed by contemporary changes, is a regular pattern of long curving garths, especially on the south side of Market Place and High Street. Although Market Weighton's growth in the nineteenth century was more modest than that of Driffield and Pocklington (the population increased from 1,200 in 1801 to 1,800 in 1901), there was nevertheless pressure upon the building space afforded by these garths. Small cottages still stand in several yards behind the street fronts; through another opening stands the early Methodist chapel (1786), though its large Victorian successor was predictably found a more prominent site by the demolition of houses on the street frontage.

Market Weighton's yards are among the features clearly shown on a pictorial plan of the town drawn in 1848 by William Watson, a surveyor of nearby Seaton Ross. A similar plan of Pocklington was drawn by Watson in 1855. Each building is drawn in elevation, together with much other topographical detail, and the names of owners and tenants are given, sometimes with occupations too. The plans provide a unique glimpse of the landscape of these Victorian market towns.[2]

Howden, the last of the market towns to be considered here, was long the centre of a parish containing a dozen townships and the focus of the Bishop of Durham's extensive liberty of Howdenshire. It was even occasionally styled a borough. It retained its markets and fairs far into the nineteenth century, among them a great horse fair which originated in a grant to the bishop in 1200. The church was made collegiate in 1267 and it was rebuilt on an impressive scale during the following fifty years, though the high crossing tower was not added until the beginning of the fifteenth century. The chancel and chapter house are now in picturesque ruins, and the remains of the episcopal manor-house stand near by.

Like all the settlements that lie close to the river Ouse, Howden was probably established where slightly rising ground offered a dry site. The shape of the town and the long curving lines of its main streets no doubt owe much to the configuration of that ridge of higher ground. Any explanation of the layout of Howden must also take account of the changing courses of rivers and streams in the area during historic times. Thus the river Derwent, which now joins the Ouse four miles west of Howden, is thought to have formerly passed close to the town on its way to a confluence with the Ouse downstream. The winding course of this or of some other long-forgotten stream may have helped to determine the shape of the settlement.

The built-up heart of the town ends abruptly at the churchyard and the manor-house grounds, the latter still containing a large moated site south of the house. The market-place may once have had an equally prominent

---

[2] Extracts from the plans are published in A. Harris, 'An East Yorkshire Land Surveyor: William Watson of Seaton Ross', *Y.A.J.*, xlv (1973), pp. 149–57; David Neave, *Pocklington, 1660–1914* (1971), p. 36.

place in the townscape, though reduced in modern times to a small space at the east end of the church where the Victorian market hall stands. There are also two other small triangular spaces in the town, and it is possible that they accommodated specialised markets when Howden's trade was thriving. In the nineteenth and twentieth centuries Howden has gradually lost its role as a local centre and has suffered from the proximity of the rapidly growing West Riding towns of Selby and Goole. After Boothferry Bridge was built near by, the town was also provided with a bypass for traffic from the south, while east–west travellers between Hull and Selby merely hasten through along the main street. Inevitably Howden has the neglected air of an obsolete market town in need of a new function.

Beverley

What is known of pre-Conquest Beverley concerns the history of the minster rather than that of the town, and the early topography remains entirely conjectural. John, Bishop of York, founded a monastery "in the wood of the men of Deira" about A.D. 705, and this doubtless attracted people to its gates, especially as the fame of John's relics spread after his burial there in 721. So came into existence the settlement at 'the beaver clearing' or 'the beaver stream'. The monastery was probably sacked by the Danes, but it later recovered and in the 930s King Athelstan refounded it as a college of secular canons, a 'minster' church to serve the district round about. Athelstan's endowment of lands and privileges, apparently including rights of sanctuary for fugitives, must have further encouraged the growth of a community to meet the needs of the minster and its visitors.

But if the Domesday commissioners found a small town at Beverley they certainly did not record it as such. Seven ploughs and 33 peasants were noted, there was a large 'pasturable wood', and streams provided power for three mills and supported a fishery of 7,000 eels. It thus sounds like a large agricultural village and nothing more, but it was a comparatively valuable one, worth £44 in 1066 to the archbishop as lord of the manor and to the canons of the minster. It is likely that tradesmen and markets existed there, too, despite the silence of the Domesday entry, and in the 1120s there is good evidence of the part played by trade in the life of the town. Henry I then authorised the archbishop and the canons to extend their annual fair from two days to five, and the archbishop granted his townsmen privileges like those of York and the right to take tolls. The growth of the town was thus assured. During the twelfth century Beverley merchants prospered by the trade in Yorkshire wool, and cloths were made in Beverley itself. By about 1150 two chapels had been built especially to serve the town, one dedicated to St Mary and the other, near Beverley Beck, to the seafarers' patron, St Nicholas.

The shape and layout of the town during these first centuries can only be surmised. The early settlement no doubt clustered around the minster, upon which converged several roads from the surrounding countryside. The chief of these roads, running from the Wolds and ultimately from York, may have led into a large triangular market-place in front of the minster, of which the present Wednesday Market is but a small remnant (Fig. 22 and Plate 33). The street pattern here certainly suggests that a market area between Eastgate and Highgate has been built over at a later date. It was mainly along this road from the north-west that the town grew in the twelfth century, and there that the great Saturday Market was laid out and St Mary's chapel (a parish church from 1269) was built (Plate 34). At the same time the town spread eastwards along Flemingate towards Beverley Beck. It is not known when the beck was

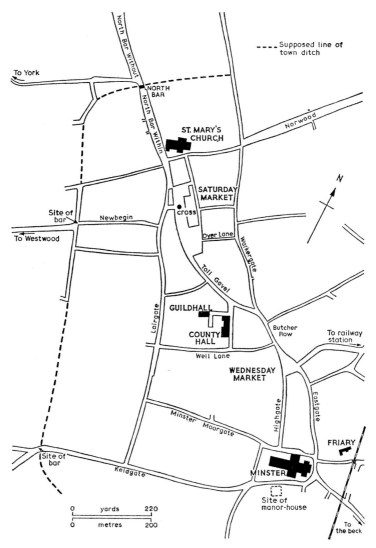

Fig. 22. The street plan of Beverley about 1900 (based on Ordnance Survey maps).

first improved, but boats were doubtless already sailing up from the river Hull in the twelfth century.

Many of the names of Beverley's thoroughfares, like those of other East Riding towns, reflect the Scandinavian settlement in the distinctive suffix -gate, deriving from the Norse *gata*, a street. Several of the early streets may have taken their gently winding courses from streams which flowed down the Wolds slopes towards the river. Both Keldgate and Walkergate certainly ran beside streams, one of them used by the walkers, or fullers of cloth. The name Minster Moorgate suggests a way leading from the church to the common pasture, though in modern times the street has stopped far short of Westwood common. This may, however, indicate the former extent of the common, which, as we shall see, was certainly being reduced by assarting in the twelfth and thirteenth centuries. Lairgate, where some of the townsmen's 'laiths' or barns stood, may have divided the crofts and garths of the town from the woodland and assarted land to the west. The minster and "the whole town" are said to have been destroyed by fire in 1188—perhaps a chronicler's exaggeration—but the old house-sites would in any case have been quickly rebuilt. Indeed, the possible extension of the town beyond Lairgate about this time is suggested by the street name Newbegin, 'the new building', which is first recorded in 1190.

By the thirteenth century, when the 'town's ditch' or 'bar ditch' was mentioned, Beverley may already have had a defensive ditch with gates or bars. But it was never a walled town, despite the royal licence to build a wall in 1321 when the Scots were raiding far into Yorkshire. Of the gateways, North Bar was rebuilt in 1409–10 and its fifteenth-century brickwork still straddles one of the main roads into Beverley; the only legacy of the connecting ditch is the line of a modern road (The Leases) on the west side of the town. There may have been a population of 5,000 and more in the late fourteenth century, before the town's medieval prosperity began to wane with the loss of its cloth industry and the decline of its trade. No doubt most of the present streets were already in existence and there were many houses outside the gates; it was to be several centuries before Beverley outgrew these medieval limits.

Except for the minster, St Mary's church, part of the Dominican friary, and North Bar, medieval buildings in Beverley are few. Only one or two overtly timber-framed houses remain from the town described by Leland in the 1530s as "well builded of wood", though some timber framing is concealed beneath later rebuilding. There are also several seventeenth-century brick houses, but the domestic and public buildings making up the modern townscape belong for the most part to the eighteenth and nineteenth centuries. In places the pattern of long garths stretching back from the streets still survives, but the houses and shops themselves have been periodically refronted or rebuilt in a great variety of styles. Already in Leland's time "the fairest part" of the town was to the north, around Saturday Market, and this remained the most fashionable district. Many of the finest Georgian houses, some of them the town houses of country gentry, lay between the town centre and Westwood or around the northern fringes of the town. Some of the larger houses had formal gardens, like those of St Mary's Manor in 1724 "which in four acres of ground contain great variety of avenues of firs, of parterres of statues; and also of arbours, seats and vases in trilliage work". Later in the century large informal gardens were created, of which a few remnants may still be seen. The most noteworthy public buildings include the handsome cross in Saturday Market, begun in 1711, the Sessions House (about 1804–14), and the Guildhall, refronted in 1832 but retaining a fine interior of the 1760s.

The Victorian well-to-do preserved the gracious and

leafy townscape around the north and west sides of Beverley, but from the middle of the nineteenth century the town's landscape was further diversified by the building of an extensive working-class suburb to the east. The railway, opened in 1846, and Beverley Beck, still much used even today, helped to stimulate a new industrial prosperity, in which tanning, ship-building, iron-founding and light engineering have all been prominent. Furthermore, to its older roles of administrative and market centre has recently been added that of dormitory town for Hull. Beverley has consequently grown in population from 5,400 in 1801 to 13,200 in 1901 and 17,100 in 1971.

The rural landscape that surrounded the town in the Middle Ages poses its own topographical problems. The number of ploughs that were worked in 1086 indicates a substantial area of arable land, and Beverley must surely have had open fields in the early medieval period. Documentary evidence is sparse, but "the fields of Beverley" were mentioned in the 1250s and there were selions (a word normally used of open-field strips) in the fourteenth century, some of them to the east of the town in "the field of Rydyng". The name ridding, as we have seen, indicates reclaimed or assarted land. Barleyholme and Maltholme, towards the beck, may also have been areas of arable land. Further evidence of former open fields is to be found in the present-day landscape, for there is much ridge-and-furrow around the town, especially on the south side. Riding Fields, to use the modern name for the area, has mostly been built upon, but even there a little ridge-and-furrow still survives (Fig. 23).[3]

The open fields must have been enclosed at an early date, divided up and in part used as meadow and pasture for the

[3] Much of the ridge-and-furrow shown on Fig. 23 still existed in 1975; some has, however, been recently levelled and some is recorded only in old air photographs.

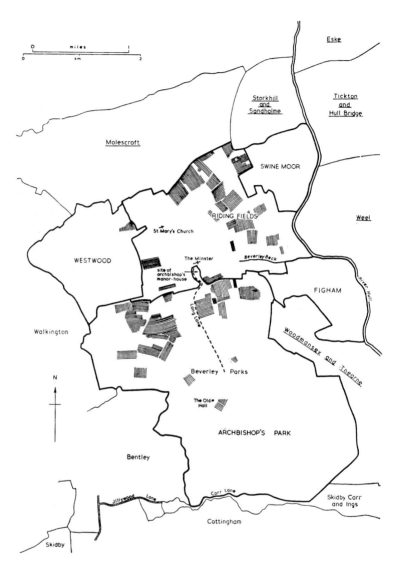

Fig. 23. Beverley. The area around the built-up town, showing the common pastures, the probable location of the former archbishop's park, and the ridge-and-furrow which suggests the extent of the old open fields. Adjoining townships lying within the liberty of Beverley are underlined.

234

townsmen's animals. It is possible that the inhabitants' rights in their common fields were converted at enclosure into the 'average', or right of pasture, which from at least the fifteenth century onwards they enjoyed in many closes and crofts around the town after hay had been mown. For the present, however, there is no documentary evidence to show when and how the enclosure of the open fields took place.

To the south of the open fields lay the archbishop's park, which was apparently created in the earlier thirteenth century. About 1258 the archbishop, as lord of Beverley, agreed with the townspeople that encroachments upon Westwood common should stop and he simultaneously granted them rights of pasture there. In return for these and other concessions the townsmen agreed to give up their rights of pasture in the park, which was then doubtless enclosed for the sole benefit of the archbishop's deer. There is good reason to believe that the park occupied only the southernmost part of Beverley's territory, stretching from Bentley in the west to the Hull–Beverley road in the east. In modern times the name Beverley Parks has been given, misleadingly, to the whole area south of the town itself, covering over 2,500 acres and embracing much of the open-field land of the Middle Ages. There are few traces of the park pale which no doubt surrounded the deer park, but a bank and ditch still to be seen along the boundary with Bentley may well have formed part of it.

The deer park long remained a prominent feature of Beverley's landscape. It was maintained by successive archbishops, in the face of constant poaching, until the manor was exchanged with the Crown in 1543. For a time it was supervised by a royal keeper, who in 1548 built a "little lodge" there, partly constructed of stone from the demolished archiepiscopal manor-house near the minster. In 1574 "certain grounds of pasture, arable land and meadow called

Beverley park" were described as lately disparked. The manor and park were, however, granted in the seventeenth century to the Warton family, who by 1688 had built a large house, the "new lodge", beside the old one. Only a fragment of the later building is to be seen in the farm-house that now stands on the site, but the massive brick walls that surrounded the Wartons' gardens still stand.

The most striking features of Beverley's rural landscape today, however, are the common pastures which together still cover some 1,200 acres. The townsmen's rights in Westwood, as already mentioned, were granted—or perhaps confirmed—in the 1250s, along with those in Figham. The third common, Swinemoor, was not then mentioned by name, though it too may already have been in existence. Later the town acquired the freehold of the commons, in the case of Westwood in 1380. The reclamation of Westwood for agricultural land stopped in the thirteenth century, but the remaining woodland was later progressively cleared and only the area of tangled trees and shrubs known as Burton Bushes still gives an impression of the medieval scene. Westwood has also for centuries provided chalk for road-making and lime-burning and clay for brick-making, and today the common is marked by extensive grass-grown and tree-filled pits. Prominent too are the stumps of three of the windmills that once stood there. The low-lying Figham and Swinemoor, beside the river Hull, lack Westwood's picturesque qualities, but on Swinemoor there survives the impressive bank and ditch which served to keep animals from straying into the lands of the adjoining hamlet of Sandholme.

Medieval new towns

The gradual and natural growth of Beverley contrasts strongly with the deliberate planting of medieval 'new towns' like Hedon and Hull. Such places were created to handle some of the flourishing trade of the twelfth and thirteenth centuries, and thus to reap profits for their founders. At Hedon the initiative was taken by the Count of Aumale, at Hull by the monks of Meaux Abbey. The landscape of new towns was frequently as dramatic as their birth. In place of the subtly winding streets in the old organic towns we find a regular layout, sometimes—as at Salisbury in Wiltshire or Winchelsea in Sussex—a truly geometric grid. At Hedon and Hull the pattern is less formal, yet it is still unmistakably planned.

Like so many new towns Hedon (Plate 35) was small in extent. It was created about 1140 by the excision of a mere 300 acres or so from the Earl of Aumale's great manor of Preston in Holderness, with its 5,000 acres and more. Trading towns did not need extensive farmlands. The stream now called Hedon Haven gave access to the Humber, nearly two miles away. On slightly rising ground near the stream—the heather-covered hill of the place-name—was in due course built the great church of St Augustine. Several roughly parallel streets led down to the haven, with others crossing them to form an irregular grid pattern. From the mid twelfth century fairs were held just outside the town, near a hospital founded by the Count of Aumale, but the town's second fair, granted in 1272, took place in and around a large market-place close by St Augustine's church.

Alongside these familiar elements of new town landscape Hedon apparently possessed other and more distinctive features, its artificial havens. Perhaps from the outset the natural stream was supplemented by a wide straight 'dock', dug parallel to the north–south streets and running up towards the rising ground. As trade prospered so before the end of the twelfth century another haven was needed, and it was then that the town was extended eastwards into Burstwick township; next to the haven was built Hedon's third church, dedicated to St Nicholas like the beckside church at Beverley.

There is no medieval documentation for these man-made havens, but the memory of them may still have lingered when Leland visited the town in the 1530s. He wrote that "the sea creeks parting about the said town did insulate it, and ships lay about the town ... it is evident to see that some places where the ships lay be overgrown with flags and reeds, and the haven is very sorely decayed". An undated map, perhaps of the seventeenth century, shows the old havens, but other modern records speak only of dikes and banks. As yet the evidence is thus inconclusive, but the impressive grass-grown depression marking the older haven seems to be adequately explained only in terms of a berthing-place for ships. The recent levelling of much of it, when a housing estate was built close by, has robbed the town of its most distinctive physical link with the past. Excavations carried out near the second haven have so far failed to uncover traces of wharves, and further archaeological investigation is clearly needed.

The regular pattern of streets—some with names recalling the craftsmen and tradesmen who lived there, like the walkers, fletchers and baxters—and the grassy market-place still recall Hedon's medieval prosperity. So does the one remaining church, the stately St Augustine's, aptly known as the 'King of Holderness' to Patrington's 'Queen'. Much of the present building dates from the thirteenth and early fourteenth centuries, with a fine tower added in the fifteenth century.

The decline and contraction of the town had reduced it by the sixteenth century to a local market centre, and in modern times it has languished in the shadow of Kingston upon Hull. The difficulty of navigating the shallow and winding Hedon Haven must have been an ever-increasing disadvantage, but it was above all the advantages of rival ports which blighted Hedon's trade. Already by 1280 it was reported that the men of Hedon "have near this two other towns, Ravenserod and the Hull, with two good harbours, growing from day to day". Of the two, Ravenserod made only a brief appearance in the landscape. It was founded by the Earl of Aumale soon after 1230 at the mouth of the Humber, standing on a sandbank and "distant from the mainland a mile or more. For access it had a sandy road no broader than an arrow's flight yet wonderfully maintained by the tides and the ebb and flow of the Humber". This could be an apt description of the present Spurn Head, but the spit on which Ravenserod stood was, in fact, two stages further back in the cycle of creation and destruction which has proceeded at Spurn.[4] The site of the borough, with its markets and fairs, numerous houses, and stores for fish, now lies beneath the sea to the east of the present spit. By the 1340s the town was already being destroyed, and by the 1360s it had gone.

It was Hull which had the greatest success of all the riding's new towns and which ultimately transformed the landscape around the confluence of the river Hull and the Humber. The town was founded by Meaux Abbey in the late twelfth century and was mentioned by name in 1193. It was known as Wyke upon Hull from the Scandinavian word *vic,* a creek, but from the first it was often called simply 'Hull'. The site for the town had only recently been acquired by Meaux. Previously the land had belonged to the hamlet of Myton, and as well as planting Wyke there the monks also established an agricultural grange near by. The town's haven lay, not in the old outlet of the Hull into the Humber, but in a new one a little to the east. Whether the river followed that new course as a result of natural changes, or was diverted to it by the monks, is one of the mysteries of Wyke's early history.

4 See p. 78.

There is plentiful evidence, however, that the town soon had a flourishing trade, and its population grew. By 1293 it contained about sixty houses, as well as nearly seventy unbuilt plots. Many of them were in Hull (later High) Street beside the haven, and in the roughly parallel Marketgate, where the weekly market and fifteen-day fair, granted to Meaux in 1279, were held. Cross streets linking Marketgate and Hull Street, and running on down to the haven, were almost certainly also elements in the early town plan. Like many new towns Wyke had no church of its own, for the chapel in Marketgate, said to have been founded in 1285, lay in the parish of Hessle, two miles away to the west. Again characteristically, Wyke was small in area for the ground contained within the medieval borough was a mere ninety acres.

Wyke prospered and its situation was clearly an advantageous one. The port consequently attracted the interest of Edward I and in 1293 he acquired it from Meaux Abbey, eventually giving the monks various properties elsewhere in exchange. Thenceforth the town was called Kingston upon Hull, and in 1299 the king raised it to the status of a borough. A programme of improvement followed the royal take-over, perhaps including an extension of the grid-like street plan started by Meaux. A new staith was built by the haven, together with a house for the king's keeper of the town and a new water-mill. Edward granted two weekly markets and a six-week fair, set up a mint and an exchange, and provided a burial ground next to Holy Trinity chapel to obviate the long and dangerous journey along the Humber shore to Hessle. A large site was also given for the friary that had already been established in Wyke.

By the middle of the fourteenth century Hull no longer had the trappings of a raw 'new town'. There were many more houses, and such public buildings as a gaol and town guildhall. The town was precocious in the use of bricks, for a brickyard was in operation close by from about 1300 until the early fifteenth century. Some went into the great church of Holy Trinity then being built, though its status was still only that of a chapelry of Hessle. A second 'church', St Mary's, was also provided, this time a chapelry of the distant parish of North Ferriby. Finally, the framework of the medieval landscape was completed by the raising of timber defences round the town in the 1320s, subsequently replaced by a brick wall. Within that wall, by the end of the century, was a population approaching 3,000, three times that of the declining Hedon. Though the marks of its new town origins persisted, Hull subsequently grew into a large commercial city and its modern landscape may justifiably be given separate consideration.

Kingston upon Hull

Throughout the Middle Ages, and indeed until the eighteenth century, Hull remained almost entirely confined within its fourteenth-century defences. The fortifications were strengthened by new works built on the east bank of the river Hull in the 1540s, and by a bank and ditch constructed beyond the medieval walls during the Civil War by the town's parliamentarian garrison. Few buildings were put up outside these limits, and within them the town grew steadily more congested. In the eighteenth century many courts of small houses were built behind the street fronts, and they were to become some of the most squalid slums of Victorian Hull. Only in the last quarter of the eighteenth century was the townscape radically changed by the breaking of the redundant defensive girdle and the development of the first substantial suburbs.

The demands of commerce made the first breach. The old harbour provided by the river Hull became increasingly congested as the port's trade expanded, and in 1774–8 the first artificial dock was dug on the site of the northern defences of the town. When further docks were opened in 1809 and 1829 along its west side, the 'Old Town' was almost completely encircled by water (Plate 37). Beyond the first dock new roads were laid out by the Dock Company and land was sold for building. Most of the houses were put up before the turn of the eighteenth century, many of them in uniform three-storeyed terraces; but they also included, in Charlotte Street, a variegated terrace of elegant and highly ornamental houses, only a sad remnant of which still stands. The proprietors of several small estates near by also began to develop them during the same period or soon after 1800, among them John Jarratt, on whose land the wide and handsome Jarratt (later Kingston) Square was laid out. An extensive suburb was thus quickly created north of the dock, in part a fashionable district for merchants and others moving out of the Old Town, but further out containing houses of a much more humble character. Several ornate public buildings lent distinction to Jarratt Street and Jarratt Square, more especially a large Roman Catholic church (1829) and new assembly rooms (1834), now a theatre. Severe bomb damage and widespread demolition since the war have left barely enough to suggest the quality of this first suburban landscape.

By the mid nineteenth century suburban development had also taken place beyond the docks on the west side of the Old Town, as well as across the river Hull in Drypool. Houses were also being built along the main roads leading from the town, many of them detached villas in leafy grounds which in due course were submerged as the land between the main roads was developed. The flat low-lying ground on which almost the whole of modern Hull is built imposed few physical restrictions upon the pattern of the town's growth. To some extent development in the later nineteenth and twentieth centuries mirrored that of the earlier period, with houses being built first along the main roads and later on filling up empty areas between the roads. The detailed story of the making of Hull's Victorian landscape, however, is one of landowners, speculators and builders, and it has yet to be unravelled.

One feature of Hull's housing which followed a practice already used in the Old Town was the building of courts behind the street fronts. Some dated from the earlier nineteenth century, but many were built after the Kingston upon Hull Act of 1854—a consequence of the cholera epidemic in 1848-9—had created by-laws to raise housing standards. It has been estimated that of the small working-class houses still occupied in Hull in 1965, nearly half stood in cul-de-sac courts of from twelve to twenty-two dwellings each, and the rest in conventional terraces. The main influence on the layout of streets and courts was the existence of a pattern of elongated rectangular fields in the countryside around the town, some of them resulting from the eighteenth-century enclosure of Myton Carr and the open fields and commons of Southcoates. Land was sold piecemeal for building, and it was often convenient to fit courts into existing fields. The term 'by-law housing' commonly implies meanness and monotony, but the Hull courts were often above the minimum standard set by the by-laws, and they exhibited great variety of layout and design. Nearly 1,500 courts were still occupied in 1965, but demolition has since much reduced this characteristic part of the town's landscape.

The Victorian and Edwardian domestic townscape still has a considerable variety of interest, from the middle-class comfort of Pearson Park and the Avenues to the few surviving working-class courts. Pearson Park, the first public park in Hull, was opened in 1860 and the large Italianate and Tudor-style houses built around it now stand in a setting of matured trees and lawns. The nearby Avenues began to be developed in the 1870s in a variety of styles;

notable features were the large and elaborate cast-iron fountains at the road junctions, two of which still stand at the
present time. Hull also possesses a garden village, begun
by the Quaker James Reckitt for his employees in 1907. Its
tree-lined roads focus upon a 'village green', and most of the
houses are in semi-detached pairs with good gardens; it also
included such community buildings as a village hall and
shopping centre. Despite war damage, slum clearance, and
the loss of redundant public buildings—among them some
fine nonconformist churches—the inner suburbs of Hull
still retain much of their original character. The uniform
terraced streets, with their variety of detail and scale,
reflecting different social pretensions, are nevertheless
slowly giving way to the new landscape of an anonymous
twentieth-century town.

The landscape of the modern port is much less apparent
to the passer-by. The ring of docks around the Old Town
was replaced in the later nineteenth and early twentieth
centuries by a string of new and less obvious docks along
the Humber bank, though their towering cranes punctuate
the southern horizon from many parts of the city. Downstream, the chemical works and petrol storage tanks at
Salt End are relatively inconspicuous, too, except when they
set the night sky ablaze with light. The vigorous growth of
industry in the nineteenth century made a more obvious
contribution to the Hull scene. The nature of the town's
industrial development was largely determined by the growing trade of the port, and many oilseed-crushing mills, paint-
works and corn mills were built, mostly along both banks
of the river Hull north of the Old Town. Two cotton mills
were also established, in 1836 and 1845, though both failed
later in the century. Shipbuilding and fishing have long been
important, too, along with the typical ancillary industries of
any big port. Several large oil and corn mills are still to be
seen, and part of one of the cotton mills also survives, but

periodic rebuilding, industrial reorganisation, and war damage have all brought changes and contributed to an air of dereliction in the older industrial districts beside the river Hull. Though the works of Reckitt and Colman Ltd are still prominent there, the newer light industries are widely scattered about the city.

The townscape of central Hull is now much scarred and in the process of being transformed (Plate 36). A new shopping area has arisen since the Second World War, but in the Old Town war damage, decay and demolition have left large open sites which are only slowly being re-developed. Some valuable buildings have, it is true, survived the inroads of friend and foe alike. They include the late-sixteenth-century grammar school; several merchants' houses in High Street, especially Wilberforce House with its splendid front of about 1660, a fragment of Crowle House (1664), and Maister House (1744); the whole Trinity House block, including several groups of almshouses (1753 and later); and most of Parliament Street, a new development of 1795–1800. But against these survivals must be set the continuing loss of the Old Town's character, and even the street plan laid down in the Middle Ages is now in jeopardy. The first of the early docks was filled in and reduced to formal gardens in 1938: the fate of the others is uncertain. Nothing would compensate the town for the loss of these expanses of open water, so evocative of its maritime life. Yet already many of the warehouses, large and small, together with the cranes, bridges and other paraphernalia of the docks, have gone or are destined to disappear before long. The old Hull landscape is tattered and torn and the new has yet to emerge, but the creation of several small conservation areas in 1973 encourages the hope that something of the past may yet be saved.

Seaside resorts

The medieval market town of Bridlington was not itself a seaside settlement, for it stood a mile inland on the lowest slopes of the Wolds. The town was dominated by the priory and its great church, the nave of which was used by the townsmen as their place of worship even before the Dissolution and has happily been maintained ever since. The only other part of the priory to survive is the fourteenth-century gatehouse, known as the Bayle. Most of the houses of the town stood along High Street, with their garths extending to two back lanes, north and south, and the street still contains a fine collection of houses and shop-fronts dating from the seventeenth to the nineteenth century. The wide straight street called Market Place is an offshoot of High Street and may have been added to the town plan some time after 1200, when the priory secured a grant of a market and fair. In modern times this part of Bridlington has come to be known as the 'Old Town'. From at least the eleventh century there was also a smaller settlement next to the harbour, a place sometimes called Castleburn in the Middle Ages and known as the 'Quay' since the sixteenth century. It is here that the Gypsey Race reaches the sea.

As a market centre Bridlington no doubt served a relatively small area, and for travellers it was a remote place. When a Crown commissioner was sent in 1537 about the suppression of the priory, he wrote that "Bridlington stands in a far corner of the shire adjoining to the sea where no resort is of strangers except such as dwell about the same that come to market there." Times change, and that distant situation by the sea was eventually to attract a great resort of strangers. Bathing by visitors to Bridlington was first commented upon in 1770, and the Quay soon became a fashionable watering-place. The cliffs of Flamborough Head enhanced its setting, while the ravine which reaches the sea at Danes' Dyke modestly satisfied the vogue of romantic scenery. The Quay was soon enlarged by the building of lodging-houses around it, but up to the mid nineteenth century Quay and Old Town remained quite distinct, despite the gradual appearance of houses on the road between them.

Further growth was encouraged by the arrival of the railway from Hull in 1846, and larger-scale building at the Quay began in the 1860s. A big hotel in an ornate Renaissance style, the Alexandra, was put up in 1863–6, and during the next twenty or thirty years a number of terraces of three- and four-storeyed lodging-houses were built near the sea. Some of the terraces were the work of G. W. Travis and the architect Joseph Earnshaw, both of whom left Sheffield to settle in Bridlington in 1869. Other estates were developed during the same period inland from the sea front, and by the turn of the century rapid growth was also taking place on the south side of the Gypsey Race, in Hilderthorpe. Old Town and Quay were now no longer distinct and separate places. During the earlier nineteenth century the combined population of the market town and the resort had grown modestly from 3,100 in 1801 to 5,200 in 1841; but by 1901 there were 9,500 people in Bridlington itself and another 2,500 in Hilderthorpe. The borough's population had reached nearly 26,800 by 1971, when it was the second largest town in the riding.

Bridlington's popularity with Hull, West Riding, and North East Midlands holiday-makers owed much to the continual provision of amenities at the Quay. Concert halls, promenades, and the like make up the typical sea-front landscape of a popular resort (Plate 38), while street after street of Victorian lodging-houses have an equally distinctive air, with their red, white, buff or bright yellow brick, their numerous floors, from basement to attic, and their regiments of bay windows. The Old Town, in contrast, has become something of a quiet backwater, and High Street has precariously retained much of its attractive Georgian character.

The fascination of Filey's landscape lies in the combination of a fine natural setting and a planned resort development of the nineteenth century (Plate 39). The wide sweep of Filey Bay is framed by a distant view of the chalk cliffs of Flamborough Head to the south and by a rocky tide-covered promontory called the Brigg, which projects from a high headland just north of the town. The old village lay alongside a deep wooded ravine, and another ravine marks the southern limit of the new resort. Between these valleys boulder clay cliffs nearly 100 feet high rise behind the sands.

Old Filey was largely a fishing community, though it never had a harbour or pier, and boats are still hauled back and forth across the beach. Most of the village houses stood along a main street (now Queen Street), and in Church Street across its landward end. The impressive twelfth- and thirteenth-century church, however, stands curiously aloof from the village, not only beyond the ravine but also—until a change made in 1889—beyond the East Riding boundary. Most of the old fishermen's houses have been demolished in recent years: they included a number of single-storeyed stone cottages in Queen Street, as well as dozens of small two-storeyed houses built in yards behind the main streets in the earlier nineteenth century. The one-time village streets nevertheless still contain an attractive assortment of seventeenth-century and later houses.

The pattern of the village began to change in the 1830s when several 'villas' and a bath-house were built on the cliff top to the south. These new houses included North Cliff Villa, built for a Hull wine merchant, William Voase, and Ravine Villa, the home of a West Riding brewer, Henry

Plate 39   Filey. An aerial view of the resort, looking north. The old fishing village lay beside the wooded ravine in the distance, with the church on its further side. Resort development began about 1830, and the stuccoed terraces of the Crescent, on the cliff-top, were built between the 1840s and 1890.

Plate 40 Eppleworth viaduct, west of Hull, on the Hull and Barnsley railway line, opened in 1885. The line has been closed and the fate of the viaduct is uncertain.

Plate 41 Melton quarry. The largest of the Wolds chalk quarries, serving a cement works near by.

Plate 42 Sutton on Hull. The old village, lying mostly along a winding main street, was gradually enlarged as a dormitory for Hull from the early nineteenth century onwards. In the present century it has been swamped. The new Hull suburb of Bransholme is seen in the distance. In the right foreground ridge-and-furrow marks part of the open fields, enclosed in 1768.

Plate 43   York University, founded in 1960, lying just outside the city at Heslington. The campus is centred on the sixteenth-century Heslington Hall, seen in the foreground with the village church. The university buildings lie around a large artificial lake. This is perhaps the best of the riding's new twentieth-century landscapes.

Plate 44   The Humber Bridge under construction. These are the north bank towers of the great suspension bridge that will eventually link the old East Riding and Lincolnshire. The golf course in the foreground has been destroyed, since the picture was taken, to make way for approach roads.

Bentley. It was, however, a Birmingham solicitor, J. W. Unett, who laid out a grid of streets and began the systematic development of the resort. By 1850 one block of stuccoed terrace houses had been built in the Crescent, overlooking the sea, together with several other rows of lodging-houses in the streets behind. Further blocks in the Crescent were put up in the 1850s, and when the whole sweep was completed in 1890 it formed the most impressive piece of resort landscape in the riding (Fig. 24). The growth of the town was encouraged by the opening of railway lines in 1846–7 linking it with Hull and York, and some of the streets of 'New Filey' were fully built-up before the end of the century. Other streets were built to unite the old village and the resort, and in the present century Filey has been growing westwards, too. The population of about 500 in 1801 was six times as large in 1901, and it had reached 5,300 by 1971. A little beyond the comfortable range of day-trippers, Filey long remained a fashionable resort, and to the present time commercial development has been far more restrained than at Bridlington. Moreover, the building of estates of bungalows and chalets, as well as a huge holiday camp, in nearby Hunmanby and Reighton has no doubt eased the pressure on Filey and helped to preserve its character.

At Hornsea the seaside resort developed from a large village lying a mile inland beside Hornsea Mere. The hamlet of Hornsea Beck, which apparently stood by the sea, had long since been washed away; Hornsea Burton seems to have suffered the same fate, and the inland hamlets of Northorpe and Southorpe had also been depopulated in the Middle Ages. Hornsea itself lay mostly along a curving main street which followed the eastern shore-line of the mere. A market and fair had been granted in the Middle Ages, and part of the main street is still known as Market Place. The plan of the village suggests, however, that there

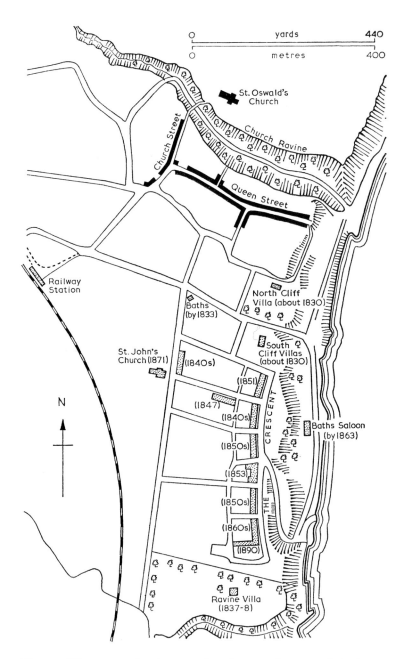

Fig. 24. Filey town plan in 1890 (based on enclosure and Ordnance Survey maps). Showing (in black) the extent of the old village in 1790, and (hatched) some of the early resort buildings.

250

may at one time have been a market-place and fairground at the western end of the street; this area had been largely built over by 1809, when a map was drawn for the enclosure commissioners (Fig. 25). The continuing need for a fairground led the commissioners to allot two acres beside the mere for the purpose, and this still remains as an open space. At the time of enclosure two or three bathing machines were already kept at the beach, and by 1822 it was said that Hornsea "has of late become a fashionable watering-place". Besides sea-bathing the village could offer boating on the 360-acre mere, and a chalybeate spring which for a few years held the promise of a 'spa'.

The first buildings put up near the sea, in the 1830s, were the large and fashionable Marine Hotel and a coffee house, and in 1850 there were also one or two lodging-houses and a baths there. From just over 500 in 1801 the population increased to about 1,000 in 1841. Most of Hornsea's visitors were from nearby Hull, and it was a family of Hull timber merchants, the Wades, who attempted to stimulate the resort's growth. John Wade built himself a house there in 1845 and Joseph Wade championed the railway from Hull which was built in 1864, terminating on Wade's own property by the sea, away from the old village. The railway not only carried trippers to the resort but also attracted Hull people as residents and commuters. By 1873 Hornsea could be described as "the quaintest mixture of a small country town and a callow sea bathing place. The better half of it is little more than a marine suburb of Hull." As a resort Hornsea subsequently attracted mainly day-trippers, and its physical expansion has been due above all to the growing influx of residents. From about 2,400 in 1901 the town's population rose to 7,000 in 1971, and it now stretches far away from the old village and disused railway station.

Withernsea's beginnings were more humble than Hornsea's, for the resort has taken the place of two straggling

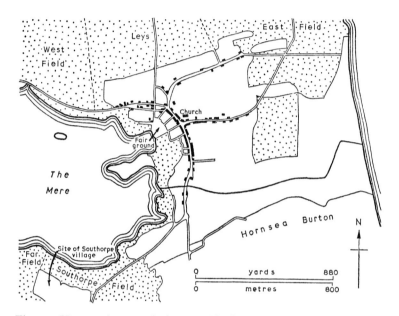

Fig. 25. Hornsea in 1809, before seaside development began (based on the enclosure map). Showing (stippled) the commonable lands enclosed that year. Most of the land between the old village and the sea has since been built over.

villages, Owthorne and Withernsea, whose combined population in 1801 was only 165. During the next thirty years erosion by the sea removed most of the houses of Owthorne, together with its church, while at Withernsea the church stood derelict a short distance inland from the cliffs. Withernsea had already lost much land to the sea, and the early village site had doubtless gone, just as the medieval church went in the fifteenth century. It was to this desolate place that a railway promoted by a Hull coal exporter, Anthony Bannister, was built in 1854, together with a splendid hotel, later the Queen's. Between 1851 and 1881 the population trebled (to a modest 872), and by 1901 it had reached about 1,500 in Owthorne and Withernsea together. As a resort Withernsea became popular with day-trippers from Hull but, unlike Hornsea, it attracted relatively few residential commuters. Today it has a population of about 6,000 and a wide sprawl of modern housing, but at the centre of the town the landscape has an air of what might have been. The former Queen's Hotel, closed soon after 1900, and the castellated entrance to the pier that was washed away about a decade later, still stand at the end of the disused railway line.

SELECT BIBLIOGRAPHY

Beresford, M. W., *New Towns of the Middle Ages* (1967).
Beresford, M. W., *History on the Ground* (2nd edn. 1971), chap. 5 (new towns).
Boyle, J. R., *Early History of Hedon* (1895).
Forster, C. A., *Court Housing in Kingston upon Hull* (University of Hull, Occasional Papers in Geography, 19, 1972).
Hall, Ivan and Elisabeth, *Historic Beverley* (1973).
MacMahon, K. A., *Beverley* (1973).

Mayoh, K. L., 'Comparative Study of the Resorts on the Coast of Holderness', unpublished M.A. thesis, University of Hull (1961).

Neave, David, *Pocklington, 1660–1914* (1971).

Ross, F., *Contributions towards a History of Driffield* (1898).

V.C.H., *Yorkshire East Riding*, I (1969) (Kingston upon Hull) and II (1974) (Bridlington and Filey).

11. The twentieth-century landscape

THE GREAT CHANGES wrought in the East Riding countryside in the late eighteenth and nineteenth centuries have no parallel in the present century, but significant alterations have nevertheless taken place, more especially since the Second World War. These recent changes sometimes involve the rapid unmaking of a landscape which is the culmination of a long and generally harmonious development. The pressures of population growth in local towns and further afield almost inevitably introduce disruptive elements, here as in so many other parts of England. Yet it ill becomes the historian of the landscape, who has delighted in centuries of change, to deplore further change now. The emerging contemporary landscape deserves his study, too. In earlier chapters the story of industry and communications, and that of the towns, were taken well into the twentieth century. A little more needs to be added on those topics, but this final chapter is more especially concerned with changes in the countryside.

The agricultural depression beginning in the 1870s no doubt had only a temporary effect on the landscape, though the large-scale import of cheap corn certainly led to a fall in the acreage under the plough in the riding and to some neglect of both buildings and land. The short-lived prosperity of the First World War, with its ploughing-up campaign, was followed by another decrease in the arable acreage during the depression of the 1920s and 1930s. The Second World War brought longer-lasting prosperity, with a permanent extension of arable farming and widespread mechanisation. The agricultural landscape of the East Riding has thus become increasingly an arable one, with ever more fields of cereals. By the mid 1950s about eighty per cent of the farmed land on the Wolds was arable, and even in the central Vale of York, where there was the highest proportion of permanent grass in the riding, the arable percentage was still sixty. One notable change everywhere has been the replacement of permanent grass by temporary leys. Sheep are still a familiar sight on the Wolds, though increasingly they are fed on ley grass rather than turnips. Beef and dairy cattle continue to be more numerous in the Vale of York and Holderness, but especially in Holderness and the Hull valley they have been joined by large numbers of pigs and poultry. East Riding farming has become more intensive, more diverse and more flexible, with many implications for the appearance of the countryside and the quality of the environment.

With the amalgamation of farms into larger and more economic units, some farmsteads have been completely demolished, like Now or Never at North Cliffe, High Drewton near South Cave, and Farberry Garth, Warter. Many isolated labourers' cottages are suffering a similar fate. Older farm buildings have often been replaced or extended in new materials, and a variety of novel buildings have been added. Scores of Dutch barns appeared between the world wars, for example, and grain bins, driers and silos have become commonplace. Aldro Farm, Birdsall, again provides a good example of such developments (Fig. 18). Tall modern silos are now to be seen everywhere, though a few older ones survive, like the decaying timber towers at Blanch and several other farms on the Warter estate. Large cattle, pig and poultry units also contribute to the concrete and steel buildings which often fit so uneasily into the landscape.

Other notable additions to the farm landscape include numerous county council smallholdings, established after the First World War, with their identical houses and outbuildings. Around Hull, another striking change has been a great extension of market-gardening. Vegetable-growing to feed the town had begun at Cottingham by at least the late eighteenth century, and in 1949 there were over 2,000 acres of market-gardens around Hull, notably in the Cottingham, Beverley, South Cave and Thorngumbald areas. What has so greatly affected the landscape has been the extension of glasshouses, prompted by Dutch growers who settled here after the imposition in 1932 of import tariffs on vegetables from Holland.

The East Riding landscape suffered from tree-felling during both wars, involving both older woodland and post-enclosure plantations. Much surviving woodland, however, is now managed by the Forestry Commission, and large-scale planting of conifers has taken place in a few districts, around Wheldrake, in the Vale of York, for example, and at Wintringham, on the Wolds escarpment. More serious for the appearance of the countryside has been the continuing removal of hedgerows, which has produced many prairie-like farms, such as Low Grange, near Market Weighton. Moreover, Dutch elm disease was spreading rapidly in the riding in 1975.

Woods and hedgerows cannot all be preserved by the necessarily businesslike farmer of today, but their disappearance is a serious loss for the interpretation of the landscape. By their character and composition, hedges can tell us much about the land-use history of an area, and work is now in progress in the riding to test the theory that they may be approximately dated by the number of species they contain. Ecologists are also showing how older woodland may be recognised from the rich assemblage of trees there and by the presence of such plants as bluebell and wood anemone, which are not found, for example, in the post-enclosure plantations on the Wolds. Woodland plants may also be useful in tracing cleared woodland, for it seems that they may survive for centuries after clearance, as for example on Westwood common, at Beverley.

R

Much other historical evidence is being lost to the landscape as the result of modern farming methods and during road improvements and new building. Earthworks and depressions of all kinds, every one with a story to tell, are continually being bulldozed and ploughed. One of the more obvious recent examples was the infilling of the old haven at Patrington which has left a former warehouse oddly standing—for the moment—at the edge of a much enlarged field. It is perhaps fair to remember that some earthworks are being preserved, like those of the deserted village at Hilderthorpe which are expected to become hazards on Bridlington's golf course.

Also arising from intensive modern farming methods are several environmental considerations of which some mention should be made. They include the threat of pollution from the disposal of pig slurry; the effects of chemical fertilisers on the water supplies contained in the chalk of the Wolds; and the consequences of stubble-burning, which is now so prominent a part of the autumn scene. Fire-blackened hedgerows and charred roadside verges are left by many an uncontrolled stubble fire, so increasing the denudation of the countryside.

Besides its influence on agriculture, the Second World War had other more immediate effects upon the landscape. Some fifteen airfields were built in the riding, for example. Only a few, like Leconfield and Holme upon Spalding Moor, are still used for flying, but crumbling runways and derelict huts are still all too apparent. At other places, such as Barmby Moor and Carnaby, hangars have been converted to industrial uses and new buildings added. Hutton Cranswick, in contrast, is an example of an airfield reclaimed for agriculture. Defence works frequently survive, too, such as the emplacements at Sunk Island and concrete blocks on the Holderness beaches. None is so prominent, however, as the single military relic of an earlier period, the fort at

Paull that was constructed in 1856. Offensive preparations had their own, albeit temporary, effects on the landscape in 1943–4, when over 10,000 acres towards the north of the Wolds were used as a tank training ground in preparation for the landings in Normandy. Not all of the scarred hedges were replaced, while deep tank tracks long persisted in some of the Wolds valleys.

Over much of the East Riding the late nineteenth and twentieth centuries, especially the periods of depression, witnessed a gradual depopulation of the countryside and a drift to the towns. In the more remote areas those trends go on, and some villages on the high Wolds, such as Langtoft and Foxholes, continue to shrink. The neglect and eventual demolition of older houses and cottages have been widespread consequences. Alongside this general depopulation there has also been an abandonment of many large country houses. Some, like Warter Priory, have been demolished, while others, such as Woodhall, near Hemingbrough, have long stood derelict. Not a few have been put to new uses: a museum at Sewerby, a school at Howsham, a nunnery at Thicket, near Thorganby. Their parks have sometimes been converted to farmland, as at Escrick, Heigholme and Osgodby. The decline of village life is to be seen, too, in numerous disused schools and chapels, a few neglected or even demolished churches, such as Leppington and Acklam respectively, and many converted parsonage houses.

In all the more accessible parts of the riding, rural depopulation has been halted at least since the Second World War, and in some districts it has been replaced by a strong movement of town dwellers into the countryside. Villages around all the larger towns now serve as dormitories for commuters and for the retired. Even comparatively remote villages, like Kilham, Middleton on the Wolds and Gilberdyke, have recently seen the building of housing estates. The phenomenon is naturally most marked near York, Hull and Beverley. South and east of York villages like Dunnington, Escrick, Riccall and Wheldrake have experienced a sudden expansion, and whether plain or pretentious, the new houses overwhelm some of the old village streets. At Heslington there was an incursion of a different kind when the University of York was established there in 1960. Centred on the old Hall and incorporating a large artificial lake, the campus provides the most satisfying piece of twentieth-century landscape in the riding (Plate 43).

Near Beverley conspicuous examples of village expansion include Cherry Burton, Leconfield and Leven. At Walkington, 180 new houses were built in the decade 1961–71 and the population rose from 830 to 1,250; and another eighty houses were added there in 1971–4. Development at Cherry Burton in the last ten years has surrounded the older nucleus with over 300 small houses, bungalows and exclusive 'Georgian style residences'. East of Hull, Thorngumbald mushroomed from 774 to 2,710 inhabitants in 1961–71, while to the west of the city such places as Willerby and Kirk Ella have been overtaken by the advancing suburbs. All the villages around the southern end of the Wolds, as far as the Caves, have seen a similar influx of commuters, and pressures are now being felt further afield, in such previously undeveloped villages as Newbald.

Hull's steadily creeping suburbs have also leapt forward in the 1970s to create a virtual 'new town', at Bransholme on the eastern bank of the river Hull (Plate 42). Other notable contributions to the suburban landscape have been made by the University of Hull, both at the campus within the city boundary and further out, at Cottingham, where impressive halls of residence have been built.

With the popular demand for a 'country life', further village expansion is inevitable. Much of it is likely to take place in the eighty-two 'minor development centres' designated in the development plan drawn up by the former East Riding county council in 1960. At that time rural depopulation was expected to continue and it was decided to restrict the provision of services to those centres. Other villages were to remain static or be allowed to decline. The detailed nature of the expansion is clearly of the greatest importance for the retention of the traditional character of so many villages. The twin threats of over-development and decay of older buildings are well illustrated by Newbald. Already in 1947 fifty-seven, or thirty per cent, of the houses there were either unfit for habitation and beyond repair at reasonable expense, or already condemned and awaiting demolition. Many have since been removed and replaced by about sixty council houses. Although it was among the minor development centres, its remoteness and lack of facilities discouraged newcomers, and only a handful of private houses were built there in 1961–71. Work on a private estate began in 1972, however, and there was subsequently a spate of planning applications. Meanwhile, decay and demolition, piecemeal rebuilding, and unsuitable modernisation of old houses have all continued. The formation of conservation areas in 1974 may help to control development here and in several other villages.

The post-war years have also seen an unprecedented descent of holiday-makers upon the coastal areas away from the older resorts. As a result, bungalows and chalets have been built at many places, most conspicuously in their hundreds alongside Filey Bay, in Hunmanby and Reighton parishes. Hunmanby can also boast a huge holiday camp. Caravan sites, too, have appeared all along the coast. The harmful visual effect of caravans on Flamborough Head was lessened by the action of the county council in the 1960s, when several sites were moved back from the edge of the cliffs. All hope of this headland forming part of our so-called 'heritage coast' would, however, be in vain if current demands for a marina at Flamborough were allowed. A new 'country park' already mars the cliff-top near Filey Brigg. The necessary expansion of leisure facilities can surely go hand-in-hand with the preservation of the best of the riding's coastal scenery, both at Flamborough and further south at Spurn Head.

Inland, leisure activities impinge only slightly upon the landscape. The first local authority picnic sites were opened on the Wolds in 1973, and the formation of a long-distance footpath, the Wolds Way, running from the Humber at North Ferriby to Filey, has proceeded slowly since 1968. Far more important to those hoping to explore the country-side is the maintenance of an extensive network of public rights of way, no mean task for county council and walkers alike in a riding that is so intensively farmed. No part of the Yorkshire Wolds has been deemed fit for designation as an 'area of outstanding natural beauty', a status which would safeguard it from harmful development, though the Lin-colnshire Wolds have surprisingly been more fortunate in this respect. The relative remoteness of the East Riding from large centres of population, as well as its own scenic limitations, have in the past limited the leisure demands made upon it, but the pressures are of course mounting now.

Growing population and traffic have brought further changes to the riding's road system, above all by the continuing improvement of the main roads leading to Hull. Most striking has been the rerouting since the 1950s of the road from the West Riding (A63) where it runs around the southern end of the Wolds. By means of several bypasses the new dual carriageway now threads its way between the expanding commuter villages for the last ten miles into the city suburbs. Only in the 1970s, however, has the motorway been introduced to the East Riding. An extension of the M62 was completed in 1976, crossing the Ouse by a long new bridge near Howden, and then partly following the course of the former Hull & Barnsley railway line before joining the improved A63 near North Cave. Long stretches of embankment on two disused railway lines have been removed for use in the foundations of the motorway. On the York–Hull road (A1079) a long series of works is still in progress, and a notable improvement on the Beverley–Bridlington road has been the bypassing of Tickton village. A new fixed bridge over the river Hull replaces the rolling bridge at Tickton, built in 1913, though the old structure is still in position.

The towns themselves present their own special road problems which will be solved only at great expense to the townscape and the adjoining countryside. The city of York has been bypassed, for example, by a new road which cuts a broad swathe through the fields of Fulford, Heslington and Dunnington. Beverley has been provided with a modest eastern bypass, with a bridge over Beverley Beck, but a long south-western bypass on the York–Hull route, still under discussion at the time of writing, might well have a great impact on the farmland in the green belt between Beverley and Hull. In Hull, new roads are planned through the city to link the docks on the eastern side of the town with the improved A63 and the motorway. Last but not least, approach roads to the Humber Bridge must be laid out in the densely populated areas immediately west of the city, for the long cherished dream of a bridge is at last reaching fulfilment. The great suspension bridge which will provide more direct access from the south, as well as linking the two banks of the new county of Humberside, is far from complete. But already the north bank towers rise to their full height above the riverside at Hessle (Plate 44).

New housing and improved communications are the most obvious results of contemporary demands on the riding's landscape, but there is a host of others. Hull's thirst for water, for example, has outstripped the supplies available from pumping stations built around the city between 1862 and 1931 to extract water from the chalk of the Wolds. Large reservoirs were therefore constructed in 1959 near Hempholme to hold water taken from the river Hull, and in future additional supplies will come from the river Derwent, where a tidal barrier is now nearing completion at Barmby on the Marsh. Other parts of Yorkshire will also benefit from this latter scheme, and it was Sheffield corporation which in the 1960s built another prominent landmark beside the Derwent, the waterworks at Elvington. A pipeline to carry the new supplies is already being laid between Barmby and Hull. There are no large power stations in the East Riding countryside, but pylons and transmission lines stand out boldly in the Vale of York and across the southern Wolds, converging on the power station at Hull.

Another pipeline, now hidden beneath the riding's fields, is that laid in the 1960s to carry North Sea gas from huge underground holders installed near Easington, on the Holderness coast. Largely unseen, too, at least in the early stages will be the surface buildings and gear of a planned new coalfield around Selby. But other projects could have far-reaching implications for the landscape, such as the reclamation for industrial development of the great bight of the Humber between Sunk Island and Spurn Head. The whole urban and industrial expansion of north Humberside, indeed, may involve the making of yet another new landscape alongside the estuary.

Whether the East Riding countryside can withstand the mounting pressures of the late twentieth century without total transformation is uncertain. For all the subdued beauty of the Wolds and the homely charm of many villages, the riding possesses a modest and little-acclaimed landscape which might not resist for long the uncontrolled advance of mechanised farming, commuter housing and modern roads and industry. The survival of much of the traditional landscape alongside the new is nevertheless a matter for concern, not only to the historian but to all who take pleasure in living in the county, be it remembered affectionately as the East Riding or acknowledged as part of Humberside.

SELECT BIBLIOGRAPHY

Agriculture, lv (no. 4) (July 1948) (Yorkshire number).

Boatman, D. J., and Harris, A., 'Burton Bushes', Hull Natural History Society *Bulletin*, 3 (no. 2) (1971).

Long, W. H., *A Survey of the Agriculture of Yorkshire* (1969).

Neave, David, *Newbald Village Study* (1974).

Neave, David, 'Conflict in Arcadia: Village Conservation and Residential Development', unpublished thesis, Diploma in Conservation Studies, University of York (1974).

Pollard, E., Hooper, M. D., and Moore, N. W., *Hedges* (1974).

Popham, J. H., 'Farm Buildings: Function and Form', unpublished thesis, Diploma in Conservation Studies, University of York (1973).

Ramsdale, G. I., 'Twenty-five Years of Agricultural Change in the East Riding, 1931–56', unpublished M.A. thesis, University of Hull (1957).

Rapier, B. J., *White Rose Base* (1972) (Yorkshire airfields).

Rubinstein, David, *The Wolds Way* (1972).

Sheppard, June A., 'Horticultural Developments in East Yorkshire', *I.B.G. Trans.*, xix (1953), pp. 73–80.

Stamp, L. D., *The Land of Britain: Yorkshire East Riding* (1942).

Index